Picturing Childhood

Picturing Childhood

The Myth of the Child in Popular Imagery

Patricia Holland

I.B. TAURIS

LONDON · NEW YORK

Reprinted in 2006 by I.B.Tauris & Co Ltd
6 Salem Road, London W2 4BU
175 Fifth Avenue, New York NY 10010
www.ibtauris.com

In the United States of America and Canada
distributed by Palgrave Macmillan, a division of St Martin's Press
175 Fifth Avenue, New York NY 10010

First published by I.B.Tauris & Co Ltd in 2004

ISBN 1 86064 775 8
EAN 978 1 86064 775 8

A full CIP record for this book is available from the British Library
A full CIP record is available from the Library of Congress

Library of Congress Catalog Card Number: available

Typeset in Minion by Dexter Haven Associates Ltd, London
Printed and bound in India by Replika Press Pvt. Ltd.

Contents

Acknowledgements

This book is the result of a long-term project of collecting and studying pictures of children. It is a sequel to *What is a Child?* (Virago, 1992), which itself grew out of an exhibition, *Children Photographed*, mounted in 1976 by the late Jo Spence and Andrew Mann of the Children's Rights Workshop, together with Christine Vincent, Diana Phillips and Arthur Lockwood of the design group Ikon. They first aroused my enthusiasm for the rich and provocative field of pictures of children, with all its implications and ramifications, and their work in collecting and discussing imagery over the intervening years made an invaluable contribution, which is now also reflected in *Picturing Childhood*. The exhibition *Seen but not Heard?* curated by Andrew Dewdney at the Watershed Gallery in Bristol in 1992 developed the ideas further.

I should like to thank Pauline Trudell and Arthur Lockwood for continuing conversations and new insights, and Arthur for his contribution to design and layout; also Vicki Annand for sharing her collection of pictures with me when I was writing *What is a Child?*; Christine Woodrow from the University of Central Queensland, Australia; Heather Montgomery and Megan Doolittle from the Open University, and Máire Messenger Davies from Cardiff University for background information, reading chapters and making comments, as well as fruitful discussions and general support. I would also like to thank all those who have invited me to give lectures and presentations on the subject in Britain and Australia. Particular thanks to students from the Early Childhood Studies Scheme at London Metropolitan University, who have enthusiastically hunted out pictures and press cuttings for me. Thanks, too, to Phillipa Brewster of I.B.Tauris for supportive and patient editing and generally making sure the book happened.

Some of the material in *Picturing Childhood* draws on my previous work published in *What is a Child?*; 'Childhood and the uses of photography', in Patricia Holland and Andrew Dewdney (eds) (1992) *Seen But Not Heard? Childhood and the Photographic Image*, Bristol: Watershed Media Centre; 'Living for libido or Child's Play 4: The imagery of childhood and the call for censorship', in Martin Barker and Julian Petley (eds) (1997) *Ill Effects, the Media/violence Debate*, London: Routledge and 'Looking at babies: pleasures and taboos', in

Catherine Fehily, Jane Fletcher and Kate Newton (eds) (2000) *I Spy: Representations of Childhood*, London: I.B.Tauris.

Finally I should like to thank all those organisations, companies and individuals who have given permission to reproduce their visual material to illustrate the arguments in this book; they are credited beside each illustration. Every effort has been made to contact the copyright holders of the visual material and we regret any errors or omissions that may inadvertently remain.

The Last Days Of Summer

www.hm.com

Catalogue cover, courtesy of H&M. Photographer Oscar Falk.

Preface

Twenty-first-century childhood and the routine spectacular

Picturing Childhood is the result of more than twenty years of interest in popular media imagery. It draws on my large and eclectic collection of pictures of children made up of postcards and greetings cards old and new, photocopies from library books, scraps compulsively ripped out of newspapers, fat copies of glossy magazines, advertisements, bedraggled packages from supermarket shelves, museum kitsch and all those brochures, catalogues, charity appeals and other printed material that come unsolicited through the letterbox. Increasingly it includes references to less tangible images on websites, or sent by e-mail. The collection continues to grow, part of an obsession I can't get rid of. Because of its ephemeral quality the older papers are yellowing and crumpled, and the whole lot is a disorderly mess. Reduced to two-dimensional surfaces, well fed, smiling babies and little girls in fairy tutus share cardboard boxes with the suffering children from international conflicts and the angry youngsters in inner-city streets. Every year I mean to put aside time to sort it out properly, but I never quite get round to it.

My collection is more serendipitous than scholarly, made purely for my own amusement, with no claims to either sociological status (no careful sampling, no systematic organisation, no key words) or artistic or antiquarian authenticity. Postcards and cheap art reproductions sit comfortably alongside originals I have casually acquired from junk shops or market stalls. I don't set particular store by age or rarity. Instead I'm fascinated by trivia, by the everyday, by common knowledge, and what I would like to describe as the 'routine spectacular'. Even so (in a sneaking fascination for the old), I do value the rose-embossed birthday card showing a toothy infant in a high chair which was sent to my elderly aunt on her first birthday in 1919, and the little girl with a fetching look and her head to one side which was published in Paris and posted in Lisbon in 1920. I am amused by the pair of sepia pictures labelled 'sorrow' and 'joy' in which a toddler in a night-cap first squats miserably over his potty, then grins with a sense of relief and achievement, and I am intrigued by a carefully staged stereograph in which a well-dressed group of women gather around a new arrival. But as far as I am concerned, a reproduction of a Victorian postcard will do as well as the original – in fact better, because it draws attention to two different historical circumstances rather than one. The social circumstances and ways of thinking in which pictures such as these originated are indeed fascinating, but what is more to my purpose is the appeal they have in the present day and the ways in which they are recycled and re-staged. The historian Raphael Samuel described this process as creating 'theatres of memory'.

My collection is roughly organised by topic and also by date, since my assess-ment of what topics are important changes and it is easier to start a new pile every now and then ('sweetness' has given way to 'sexiness'; 'free schooling' to 'tests and examinations'). However, from the top of a recent pile I pick, pretty well at random, the 2001 autumn catalogue for the fashion chain H&M, and am reassured that contemporary childhood is indeed a blissful affair. The children pictured in these pages are active, out of doors, fascinated by the world around them (a boy peers at a frog in a jar), windswept, heterogeneous (there are boys and girls, a child of apparently mixed-race origin, a child of oriental origin), all bursting with health and energy. And, of course, they are beautifully dressed in a varied wardrobe of clothes that are warm, hard-wearing, good quality and stylish. What more could anyone want?

Picturing Childhood starts from the pleasure I continue to take in my collection, and draws out from this minor amusement what I hope will be a more serious commentary on the nature of childhood itself. Despite a twenty-first-century mood of cynical iconoclasm, I do not want to defuse the pleasure of these images but to try to make sense of that pleasure. This is not primarily an academic book. It does not observe academic conventions, and tries to avoid academic language. I hope it will appeal to all readers who are concerned about childhood and contemporary debates around pictures of children. However, it is written in the context of two newish academic disciplines: a 'new' sociology of childhood, which considers childhood as a social phenomenon freed from the value-laden, instrumental preoccupations of developmental and educational approaches; and a burgeoning literature on visual culture, which specifically detaches a study of the visual from its art historical roots, and celebrates the proliferation of popular visual forms. In that spirit, pictures that are made specifically as works of art will not be the central focus of my discussion. I am more interested in those little treats or shocks which we encounter everyday than in the one-off and deliberately remarkable.

Picturing Childhood is an updated version of *What is a Child?*, published more than a decade ago. When that book was first conceived, the 'new' sociology of childhood was in its early days, influenced by a clamour of voices from outside the academy which demanded a demystification of received ideas and an unprejudiced way of looking at children and childhood. Voices came from the free schooling movement, the children's rights movement, the student movement. The discipline was influenced by academic radicalism, 1970s feminism and a growing sensitivity to cultural diversity. At the same time, a number of social historians were setting out to write history 'from below' – grounded in the everyday experience of ordinary people – and had begun to research a specific history of childhood itself, separate from the histories of education or 'the family'. A history of children's daily experiences has been extremely difficult to trace, since children themselves have had little or no access to those public forms of expression that last down the ages. It became necessary to make a distinction between a history of *children* and children's experiences, and a history of '*childhood*' – which is effectively an account of *adult* views of what children are and how they should be. Such views have gone through many transformations, and the imagery of childhood reflects those changes. Phillipe Aries's controversial claim that childhood is a slippery thing and a recent, Western invention was based on his study of the Western art tradition. *Picturing Childhood* takes as its subject matter those debates and mythologies which have circulated in Britain from the 1970s up to the present, with an occasional glance further back into history. It accepts that the study of childhood includes a re-evaluation of children's place in society as well as an assessment of adults' changing attitudes to children.

Despite the optimism and child-centred nature of the new approach, calling the nature of childhood into question has given rise to a complex of new fears. Alongside the joyous images from advertising and consumer magazines, many contemporary narratives of childhood are bleak and deeply disturbing. Amidst the unprecedented prosperity of the Western world, we are told stories of children who are dangerous and who are themselves in deadly danger; we hear of children who are both damaged and damaging; of children who are sexually or intellectually precocious, and of others who are aggressive, assertive or out of control. The children who murdered the toddler James Bulger; the 'Rambo Boys' who massacred their classmates in Jonesboro, Arkansas; Jon-Benet Ramsey, the six-year-old beauty queen in lipstick and high heels who was herself murdered; the Palestinian baby dressed as a suicide bomber; the wild children, like 'Balaclava Boy', who terrorise inner-city estates; these children seem to have rejected childish qualities. If children represent the future, there seems to be little faith in what that future might bring.

And the imagery itself has become a focus of concern. What sort of exploitation is involved when children, the most powerless group in society, are pictured for the pleasure and delight of adults who potentially have total control over them? When I look at my collection of postcard children, made up of purely hedonistic images, I now find myself looking with the jaundiced eyes of an age which no longer draws strength from mythology and is acutely aware of the darker side of fantasy. Contemporary debate has drawn attention to illicit adult desires which lurk below the surface, and suggests that the most innocent-seeming image may feed or provoke them. Across the appreciation of every chubby infant falls the shadow of other pictured children – particularly those sexualised children whose images are circulated on the Internet. Can an adult man in this day and age enjoy an image of a naked baby, a pre-pubescent girl or a feminised boy without fearing an accusation of paedophilia? If the clear eye of the catalogue baby or the cheeky smile on the picture postcard is created by a lascivious adult or is provoked by a callous photographer, does that alter our enjoyment of it?

We live in an age which has learned not to trust its reactions, afraid of being exploitative and of being exploited. The tendency in the press and in everyday conversation is towards cynicism. The urge is always to deconstruct, to search behind every attractive surface in order to avoid being deceived. Should we interpret that smiling boy on the travel advertisement as an invitation to sex tourists – even an unconscious one? My news cuttings include many items concerning moral debates around such pictures. In March 2001 the police threatened to shut down an exhibition because of Tierney Gearon's oversized, brightly coloured snapshots of her children, particularly one in which they flaunt their nakedness, their faces, disturbingly, covered by masks; in 1995 a British newsreader was arrested when the processing laboratory reported the family snaps of her seven-year-old daughter in the bath as 'indecent'; the society photographer Ron Oliver had his negatives confiscated by the Obscene Publications Squad and was threatened with prosecution because he photographed other people's children naked; the respected artist and historian Graham Ovenden was suspected of being part of a child pornography ring, partly because of his collection of Victorian photographs. In the light of such concerns, when we look at everyday mass-produced and mass-circulated pictures of children, should we always be troubled rather than charmed or delighted? These will be amongst the questions addressed by this book.

Many present-day images knowingly trespass on dangerous ground. In the art world and in news and advertising, there has been growth in imagery that deliberately sets out to shock, in an undisguised attempt to cut though the visual babble of the everyday urban scene. In the face of critique, rather than creating works that are more 'realistic' or restrained, some artists have sought themes that are even more outrageous and exuberant. Childhood has become an overt focus for challenging taboos, and artists such as the Chapman brothers, whose work includes models of children in obscene and sexual poses, and Paula Rego, whose frank exploration of the darker side of familiar nursery rhymes deals with violence, pain and sexuality, go straight to the heart of contemporary fears. The scandalous image suggests that children may well be corrupt after all.

There seems to be a *need* to violate innocence – or perhaps it is a recognition that innocence will in any case be violated, and that dreaded moment must be rehearsed in fantasy and imagery. Childhood has come to embody the thrill of the forbidden and the excitement of taboo. It was Sigmund Freud who taught us that a horror story about childhood is at the roots of our self-awareness. Such a horror story needs forms of expression that go beyond everyday realism.

There is something very odd about taboos. They do not warn us off a topic, as is normally thought; they attract us to it. They signal with bright and flashing lights that here is something we will all be fascinated by, and then (as in the 1997 London Royal Academy *Sensations* exhibition, where controversial work by the Chapman brothers and others was put in a 'special room' which visitors were warned was not suitable for children) they hide it away to tantalise their audience further. Instead of averting our eyes, we rush to see, but our looking is of a special sort, tempered by fear. Taboos are badly kept secrets. Attention is drawn to a taboo act through the proliferation of taboo speech: on television, in the newspapers, on the Internet – everywhere. Taboos are temptations, but breaking one does not serve to dissolve it or make it disappear. It merely heightens the moral and cultural dilemmas that generated it in the first place. To challenge a taboo is to strengthen it and to reinforce its power.

The shiver of horror that Freud described as characteristic of taboo may come from an appraisal of the content of an image, but it also lurks in fears of what that image may conceal, and the emotions and forbidden desires that the image may provoke. The lamented loss of innocence is not only the innocence of childhood, but the innocence of the adult gaze. At the dawn of the twenty-first century, the revelation of impurities at the heart of our popular pleasures has led to a crisis of looking. The use of the Internet and the proliferation of digital technologies has increased the fears which our culture brings to the manner in which we do our looking, aware of the myriad uncontrollable ways in which it is possible to respond to any image.

What are we to make of this strange new mood? Must we reject its easy pleasures and condemn its risky explorations? Out of respect for children, must we all become puritans or moralists? The crisis over childhood, reflected in the popular media, is real. Children *are* getting older younger. But it could also be seen as a crisis over what it means to be an adult at a time of rapid social change. In my view, repressive attitudes may well represent a panic-stricken and some-times vicious response to the increasing power and visibility of children in the public world. Examples of such changes include: long-standing abuses against children being brought to light and abusers forced to face the costs; a questioning of the automatic power of those in authority over children – whether teachers, parents, social workers or school bullies; the fact that children are listened to with greater respect by journalists and in television programmes; and the moderate success that has been achieved by campaigns for children's participation in many different fields.

Picturing Childhood is about construction rather than deconstruction. I want to make it clear that when I speak of 'imagery' and 'mythologies' I am not asserting that these things are necessarily wrong or untrue. Sometimes the grimmest of fantasies reflect the real world only too well. Sometimes an image may be stereotyped or biased, but even pictures which are not an accurate representation of the ways things are, I will argue, express important realities about contemporary life. Rather than pointing out how images mislead or deceive, this book will be looking at the attitudes and ideas which *construct* the image, and how those attitudes and images together put pressure on real flesh-and-blood children. *Picturing Childhood* seeks to explore the ways in which the popular imagery of recent history has influenced contemporary definitions of childhood. This means that a clear distinction needs to be made between the study of the lives of real flesh-and-blood children and a study of the history and influence of the *concept* of childhood, to which images have made a powerful contribution. Rather than seeking to criticise and control the content of an image, we should be asking what the circumstances are within which pictures are created, and why they are greeted with pleasure or judged unacceptable.

We must always remember that while individual pictures may portray real *children* – each child unique and individual – the imagery shows us an abstract, shifting and heavily ideological *concept*. This book looks at the ways in which the imagery of childhood moves beyond pictures of children to tell stories, spin mythologies, and bring its own visual delight. As both routine and spectacular, it tells of the dream of childhood and its persistent nightmare.

Notes on Preface

p.x   **Raphael Samuel:** (1994) *Theatres of Memory,* Vol.1: *Past and Present in Contemporary Culture,* London: Verso.

visual culture: Nicholas Mirzoeff (1999) *An Introduction to Visual Culture,* London: Routledge.

p.xi   **the 'new' sociology of childhood:** Allison James and Alan Prout (eds) (1990) *Constructing Reconstructing Childhood: Contemporary Issues in the Sociological Study of Childhood,* London: Falmer.

a history of '*childhood*': Hugh Cunningham (1995) *Children and Childhood in Western Society since 1500,* London: Longman.

Phillipe Aries's controversial claim: Phillipe Aries (1960/1973) *Centuries of Childhood,* Harmondsworth: Penguin.

James Bulger: murdered by two 10-year-olds in 1992. See Chapter 5.

'Rambo Boys': this was how the *Mirror* labelled 11-year-old Andrew Golden and 13-year-old Mitchell Johnson. 26 March 1998.

Jon-Benet Ramsey: murdered in 1996. See Chapter 7.

the Palestinian baby: a picture found by Israeli soldiers in July 2002. *Guardian,* 28 June 2002.

p.xii   **'Balaclava Boy':** *Guardian,* 15 May 2000. See p.122 and Chapter 5.

images are circulated on the Internet: see Chapter 6.

Tierney Gearon: *Guardian,* 10 March 2001. See p.123

a British newsreader: *Independent,* 6 November 1995.

Ron Oliver: Alex Bellos, *Guardian,* 5 February 1994.

Graham Ovenden: and Robert Melville (1972) *Victorian Children,* London: Academy Editions. On child photography and the law, see David Newnham and Chris Townsend, 'Pictures of innocence', *Guardian* 'Weekend', 13 January 1996.

p.xiii   **Paula Rego:** (1994) *Nursery Rhymes,* London: Thames and Hudson.

Freud described as characteristic of taboo: Sigmund Freud (1913/1985) *Totem and Taboo,* Harmondsworth: Penguin Freud Library.

p.xiv   *Getting Older Younger:* the title of a television programme dealing with advertising to children. BBC Bristol for BBC2 (1999).

Illuminated poster advertising *Daily Telegraph*, mid-1990s.

Introduction

Pictures of children: images of childhood

PART 1: THE IMAGE WORLD: SENSE AND SENSUALITY FOR OUR TIMES

The ecstasy of communication

In contemporary society, images of children are part of a populous world of two dimensions that threads through the living world of flesh and blood. Especially in the metropolitan centres of globalised society, every individual is surrounded by representations and images which stand as an arrogant assertion of social wealth. Pictures on the page or screen; advertisements on street hoardings or the sides of buses; posters in the underground; front pages on newsagents' stands; jokes in the card shop; packaging in the supermarket: these are public pictures designed for public spaces, whether in decaying inner cities, spruced-up country towns or suburban shopping parades. (The Henley Centre for Forecasting estimated that an average 'mobile citizen' could expect to see 1300 advertisements in a day.) In addition, television, video recorders, computers, mobile phones and digital technology bring public images into the private spaces of the home, causing the boundaries between public and private to shift and blur. These are *available* pictures, which feed comfortably into the consciousness of the age. The modern communications industries provide a repertoire of visual excitement that is at the same time both dazzling and absolutely mundane and taken for granted. Occasionally it is remarkable and shocking; more often, it is easy and unemphatic in its omnipresence and attractiveness. Childhood lends itself both to spectacular presentation and to the sort of comforting and engaging routine imagery that attracts readers to a newspaper, or to *Parents* magazine, or to a hurriedly chosen postcard for a friend.

When urban dwellers look around themselves they see material phenomena – buildings, traffic and other people – and two-dimensional *reproductions* of material phenomena – *pictures* of buildings, traffic and other people. Many writers have argued that the persistence of this second world of images represents an unprecedented shift in human experience and modes of perception. The fact of being surrounded by – permeated by – imagery has radically changed the ways in which the world is perceived, and the ways in which individuals relate to each other. Jean Baudrillard called it an 'ecstasy of communication'. And this is not a system we can detach ourselves from or step outside, since its meanings touch our very sense of ourselves and our place in the world. In the following chapters I shall be tracing the presence of children in this image-world, specifically in relation to institutions – the family and the school – and to some of those ideologies which have attached themselves to childhood, playfulness, innocence, victimisation and bad behaviour. But first, in order to give a grounding to those discussions, I want to use this introduction to consider more closely the available imagery of childhood itself, and to lay out the ways in which I intend to approach it.

In this first section I shall be looking at the special nature of public available imagery, and at how it both creates conceptual meanings and carries a powerful emotional charge (its sense *and* its sensuality). My focus will be on imagery *in use*. In the second section I shall consider childhood in relation to those visual technologies which have characterised modernity and post-modernity – in particular photography and digital media; the first constructing a version of innocence, the second decisively undermining it. Finally I shall be considering contemporary fears around the concept of childhood itself, and its challenge to established boundaries between adults and children.

Contemporary imagery has a sort of double presence, in which the image is at the same time both ephemeral and persistent. Routine imagery is not designed to be looked at with particular attention. Its nature demands that it should be treated with careless disregard – caught sight of rather than stared at. Magazines, sweet wrappers, greetings cards are waste paper that is screwed up in the hand or discarded in the dustbin. Advertising hoardings are whisked past at car-speed or hurried by on foot with hardly a glance. The pictures on a website scroll swiftly past at the touch of a mouse. Yet, despite its disposability, the imagery has a curious continuity. Just as one picture is thrown away – a newspaper goes into the nearest bin, the packaging is torn off a new toy – another newspaper, more packaging, a new magazine, with similar if not identical pictures, will come instantly to hand. A specific picture may be half remembered, lingering in the mind as an impression only and difficult to find again once lost, yet many a key image remains as familiar as if it were always present. So, when we isolate a single birthday card or advertisement for critical comment, it can rarely bear the weight of the study. In any case, to select out a single picture changes the nature of the experience. How can one or even a dozen pictures represent that massive flow which permeates contemporary existence? I intend to consider public imagery as a total phenomenon, something that is made up not of singular, precious pictures, but of multiples in time and space. I am interested in those pictures which are duplicated thousands, if not millions, of times, and in the spread of imagery as it is repeated in many different contexts. I will be following certain *resonant* images as they circulate through the media, and observing the ways in which they mutate as they are reflected back and forth between newspapers and advertisements, from the pages of magazines to picture postcards, packaging, wrapping paper and so on. Focusing on still imagery rather than moving pictures, I shall be drawing attention to key images, resonant images and sets of images.

Imagery in use

My discussion will be less concerned with the accuracy or otherwise of pictures of children than with their place in this handy universe of images. Pictures of children contribute to a set of narratives about childhood which are threaded through different cultural forms, drawing on every possible source to construct stories that become part of cultural competence. These stories without a single author explore the potent themes I am taking up in this book – family relationships, sexuality, nature, schooling and education, violence and the very limits of humanity itself. They organise patterns of expectation which sediment into a broader set of public meanings and become an active part of the mapping of social, political and emotional worlds. They make it possible for daily lives to continue and meaningful actions to be undertaken, as we half-consciously refer to them for guidance on behaviour and relationships. Viewers of the pictures become joint authors of the stories through the pleasures of recognition and re-use. Even the most personal forms of experience and the tales we tell about ourselves are partly shaped by public imagery and publicly available narratives. These pictures become our pictures, these stories our stories. This is imagery *in use*.

Much effort has been wasted in pointing to the gap between image and reality, or in arguing that representations are not accurate, or are stereotyped, or do not portray life as it is. But I shall not be looking for resemblances (as we would if looking at family photographs), since advertisements, greetings cards and the rest seldom represent real children in the real world. Instead, I will give an account of a more interactive approach, in which contemporary meanings are a way of responding to the modern environment. I do not plan to discuss a picture as a passive portrayal, but to see it as a contribution to an imagery which is always dynamic, in which meanings are created *between* an image and its makers and its users. I shall be asking who has the resources to produce these images? Who constructs their meanings? What sort of claim do they make to *authenticity* – to some sort of rooting in the realities of life (as opposed to being an accurate copy)? I shall be asking questions about the context within which a picture is circulated, and about the multitude of different ways in which it can be dealt with and interpreted by its viewers and handlers.

Above all, I shall be drawing attention to *images* rather than concentrating on individual *pictures*. I use 'image' in this context to refer to a repeated, generalised representation, which can be teased out of a sequence of pictures or traced across multiples of similar pictures which appear in different media. As they move between definite social contexts, individual pictures frequently float away from their origins to be re-used in a variety of different narratives. Advertisements imitate a family snap; a cherub is reproduced on wrapping paper and also appears on a Christmas card or is mocked in a cartoon. The 'family image' or the 'cherubic image' both have their own well-worked history to which each new context refers. My aim is to trace key images of children as they are made publicly available in this way, and become *resonant* images, repeatedly reflected through many different pictures.

Making sense

Public imagery is 'available' in two senses: its physical accessibility and its conceptual utility as a ready reference, making an easy contribution to the construction of contemporary thoughts and ideas. Pictures on a page linger as images in our minds, so that a mental construct such as that of 'childhood' is always partly visual. A resonant mental 'image' may generate new 'pictures' for our use. Within this system a familiar typology of childhood has evolved creating a cultural-image-bank – a sort of quick-access pictorial vocabulary. Key images emerge which resonate between the different media, condensing into them-selves the most emphatic of repeated meanings. These include the wide eyes of the appealing child; the crouched body of the abused child; the structured placing of the child within the family; the ambiguous sexuality of the pre-pubescent girl; the ignorant child in need of education; the playful child in the home and the violent boys on the streets. I will be exploring the ways in which some of these key images make sense in the following chapters.

Presentations of public imagery characteristically combine pictures and text, relying on the exchange of meanings between the two (I use the word 'present-ation' to refer to the overall combination of pictures and words in, for example, an advertisement, a newspaper page, or a birthday card). A single picture may be difficult to make sense of without language to direct its viewers towards a range of possible meanings (the caption on the news photograph, the punning slogan on the advertisement). But when a picture reflects one of the key images, it may also act to concretise and give substance to the meanings evoked by the words (of course those catalogue children are pleased with their new clothes – their smiles and their body language confirm it). The definiteness and visible presence of a picture may well appear to halt the slipperiness of language, to pull meanings together and bind them so that they appear natural and irresistible.

This imagery obsessively sorts and classifies, as if afraid of interpretations which might run out of control. With absolute conviction it stresses those visual indications which separate children from adults, work from play, happiness from unhappiness, appropriate from inappropriate appearance and behaviour. Sometimes pictures differentiate sharply between girls and boys; at other times the signifiers of age dominate those of gender. I shall be tracing their meanings through these contrasts and demarcations. I shall also be looking for inter-relationships between sets of pictures. As they cluster together, pictures gain meaning from their proximity to each other – the advertisements in a baby magazine influence the glossy features; the newspaper photograph of the child who has been abused gives rise to anxieties about the pert pre-teen in the catalogue. The significance of any single picture or visual representation is never complete, because it always refers to other pictures or other texts.

A proliferation of imagery does not mean a proliferation of sense. Instead of expanding meanings, the imagery frequently strives to fix and limit them. In the following chapters we will sometimes find a pictorial attempt to buttonhole the viewer, to pin them down, as it were, and trap them within a restricted field of meaning – 'school' is so often indicated by children in uniform with their hands raised that it is difficult to imagine in any other way; a group that contains a man, a woman and a couple of children is instantly read as a 'family', however they may be arranged within the frame. The exciting variety of the visual surface may well turn out to be a distraction from what is effectively an insistent repetition of the same conceptual message. Instead of allowing space for understanding to develop, all too often images appear to secure meanings within a structure of power which sets out to establish its own regimes of truth.

Yet meanings remain slippery things which can never be finally established. Pictures can always be recycled in a new context, and different individuals and social groups will set out to make sense of them in a variety of ways. Public imagery carries its meanings within a total environment – but the environment itself is always in flux. The imagery is an important part of *negotiations* around social meanings, continuously creating new versions of contentious concepts such as 'childhood'. This tension between the fixing of meanings and the potential for richness and ambiguity will be illustrated in the following chapters, as we observe the flexible manipulability of the image-vocabulary, and trace the changes that have occurred over the last decades.

Sensuality and spectacle

However, I do not want to be carried away by the semiotics of images and the construction of meanings; instead I intend to keep a balance between sense and sensuality. Whatever the conceptual meanings that engage the mind, there is always something more, which Roland Barthes described as an erotics of the text. Although Barthes was discussing literary texts, the point applies even more strongly to the visual, which enables a static moment to interrupt the eager flow of narrative and the incessant demands of understanding. Visual imagery gives us pause. It offers a time out, however short, from the onward movement of rational thought. The emotional charge can open up unpredictable vistas. It may be a moment of celebration, of unquestioning affirmation, or it may be a moment of hesitation and disturbance, allowing the otherwise inexpressible to be hinted at. The power of the visual may resist attempts to reduce it to verbal sense and can put pressure on understanding in ways that seem beyond language. Always offering something more, always reaching towards the unconscious, the work of the visual cannot easily be accounted for.

Pictures offer both reality and illusion. They are both more representational than language and more fantastic. A picture can pull a moment out from the passage of time and hold it static for our delight. It can offer us visions – of places we have never visited, people we will never meet, experiences we have only dreamt of, fantasies the more powerful for their seeming reality. Pictures act in what appear to be contradictory ways. Sometimes they seem like a window on the world, separating us from it, enabling us to observe and hence control it (and we will observe many ways in which the imagery of childhood is constructed as a way of controlling that difficult state). At other times they are more like a mirror in which we see ourselves reflected, so that we seem to become part of the scene in front of us. An anonymous child laughing on the front page of a toy catalogue may on some occasions seem like an indulgent view of our earlier selves, on others like an obstreperous son or daughter pushing their luck. (A cover of *The Parents' Guide* plays on this ambivalence, captioning a curly haired, wide-eyed cover-child 'Tantrums. How to keep your cool'.) In public pictures a 'model' – an abstract individual, pictured in an advertisement or a magazine spread, who represents no one in the real world – may serve very well for an ideal self, and help us imagine ourselves as we would love to be – part of that tanned family on the holiday beach, say, or the modern mother with the perfect baby, suave, competent and glamorous.

Most of the images I shall be discussing here are *desired* images. They are the images which viewers long to see, and which give back a sense of stimulation or well-being. Many writers have tried to enumerate or identify these intangible pleasures – Barthes's alphabetic list in *The Pleasure of the Text* is one attempt to grasp at the unsayable and ungraspable. Sergei Eisenstein wrote that he constructed his films as a 'montage of attractions', with each shot exhibiting a feature which will shock or amaze the audience, so that nothing is redundant. In one of her books on fairy stories, Marina Warner notes a Sanskrit critic who identified nine *rasas* which give power to a text. They are 'wonder, joy, sexual pleasure, pity, anguish, anger, terror, disgust and laughter'. In looking at the details of the spectacular presentation of pictures of children I shall be looking for their attractions, their *rasas* and their specific pleasures – even if they are forbidden images and the pleasures are guilty ones.

As we have seen, there is a sense in which pictures appear to pin down and concretise language. The powerful affirmative quality of a picture may pre-empt questioning and offer a positive assurance that accompanying words seem powerless to contradict. But in another sense they add an irreducible ambiguity. The appealing eyes and puckered mouths of the children in the baby magazines stir a different part of our consciousness. Conceptual meanings cannot be constructed without the repression of the inconvenient, the contradictory, and of that which is too disturbing. The spectacular allows such material to be *expressed*, without necessarily demanding to be *recognised*. It ensures that, even in their realist modes, pictures never merely reflect the material world. The imagery always draws on and nourishes the fantasy world of human longings. It mediates between memory and dreams. The nostalgia of imagery is part of the nostalgia each of us feels for a lost moment of satisfaction and a longing for a future of reconciliation and peace. This is a powerful theme in the imagery of childhood which we will be exploring in later chapters.

PART 2: THE INNOCENT EYE
AND THE CRISIS OF LOOKING

The innocent eye in search of the innocent subject

It is not possible to make sense of the contemporary imagery of childhood without looking back more than 150 years to the mid-nineteenth century, when the ideal of a protected childhood was taking hold amongst the newly prosperous middle classes. 'Childhood' was part of a more comfortable lifestyle based on an ideal of domesticity and privacy. In the newly built suburbs, middle-class children could be kept apart from the turbulent world of commerce and toil, and spending time with your children could become an enjoyable leisure activity. Such domestic pleasure would be all the greater if childish qualities denied to adults were actively cultivated in children. The moral purity campaigner Mary Whitehouse echoed a nineteenth-century spirit when she characterised the qualities of childhood as 'joy and guileless innocence'. Raymond Williams has pointed out that at any point in time there exist 'residual' cultural forms, which

Back of a *carte-de-visite*, London, 1901.

linger from a previous age and are concurrent with 'emergent' forms in which new styles develop. As we will see in the coming chapters, many contemporary attitudes and expectations still refer back to that lingering nineteenth-century moment when the cult of childhood blossomed in literature and the visual media. John Tenniel's illustrations for Carroll's *Alice in Wonderland* and *Through the Looking Glass*; John Everett Millais's *Cherry Ripe*, the most reproduced painting of the nineteenth century; Little Lord Fauntleroy in his velvet suit and lacy collar; Julia Margaret Cameron's misty photographs of cherubic infants all continue to carry a powerful visual reference as the quintessence of childhood.

It was a time when the new technology of photography was becoming ever more accessible. The ability to record with an apparently unmediated accuracy developed in parallel with the cultivation of a romantic sensibility, which rejected the ugliness and functionality of industrialisation. Both were visible in attitudes to children and childhood – a new rationalism, which set out to record and improve children's objective conditions, and a romantic notion of childhood as a holy state, undistorted by contact with adult sexuality or commerce. The claims made by the photographic image to innocence, authenticity and simplicity paralleled the establishment of innocence as a quality of childhood. Julia Margaret Cameron and Oscar Rejlander both made allegorical pictures showing 'photography' as an infant art. High-street photographers decorated the backs of their portrait cards with chubby cherubs, sometimes, as in Rejlander's *Infant Photography*, wielding an artist's brush, demonstrating the continuity between photography and painting, at other times operating a camera themselves.

'Unlike adults, children face the camera innocent of all but the present moment, and often with a striking purity of motive,' wrote Susan Kismaric, curator of a 1980s exhibition at the New York Museum of Art. Just as the innocent camera asserts the right to record things 'as they are', regardless of the subject's wishes, 'innocent' subjects are those who make no attempt to shape their own image. They relinquish control not only to the photographer, but also to the technical and industrial structures that determine what type of photography is possible. Given this unequal relationship, it is hardly surprising that children, the least powerful of all social groups, have made ideal subjects. All too often, the adult gaze seeks to put children in their place and to conform their image to expected patterns. The look is a dual one of power and pleasure: the power which comes from adults' superior knowledge of their subject, the pleasure of the beauty and seductiveness of childhood. Subject to an adult gaze, children must accept that power and grant that pleasure. They must allow their 'innocence' to shine through. But, as it will become clear throughout this book, the innocence of the child and that of the photographic image have proved equally deceptive.

Exploiting innocence?

Photography and photographic technologies brought a new precision to documentation, while the amazing accuracy of the photographic record changed the ways in which memory and observation could operate. In the words of a Nikon advertisement, we could now 'make today's moments tomorrow's memories', and family albums could preserve a visible trace of earlier generations. But that same nineteenth-century moment brought other, less intimate changes to the ways in which the world is perceived. In this respect technology was brash and commercial rather than pure and innocent. The nineteenth century already had a thriving market in prints, especially copies of popular paintings made from engravings or woodcuts, but photographic technologies provided the means by which image-making could become a modern industry. Many different types of pictures could now become cheaply available for commerce and entertainment. The mass culture that is a central feature of the modern world would be unthinkable without the industrialised production of photographic images.

Even before the coming of such twentieth-century phenomena as the snapshot, the paparazzi and the glossy consumer magazine, photography was an unashamedly populist medium. It brought a multitude of small, accessible amusements, which appealed beyond the ranks of the respectable middle classes. Photographic cards showing celebrities were mass-produced from the 1860s for collecting in albums or giving to friends. A picture of Queen Victoria's daughter-in-law, the Princess of Wales – the Princess Diana of her day – carrying one of her children piggyback, was amongst the most popular, selling over 500,000 copies. The aim was instant appeal, and, of course, children were the most appealing of all.

This imagery of easy access and undemanding format outraged the modernists of the first half of the twentieth century. Pictures which were reproductions, mass-produced and appreciated purely for pleasure brought condemnation from intellectuals as fake art, debased taste or kitsch. Widely distributed popular art needed to be 'pretty and elegant' according to Alexis de Tocqueville, who first described the phenomenon in America in the 1830s. And 'pretty and elegant' pictures of children continued to enjoy a huge popularity, ranging from reproductions of paintings (Millais's doe-eyed and frilly-bonneted *Cherry Ripe*) to

Photographic postcard, Lisbon, 1920.

carefully staged picture postcards like the one I bought in a Lisbon junk shop, showing an 'angel' with feathery wings watching over a child doing her best to ignore the photographer and pretending to be asleep. Matei Calinescu describes kitsch as 'efficient' art and as 'hedonistic': an art that easily produces its effects of sentiment and pleasure. 'Beauty', he notes, 'turns out to be rather easy to fabricate'. For the critics of kitsch, adherence to an austere artistic modernism meant rejecting that other more pervasive form of modernity, the democratic modernity of mass availability and popular appeal. Kitsch art, including popular pictures of children, was a form of visual pleasure which could easily slide into a working-class front parlour. Kitsch combined brash vulgarity with what some saw as the embarrassing pretentiousness of the aspirant classes. But hedonistic pictures of children could be seen as containing elements of the rational as well as the romantic. They were one way of expressing a longing for a better world, and part of a more indulgent attitude towards real-life children. Shorter working hours and increasing prosperity meant that by the last decades of the nineteenth century a greater proportion of the population of Western nations had time for recreations that were previously confined to the middle classes – and more time for their children. Kitsch was both a central aspect of modernity and part of the widening cult of domesticity which put children at its centre.

But the decisive development in the commercialisation of public imagery was the development of an advertising industry serving an economy increasingly based on mass consumption. The proliferation of public promotional images went hand in hand with the expansion of the private domestic realm as a site of consumption. Advertisers, publicists and marketing companies soon became the prime producers and distributors of pictures, anxious to latch on to, and also to exaggerate, the tastes of the era. In the 1890s the Pears Company bought the reproduction rights to *Cherry Ripe*, while another of Millais's hugely popular child paintings, the ethereal *Bubbles* (originally entitled *A Child's World*), was used to advertise that important domestic convenience – soap. The image of innocence was an eminently exploitable commodity. It could be associated with cleanliness and purity, and could contribute to the new marketing technique of branding. Promotional culture meant that viewing an image now required increased sophistication. The viewer must learn to separate the attractive content (sweet child) and the promotional message (buy this soap). It was becoming difficult to take any picture simply at its face value; the seeds of cynicism and irony had been planted.

Photography, digital imaging and the crisis of looking

A set of residual images which hark back to the nineteenth century linger as a backdrop to the dominant imagery of the twenty-first century. But the romantic cult of innocence has given way to an anxiety about childhood corruption which verges on the hysterical, while the rational investigation of children's lives across the globe daily reveals conditions which are often degrading and deeply shocking. 'Childhood' is valued, possibly more than ever before, but it is perceived to be either in crisis or dying.

In the photographic media, too, any residual claims to innocence have finally disappeared as digital technologies reinforce a view long argued by critics, that no picture is independent of human intention. Kitsch has been replaced by irony, 'bad taste' by camp cultivation of bad taste, romanticism by nostalgia, and there is an acute awareness of the sales pitch behind every commercial image, however engaging. While the fantasy of a carefree and appealing childhood continues to generate a rich and gratifying body of hedonistic imagery, the image has become a playful one, exploiting the contemporary delight in pastiche, uninterested in accurate representation and unashamed of digital manipulation. In later chapters we will be considering various ways in which digital technologies have transformed available imagery. In particular they have given increased control to the producers of a picture, since computer technologies make it possible to eliminate chance and to create a photographic image that is 'just right'. Computer-generated pictures may have no single referent in the world; they may be constructed from fragments, representing nothing but the buzzing and interrelation of many historical images. Faced with such intricate mechanisms of control, visually sophisticated viewers move between mistrust and cynicism – a crisis of looking. However convincing a picture, there is either a fear of being taken in by its deceptive techniques or a conviction that anything can be enjoyed – whatever the content – since nothing refers beyond itself.

Paradoxically, at the same time, particularly in press photography, there has been a renewed drive towards documentary realism. Possibly as a reaction to this digital instability, there is an urge to get *behind* this too-perfect image, backed up by a continued conviction that photography really *can* probe and record actual conditions, and *can* reveal the ways in which the lives of real children fall short of the ideal. There are ways in which a photograph still attaches itself to the world in ways that are unmatched by any other visual medium. A photograph of a child, however manipulated, however artfully formed, means that at some point in time a real child was in front of the camera. So when pornographic photographs of children are distributed via the Internet, the fact that their distribution is via digital technology does not detract from public outrage. The public is convinced that these pictured abuses really happened. In investigating child pornography, police officers have said that they are not considering an image, but evidence of a crime. It is still possible to look at a photograph in this literal way, to peer *through* the picture, as if through a window, to see the pictured child.

The nineteenth-century rationalist legacy of scientific observation which photographic techniques made possible (possibly best exemplified by Charles Darwin's photographic cataloguing of the human emotions, and his minute daily observations of his own child) has been pushed even further by the technologies of the twentieth and twenty-first centuries. The most mundane of minute-by-minute moments of everyday life can be recorded on CCTV, or with concealed cameras or by night imaging. Children's behaviour and their interaction with their parents is scrutinised as never before – and made publicly available on television or in the newspapers. The drive for objective scientific knowledge has dissolved the boundaries of the human body and recorded the earliest moments of conception and foetal development. Improved X-ray techniques and magnetic resonance imaging have made bodily structures and internal damage visible. 'Science' has renewed its nineteenth-century claims.

In the meanwhile, children have begun to take the initiative for themselves. In striking contrast to those 'pretty and elegant' children who passively presented themselves to be looked at, concerns now centre on children's own looking. Television, video, the Internet and other unpredictible digital technologies have all been described as a corrupting influence. The worries have increased as screen media have become ever more accessible and, above all, interactive. Children may appear immobile in front of the small screen (risking 'mouse elbow' and 'video eyes' according to one report), but the fear is that their activity may be intense. Perhaps the Internet is putting them in touch with a huge network of unknown influences beyond adult supervision, or perhaps, with fingers on the games console, they are effectively entering a violent three-dimensional world which responds to their actions. The identity of a far-from-innocent twenty-first-century child seems to merge with those strange luminous identities created on the screen.

Every public picture is directed at a specific audience and carries an expectation of who its viewers will be. The space in front of the picture frame – whether on a screen or a printed page – was originally occupied by the picture-*maker* – photographer, artist, web designer, advertiser – and is designed for occupation by the picture-*viewer*, who may be projected in a variety of different roles: as caring parent, censorious critic, charitable donor, anxious teacher, eager consumer – or even a child. A complex structure of looking is brought to any picture, whatever technology has been used to construct it, which always involves doubts, judgements and uncertainties about the status of the image and about its subject. It may well leave little room for manoeuvre by those subjects – particularly when they are children.

PART 3: CHEATED OF CHILDHOOD?

Blurring the boundaries

As I flick through my collection of news cuttings, a glance at the headlines demonstrates the concern that children's 'childhood' can all too easily be taken from them. 'The end of childhood?' signalled 'parents' hopes and fears for the schools revolution'; 'Give children the chance of being children' headed a letter about upbringing; 'The corporatisation of childhood' was an article on consumerism; 'So old and yet so young, pity our lost children', on teenage parents; 'Let our kids enjoy childhood' introduced a speech in which 'the world of TV, media and the pop music industry were blamed for conniving in the encouragement of a premature pseudo-sophistication which cut short the span of a child's innocence that could never be retrieved'; and the first article by Rowan Williams, after his appointment as Archbishop of Canterbury, was headed 'The loss of childhood: why we must preserve innocence'.

When the categories of childhood and adulthood are confused, it seems, disaster ensues. Those who 'blur the boundary...may be cheating children of childhood itself,' wrote Mary Whitehouse. 'In failing to treasure our children's childhood we are destroying not only their future but our own. We are like lemmings. We've got a death wish on us.' In the games played with the public image, this death wish is both challenged and kept at bay. In the following chapters we will be observing some different contexts within which the boundaries between 'adult' and 'child' are constantly challenged and re-negotiated.

One consequence of firm boundary maintenance is to create a childhood which is not only different from adulthood, but is also its obverse. In this view, childhood should be everything adulthood is not: children are powerless and dependent on adults; they are without knowledge and need to be educated; economic and sexual activity is prohibited for them – and so on. Yet these negative definitions allow abstract 'childhood' to become a depository for many precious qualities that 'adulthood' needs but which are incompatible with adult status; qualities such as impulsiveness, playfulness, emotional expressiveness, indulgence in fantasy, sexual innocence. Hence the dichotomy child/adult parallels other dichotomies which have characterised Western discourse: nature/culture, primitive/civilised, emotion/reason. In each pair the dominant term seeks to understand and control the subordinate, keeping it separate but using it for its own enrichment.

The child in the picture opens a door to a libidinous existence, a life without constraints, a life of possibilities now forbidden. When children accompany adults in a picture, it is they who display what Barthes described as 'euphoric values'. Their expressiveness invites a reciprocal expressiveness from adults who look at them. They are a signal for a release of emotions. But together with ecstatic fulfilment comes the threat of total disruption. Childhood poses a challenge to the hard-won stability of adulthood. From the engaging innocents in the baby books to the clued-up kids of contemporary advertising, behind many an attractive picture of a child lies the desire to use childhood to secure the status of adulthood – all too frequently at the expense of children themselves.

One argument developed throughout this book will be that the uses of public imagery are part of a continuous adult effort to gain control over childhood and its implications – both over actual children and over a personal childhood which adults must constantly mourn and constantly reinvent. The effort that goes into negotiating the difficult distinction between adult and child is both social and psychical. The interplay between the two dimensions means that adult dominance over children is likely to be accompanied by a particular pleasure of achievement, since it also implies gaining control over one's *own* persistent and troublesome childhood. Children bear the burden of a nostalgia for a remembered childish, impulsive self – an ambivalent nostalgia which becomes clear in the recurring moral panics around the potential uncontrollability of real children. Crises of childhood usually turn out to be crises which are all too adult.

Ultimately, childhood cannot be contained, the boundaries will not hold. The relationship between childhood and adulthood is not a dichotomy but a variety of fluctuating states, constantly under negotiation. The presence of a child – with its potential for blurring boundaries and confusing meanings – can all too easily upset an adult search for stability. While pictures remind us that childhood is never fully left behind, we are also reminded that adults' inner childhood is nothing like these delightful images. Wishful desire is balanced against realistic disappointment. To quieten the anxiety, the image continues to be smoothed over and beautified. For all its modernisation, the imagery of childhood retains a powerful nostalgia, which refers to a harmonious and comfortable world before industrial civilisation, when plenty did not depend on work or wealth. In a set of images which will recur throughout the book, we will find a rural idyll still celebrated on milk cartons, bread wrappers, supermarket labels, advertisements for foodstuffs and in high-gloss magazines about country living. We will find a domesticated nature which provides for the needs of culture – where civilisation is firmly in control. Imagery made possible by the most highly developed technology re-creates pre-technological values, scarring over the wounds. In the constant renewal of childhood, this lost harmonious past remains forever present and promises a future in which innocence may be regained; in a world dominated by commercial imagery, a child claims to be outside commerce; in a world of rapid change, a child can be shown as unchanging; in a world of social and political conflict, a child may be damaged but remains untainted.

But as the image of a child promises a richer world, in the same moment it threatens the security of the world we have. Children introduce disorder and pollution into a comfortable everyday life, and this theme runs alongside the idyllic beauty of childhood. The bodies of young children are leaky; they do not respect established boundaries. They wet the bed, spew up their food, have no respect for tidy kitchens or hoovered carpets. They roll in mud, have uncontrollable tantrums, cover themselves in paint and bloody their hands and knees in falls and fights. Even worse, they spill out onto the streets, where their behaviour is threatening and sometimes dangerous. We will be looking more closely at a powerful set of public narratives which speaks of little monsters, threatening their parents, refusing all constraints and calling for extremes of punishment and control. Consumer imagery of mini-gangsters and precocious temptresses plays with the danger, taunting it, keeping it at bay. But when the paradoxes of the 'natural' are replaced by the paradoxes of civilisation, when children move beyond constraint and surveillance and run together in the urban streets, the fear is genuine. This is where we will find the terrifying image of youth, of children alone together beyond the reach of family or school, sufficient in each other's company. Such an image creates a mythological conflict between spontaneity and control.

At some points, in posing questions about rationality and order, the image is able to leave aside the distinction between child and adult, and scrutinise the margins of humanity itself. Misbehaving children are compared to animals or said to be close to madness. They may be described as inexplicably evil. By persistently drawing attention to the boundary between the natural and the human, and throwing up questions about the legitimacy of control, the presence of a child holds the potential to throw adult civilisation itself into question.

Creating a child-shaped space

Turning from the psychical to the social and historical dimensions of the relations between children and adults, it becomes clear that definitions of 'childhood' have been constructed and maintained through a firm *institutional* separation from the adult world. From the turn of the twentieth century, as a protected childhood gradually became possible for almost all children in the prosperous West, children were gradually expelled from public spaces, where they had had a raucous independent presence, and confined to spaces designed especially for them. Compulsory education in purpose-built schools came to occupy their days; homes became increasingly child-centred as the domestic ideal spread throughout the population; an enlarged state intervened more actively in their welfare, and provided health care in clinics and hospitals. The public imagery of childhood discussed in this book has been institution-based, and, in turn, the physical spaces of the institutions have been affected by the prevalent image of childhood. As specially designed locations – schools, nurseries, adventure playgrounds – have been created, the layout and equipment provided, together with the codes of behaviour deemed suitable, have also indicated a *conceptual* space and suggested a particular view of childish lives. The institutions of childhood have established a set of overlapping but socially workable definitions. As we will see, the imagery which accompanies them frequently seems more concerned with the construction of a suitably child-shaped space than with the individuality of the child who is slotted into it. A child-shaped space may be resented by real-life children who resist being squeezed into a mould, but children's lives are inevitably constituted in interaction with the expectations created.

Imagery may well aspire to an abstract universal concept of childhood, but it is inevitably placed within a specific historical moment, and itself contributes to political and social contestation. An institutionally based image of childhood, central to a rational, modernist, structured society had its apogee in the mid-twentieth century, but it was increasingly challenged by a more fluid and subversive set of images. As we have seen, by the end of the century the most fertile source of public imagery of children was produced as a necessary part of a prosperous consumer-based economy. The ecstatic smiles of the children who sell toy animals, talking dolls, plastic building bricks, designer baby clothes, party gear, breakfast cereals, illustrated books, bouncy castles, miniature cars and dumper trucks, Barbie tricycles, soft drinks, video games, dressing-up sets, fairy wings, trainers that flash with coloured lights, Pingu videos and the rest of the exotic

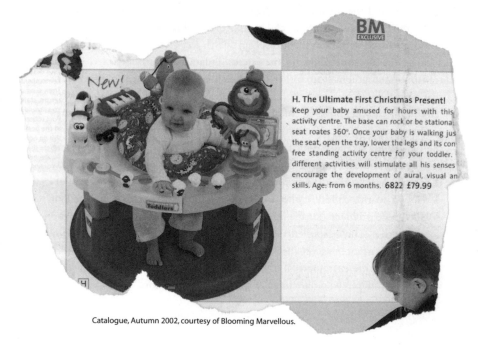

Catalogue, Autumn 2002, courtesy of Blooming Marvellous.

paraphernalia of contemporary childhood are familiar from display advertisements, catalogues, supermarket posters, flyers, mail-order brochures, pop-up ads on websites and a mass of other promotional outlets. And, of course, children feature prominently in advertisements for cars, household goods, computers and innumerable other products intended for adult use. The commercial image follows its own laws and acknowledges no limits beyond itself. It envisages a blissful world of plenty in which pictures of children are commodities which enhance the desirability of other commodities, and in which children are increasingly targeted as consumers with money to spend. At points the children themselves seem lost amongst their possessions. With its prosperity, its resources and its unashamed hedonism, the consumer image has invaded the institutional spaces of schools, hospitals and welfare advice as well as expanding the possibilities of childish play, fashion, food and other pleasures. At points it even seems to have achieved the impossible task of preserving free-flowing, libidinous, childish values throughout adulthood.

But the gap between wishful desire and realistic disappointment has intensified. While the consumer image has become ever more euphoric, in stark contrast the image of a child suffering from harsh conditions or damaged at the hands of adults has been pushed into public consciousness through the national press. The new realism in photojournalism has highlighted children who have moved beyond the institutions designed for them – children sleeping rough, drug abuse amongst children, children as the victims of physical and sexual abuse (pictured with their identities concealed), and violent youngsters posing a danger in the streets and on the estates. Enhanced ability to travel and to transmit photographs from hitherto inaccessible parts of the world have meant that major disasters across the world have become painfully visible. In wars, famines or extreme poverty, children have been the first to suffer, and pictures of emaciated children close to death have become the symbols through which the magnitude of those disasters have penetrated Western media. This group of suffering children are not placed within a neat institutional context, nor are they of any use to the driving forces of commerce. Children from the underdeveloped world, children who are poor, children who are sick, harmed or disabled pose problems for the dominant image, yet they are, in a curious way, necessary to it. Their experience means that they cannot be the bearers of joy and guileless innocence, yet their weakness is an essential part of childhood. They are extreme exemplars of children's dependent status. They stand as a warning to children who dare to resist their childish position.

Behind the childhood masquerade

The imagery of children/childhood is part of an elaborate drama in which children perform well-known roles. Girl children in particular are expected to present themselves as an image, and to learn a special sort of exhibitionism in order to act out the charming 'childish' qualities adults long to see. Refusal to co-operate – grumpy behaviour, rudeness to adults – may well invite punishment and a forced return to childishness in tears and humiliation. The child models who people advertisements are experts in this role, but they are treading on delicate ground. Children are in a double bind. When they knowingly invite the adult gaze, when their beauty is no longer self-absorbed, and when they deliberately put themselves on display, the result is a loss of innocence and of childishness itself. Engaging in a tactful masquerade for the benefit of those who aim to control and enjoy them, the children in the advertisements may well pose the question who has the right to look and under what circumstances?

The image of childhood poses the problem of generations, of continuity and renewal. Children are expected to mature into the established patriarchal order, yet they stand as a threat to that order. Their challenge may be interpreted as an instability which must be repressed in the interests of civilisation, or it may be seen as a challenge in the name of a better society. Paul Goodman, whose *Growing up Absurd* was first published in 1956, is amongst many who have argued that 'childlike' values should permeate and improve society as a whole. Children would retain their 'right to wildness' and relations between children and adults would cease to be based on coercion and domination. But any right is meaningless if it is merely expressed by adults on behalf of children. The point when the popular concept of childhood breaks down is when it runs up against children's own expression. This is not because children's expressions have special qualities which differ from those of adults, but because they come from a radically different perspective with very little outlet in contemporary media. When spaces have been found for children's voices, they pose a very different challenge to the boundary between childhood and adulthood than the death wish envisaged by Mary Whitehouse.

Over history, children have been the objects of imagery, very rarely its makers. Their voices have had only limited access to the channels that produce public meanings, and even then the tools that are available to them have been inevitably honed by adults. Like all groups without power, they suffer the indignity of being unable to present themselves as they would want to be seen or, indeed, of even considering how they might want to be seen. Until very recently they have been defined as incapable of meaningful expression. They have not been in a position to manufacture a public image for themselves, and have had little control over the image others make of them. Children are, in the words of James and Prout, a 'muted group'. They may say of adults, as the great Caribbean writer Franz Fanon wrote of 'the white man', that he 'had woven me out of a thousand details, anecdotes, stories'. Without any input from children themselves, childhood can only remain an impossible concept, always mediated by adulthood, its 'guileless innocence' searched for but never found.

When children's voices are effective, adults' definitions are of necessity less rigid. They are not necessarily replaced by other definitions but by an approach that is sensitive to the ever-shifting perspectives of meaning. (The aid agency Save the Children concluded their guidelines for journalists and photographers with a picture of a boy with a video camera pointing back at the viewer.) In such a context an imagery of childhood can reach beyond the adult attempt to dominate and define. The boundaries are challenged, not in the name of rigidity and death, but of change, development, flexibility and life.

NOTES ON INTRODUCTION

p. 1   **The ecstasy of communication**: 'That's the ecstasy of communication: All secrets, spaces and scenes abolished in a single dimension of information', Jean Baudrillard in Hal Foster (ed.) (1985) *Postmodern Culture*, London: Pluto, p.131. **Henley Centre**: Nick Cohen, 'Class struggle', *Observer*, 9 September 2001.

p. 2   **imagery *in use***: in a similar spirit Sarah Kember focuses on the 'social and psychological investment' in the new technologies she discusses in *Virtual Anxiety*, Manchester: Manchester University Press, 1998.

p. 4   **images in our minds**: see W.J.T Mitchell (1986) *Iconology: Image, Text, Ideology*, Chicago: University of Chicago Press, Chapter 1, 'What is an image?'.

p. 5   **A single picture may be difficult to make sense of**: Roland Barthes wrote of press photographs, 'the text loads the image, burdening it with a culture, a moral, an imagination'. Writing of advertising photography, he notes two functions of the linguistic message in relation to the iconic (representational) message, that of 'anchorage' and that of 'relay'. Roland Barthes (1977) *Image, Music, Text*, trans. Stephen Heath, London: Fontana, pp.26, 38. Victor Burgin expanded on the point: 'Visual and non-visual codes interpenetrate each other in very extensive and complex ways', Victor Burgin (ed.) (1982) *Thinking Photography*, London: Macmillan, p.83.
obsessively sorts and classifies: Mary Douglas (1966) *Purity and Danger: an Analysis of the Concepts of Pollution and Taboo*, London: Routledge & Kegan Paul, on the cultural significance of the classification process, in which things out of place are perceived as 'dirt'.

p. 6   **semiotics of images**: Umberto Eco (1977) *A Theory of Semiotics*, London: Macmillan; Mitchell (1986) above.
an erotics of the text: Roland Barthes (1976) *The Pleasure of the Text*, trans. Richard Miller, London: Jonathan Cape.

p. 7   *The Parents' Guide*: May–June 2001.

'**montage of attractions**': Sergei Eisenstein (1943/1986) *The Film Sense*, trans. Jay Leyda, London: Faber and Faber, pp.181–83.

Marina Warner: (1998) *No Go the Bogeyman: Scaring, Lulling and Making Mock*, London: Chatto and Windus, p.7.

p.8   **an ideal of domesticity and privacy**: Leonore Davidoff and Catherine Hall (1976) 'The charmed circle of home', in J. Mitchell and A. Oakley (eds) *The Rights and Wrongs of Women*, Harmondsworth: Penguin; F.M.L. Thompson (ed.) (1990) *The Cambridge Social History of Britain 1750–1850*, Vol. 2, *People and their Environment*, Cambridge: Cambridge University Press; Witold Rybczynski (1986) *Home*, London: Penguin.

'**joy and guileless innocence**': Mary Whitehouse, 'Today's children are deprived – of their childhood', *Daily Express*, 1970s.

Raymond Williams: (1981) *Culture*, London: Fontana, p.204.

p.9   **John Tenniel's illustrations**: these examples and the nineteenth-century visual image of childhood are discussed by Anne Higonnet (1998) *Pictures of Innocence: the History and Crisis of Ideal Childhood*, London: Thames and Hudson; for the literary image, see Peter Coveney (1967) *The Image of Childhood*, Harmondsworth: Peregrine; Jackie Wullschlager (revised 2001) *Inventing Wonderland: the Lives of Lewis Carroll, Edward Lear, J.M. Barrie, Kenneth Grahame and A.A. Milne*, London: Methuen, Chapter 1.

Rejlander's *Infant Photography*: (1856) and Cameron's *Cupid's Pencil of Light* (1870) are discussed by Lindsay Smith in *The Politics of Focus: Women, Children and Nineteenth Century Photography*, Manchester: Manchester University Press, 1998, p.88–92.

p.10   **the ways in which memory and observation could operate**: Jonathan Crary (1990) *Techniques of the Observer: on Vision and Modernity in the 19th century*, London: MIT Press; John Tagg (1988) *The Burden of Representation*, London: Macmillan; Walter Benjamin (1936) 'The work of art in the age of mechanical reproduction', in Hannah Arendt (ed.) (1999) *Illuminations*, London: Pimlico.

Photographic cards showing celebrities were mass-produced: Audrey Linkman (1993) *The Victorians: Photographic Portraits*, London: Tauris Parke. The Princess of Wales with her baby is on p.68.

p.11   **picture postcards**: became possible with the introduction of the postage stamp and the development of printing techniques. They first went on sale in the 1870s and gained huge popularity from the 1890s. Martin Willoughby (1992) *A History of Postcards*, London: Studio Editions.

rather easy to fabricate: quoted by Matei Calinescu (1987) *Five Faces of Modernity*, Durham, US: Duke University Press, p.230.

p.12   ***Bubbles***: see p.196. The picture was sold to the Pears Company in 1886 for £2200. In the age of high colonialism, soap also signified 'whiteness'. Anne McLintock (1995) describes Pears' promotion as 'commodity racism': 'Soft-soaping Empire: commodity racism and imperial advertising', in *Imperial Leather: Race, Gender and Sexuality in the Colonial Conquest*, London: Routledge.

either in crisis or dying: Phil Scraton (ed.) (1997) *Childhood in Crisis*, London: UCL Press; Neil Postman (1983) *The Disappearance of Childhood*, London: W.H. Allen; David Buckingham (2000) *After the Death of Childhood: Growing up in the Age of Electronic Media*, Cambridge: Polity, Chapter 2.

digital technologies reinforce a view: Martin Lister (ed.) (1995) *The Photographic Image in Digital Culture*, London: Routledge.

p.13   **In investigating child pornography**: see Chapter 7 for a further discussion of this point.

Charles Darwin: 'My first child was born on December 27th 1839 and I at once commenced to make notes on the first dawn of the various expressions which he exhibited'. Darwin's observations were published as 'Biographical sketch of an infant', in *Mind*, 1877. See Christina Hardyment (1993) *Dream Babies: Childcare from Locke to Spock*, London: Jonathan Cape, pp.104–5.

CCTV: see Chapter 5 for a further discussion of the James Bulger case. Also Kember (1998) above, Chapter 3. She discusses magnetic resonance imaging in Chapter 4.

their interaction with their parents is scrutinised: in television programmes such as Professor Robert Winston's *Child of Our Time*, which follows children born in the year 2000 (BBC 2000, 2001, 2002).

p.14 **'mouse elbow' and 'video eyes'**: a report from the medical journal *Paediatrics International*, quoted in *Independent*, 17 February 2002. Photograph: John Lawrence. See Buckingham (2000) above.

'The end of childhood?': *Guardian* 'Education', 29 February 2000.

Give children the chance: *Metro*, 6 December 2000.

'The corporatisation of childhood': Deborah Orr, *Independent*, 2 November 1999.

'So old and yet so young': *Express on Sunday*, 24 August 1997.

p.15 **'Let our kids enjoy childhood'**: *Westminster Record*, June 2002.

Rowan Williams: *Times*, 23 July 2002.

primitive/civilised, emotion/reason: Richard Appignesi, 'Some thoughts on Freud's discovery of childhood', in Martin Hoyles (ed.) (1979) *Changing Childhood*, London: Writers and Readers.

'euphoric values': Roland Barthes (1977) 'Rhetoric of the image', in Barthes (1977) above, p.34.

p.16 **Wishful desire is balanced against realistic disappointment**: Adam Phillips (1998) *The Beast in the Nursery*, London: Faber and Faber, p.3.

p.17 **little monsters**: Marina Warner (1994) *Managing Monsters*, London: Vintage. See Chapter 5 for a further discussion of 'bad' children and the image of youth.

they had had a raucous independent presence: James Walvin (1982) *A Child's World: Social History of English Childhood 1800–1914*, Harmondsworth: Pelican; Hugh Cunningham (1991) *Children of the Poor*, Oxford: Blackwell; Anna Davin (1996) *Growing Up Poor*, London: Rivers Oram.

confined to spaces designed especially for them: Allison James, Chris Jenks and Alan Prout (1998) *Theorising Childhood*, Cambridge: Polity, Chapter 3, 'Childhood in social space'; Douglas (1966) above; Michel Foucault (1977) *Discipline and Punish*, London: Allen Lane. See also the dispute over the layout of primary classrooms discussed in Chapter 3.

p.20 **Paul Goodman**: (1956) *Growing up Absurd*, New York: Random House.

When spaces have been found for children's voices: Bob Franklin (ed.) (2002) *The New Handbook of Children's Rights: Comparative Policy and Practice*, London: Routledge.

p.21 **'muted group'**: Allison James and Alan Prout (eds) (1990) *Constructing and Re-constructing Childhood: Contemporary Issues in the Sociological Study of Childhood*, London: Falmer, p.7.

a thousand details, anecdotes, stories: Franz Fanon (1952/1970) *Black Skin, White Masks*, London: Paladin, p.79.

Save the Children: *Focus on Images*, 1991. See Chapter 6 and p.206.

'Tea for two', greetings card, USA, 2000. Photograph © Valerie Tabor Smith, used with permission of Art Impressions, Inc.

1

There's no such thing as a baby
... or is there?

Hedonistic babies: kitsch and taboo

Babies are probably the last group of children whose image may be enjoyed
without guilt for their purely sensual pleasure. A huge amount of money, time
and effort goes into producing luscious, luminous pictures, widely distributed
and desired by many. Yet the contemporary image of babyhood does not speak
of nature, but of sophistication and artifice.

'When I first put a baby in a flower pot I thought, "isn't that just divine.
Just look at them!"' says photographer Anne Geddes. Her colour-saturated
greetings cards show quaint babies and sugary-sweet babies, naked babies and
babies in fantastic costumes. Here's one on a bed of roses; here's another
curled up asleep, wearing cherubic wings, apparently part of a statue; here are
three chubby infants peeping out of a nest like newly hatched chicks. In one
of her most popular pictures no less than one hundred babies peer out of
terracotta flower pots, their fleshy pinkness reflecting the earthy pinkness of
the pots. Frequently the faces show blank astonishment, and the effectiveness
of an image depends on their cuddly helplessness. Anne Geddes's work is
prolific and her inventiveness is endless, but she is not the only contemporary
photographer who has dragged babies into the realms of the bizarre and
grotesque. Despite the softness of babyhood, many contemporary pictures are
hard-edged. Their carefully controlled effects stand as a tribute to present-day
knowingness and cynicism. My postcard collection includes babies in
sunglasses, babies dressed up as adults, babies whose captured expressions
provoke adult laughter, as well as sugary-sweet babies decked out with wings

and surrounded by flowers. In this manipulated world, sentiment and whimsy is frequently tinged with irony.

Yet, walking the streets, city-dwellers may raise their eyes just a bit above the level of the crowds and traffic jams and enjoy the sight of many babies from an earlier era whose sensuality is less self-conscious. These babies embellish statues of dignitaries and decorate the facades of important buildings. With plump little stomachs and unashamed nakedness they support medallions, nuzzle up to the curving stonework and romp across decorative friezes. Their irreverence softens the formality of public spaces. Some of them have wickedly impish faces, reminding us of the Victorian cult of goblins and fairies, of paintings by Richard Dadd, illustrations by Arthur Rackham and Christina Rossetti's eerie poem 'Goblin Market'. Even though they are made of stone, these babies are warmly associated with bodily pleasures. They are placed amongst swags of foliage, grapes, curling acanthus leaves and other reminders of natural abundance. Classical themes evoke sunshine, relaxation, good food and endless playfulness, as if the dignified architecture of civic pride has met up with the era of the Mediterranean holiday.

The addition of wings raises to mythological status creatures who might otherwise seem too cuddly and domestic. Wings confirm the place of babies in the dignified history of Art with a capital 'A'. From the Renaissance to the nineteenth century, putti, cherubs and other mythological babies have acted as fleshy and secular observers to the painted as well as the sculpted drama, distanced from the gutsy activities of the adults, they puff across the sky in a cloud or gather in clusters in the corner of a canvas. Of course, classical art also turned loveable babies into the mischievously sexual Eros and the more domesticated Cupid, aiming at vulnerable lovers with bow and quiver. The similarity of Eros to the holy cherub has provided a visual vocabulary which keeps sexuality hovering on the borders of consciousness. When a mythological baby is carved or painted it can be given an adult knowingness and facial expressions difficult to achieve with photography. These mythological babies have a virile independence, with no apparent need for parenting or protection.

Pictures of babies continue to provide an excuse for what Phillipe Aries was happy to call 'ornamental nudity', and the energetic image of babyhood which dignifies public life has long been a resource for popular image-making. As technological developments enabled the mass distribution of prints and postcards, celebrated works gained notoriety through multiple reproductions, and baby pictures became an indispensable part of kitsch modernity. From Victorian lacy greetings cards and prints in illustrated magazines to twenty-first-century Christmas cards, the image of a quasi-mythological baby has been part of everyday enjoyment. The tourist and heritage industries have taken up the task with enthusiasm. The Victoria and Albert Museum greeted the millennium with a calendar for the year 2000 featuring cherubs lifted from classical and religious paintings, including Raphael's familiar pair from the base of the Sistine Madonna. Chin on hand, their expressions testify to a tolerant detachment from the curious eccentricities of the adult world. They have become some of the best-known pictured infants, reproduced and recreated many times over the years – from Oscar Rejlander's reconstruction made in 1857 (a copy was bought by Prince Albert), to a US postage stamp, and an irresistible 1995 television commercial for St Ivel baby and toddler yoghurt, 'pure enough for little angels'.

My collection of babies includes the curious, the nostalgic and the everyday: curiosities such as a photomontage published in 1880 which assembles fifty howling mouths and scrunched-up eyes, captioned 'Good night', and Douglas Tempest's suggestively captioned toddlers for comic seaside postcards in the 1920s. The nostalgic include Rose O'Neill's 'kewpie' – a saucer-eyed little thing, with chubby stomach, a pointed wisp of hair on top of its head and tiny blue wings just behind its neck – a hedonistic baby if ever there was one. Hovering between playful realism and complete fantasy, the kewpie was one of the earliest baby dolls to be mass produced. Amongst the everyday babies there are those who have sold products over the years, such as the Fairy Liquid infant who strides around the container with great assertiveness, despite his old-fashioned fluffy nappy. Packages such as Cow and Gate baby food and Johnson's baby powder are a testament to the long-standing importance of baby appeal to calculated marketing.

In Western countries at the beginning of the twentieth century, there was a notable gap between the hedonistic image and the lives of the vast majority of children. A move towards representations that were closer to everyday life was driven by the use of photography both as a record and a campaigning tool. Photographs from the 1910s and 1920s document mother-and-baby clinics and illustrate campaigns around mother and infant welfare. The babies in these pictures are frequently thin and sickly – less a chubby cherub than a creature with physical needs. By the beginning of the twenty-first century, the romantic and the realistic had come together to create a contemporary image in which glowing health and physical beauty are taken for granted. My contemporary pictures are as luscious and delectable as the cherubs from an earlier age, but are presented as real-life not fantasy babies, most of them pulled from the glossy pages of publications for parents. The glorious colour and the comfortable lifestyle they evoke is balanced by practical advice on problems such as sleepless nights and teething. These are *consuming* babies, their image directed at parents for whom there appears a real possibility that reality may match the ideal.

Hedonistic babies have cheerfully addressed a diverse audience. Decorative infants such as Anne Geddes's fantasies, architectural stone babies and Raphael's reproduced cherubs are designed to give pleasure to all who make use of public spaces. But consumer pictures are more precisely directed and more individually based. They carry powerful messages about the social positioning of babyhood, about the nature of the home, and above all about those who are expected to care for babies, in particular their mothers. Unlike the image of the ornamental cherub, contemporary babyhood is rarely imagined as resilient and independent.

Balancing between the public and the private, the imagery of babyhood runs straight up against major questions about the limits of human life itself. Babies may be central to the image of a domestic haven, but they bring a hint of insecurity to this very safe place with their nakedness, their closeness to the unspeakable moments of life and death, and their ability to drag humanity away from civilisation and back to the earthy reality of bodily functions. In the photographic image, nakedness has itself become suspect, vulnerability more obvious, and the possibility of exploitation only too real. Hedonism and kitsch have come up against the electric atmosphere of taboo, in a strange overlap between pleasures and fears. Political dramas and moral dilemmas around conception, pregnancy and birth run as a disturbing undertow to the long-standing image of babyhood designed purely for pleasure.

Making babies: the unborn

Photographic technology has revolutionised the concept of the beginning of life by providing a visual image of a human creature from the very moment of conception. The records in the family album now begin before birth with the image of an ultrasound scan. Lennart Nilsson's celebrated photographs of the foetus floating as if in space were first published in *Life* magazine in 1965; 25 years later, the *Sunday Times* devoted a colour spread to the same photographer's vastly magnified images of the instant when a sperm pierces an egg. Those strange, convoluted landscapes hold an abstract beauty, but the now familiar image of a young human months before birth carries a more personal power. Life in the womb can stand for total satisfaction. The curled-up foetus suggests perfect peace and security, surrounded by its supernatural aura, revelling in its nakedness and fluidity. 'For nine months he gets everything he needs from one place,' declared the caption of a 1990s advertisement for the superstore Children's World, beneath an image of a thumb-sucking tranquil creature, 'Why change the habit of a lifetime?'

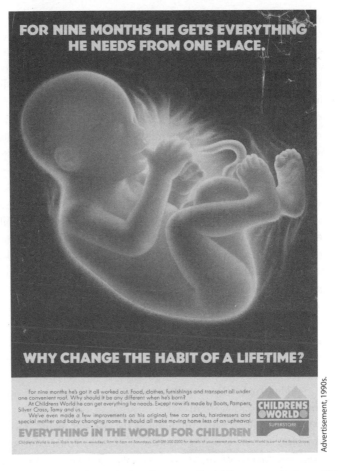

Yet the peace of the image belies the turmoil which surrounds the realities of conception and birth, as well as the political and technological disputes within which they are embedded. As the visible foetus gained a new public presence, its luminous image floated calmly at the heart of one of the most intense disputes of the last quarter of the twentieth century, and posed impossible questions about the status of life itself. To whom does this foetus belong? The Children's World advertisement referred to the mother in oblique and humorous terms ('For nine months he's got it all worked out. Food, clothes, furnishings and transport all under one convenient roof'). No maternal container was visible around the floating infant. Feminists of the 1970s were not satisfied to be an invisible 'convenient roof'. They saw enforced pregnancy and motherhood as one of the shackles from which women must be freed. For them the unborn child is clearly part of the body of the mother. The 'pro-life' opposition argued that the child belonged either to god or to society – but either way it had a separate existence which must be protected, if necessary, against the interests of the woman who bore it. As more information came into the public realm concerning the intricate development of the child prior to birth, the early feminist demand for abortion on demand developed into a more complex argument around reproductive rights – for a woman's right to control her own body and make her own decisions on her fertility. But for anti-abortion campaigners, the humanity of the foetal image has continued to be a highly charged emotional centre. 'A foetus is a baby – don't forget' was the caption on a 1970s leaflet showing a bin bag apparently full of aborted babies. In 2002 the ProLife Alliance sought to base a party political broadcast on a series of bloody and emotive pictures of aborted foetuses. Both the BBC and ITV argued that the pictures were unacceptable and transmitted the broadcast without them. However, a Court of Appeal ruled that the decision not to transmit the pictures was 'censorship' and the pictures rapidly entered the public domain via the Internet.

Although the rights of the unborn child have been a rallying cry for those who would define women primarily as mothers, technological developments have, in effect, begun to remove the foetus from the 'possession' of the woman who bears it. A view of the beginning of life as mystical and natural has been shaken by the ability to separate insemination from conception and pregnancy from motherhood. In a confusion of parental bodies, *in vitro* fertilisation, artificial insemination by donor (AID), surrogacy, egg sharing and other developments in genetic science mean that the creation of a child may be a carefully controlled process in which the producer of the egg and the producer of the sperm do not automatically become mother and father of the resulting child. In this context, the images of sperm and egg take on a new meaning and the solitary foetus must now be reinterpreted as an isolated creature who is, almost literally, up for grabs. Aminatta Forma writes of the shifting definitions of 'motherhood'; in surrogacy the 'natural' mother is the one who donates, while the surrogate mother is devalued, whereas in an 'egg donation programme' the woman donating the genetic material has no rights over the future child. In both cases it is the woman who is using her body as a source of income – often from a poorer society – who forfeits the right to 'motherhood'.

The consequence of consumer choice in reproduction is that the possibility of purchasing the perfect baby has come closer. Just as digital imaging can produce a perfect picture, headlines predict a future in which all babies will be designer babies, constructed out of carefully selected genes. News items describe prospective parents choosing the sex of their child, or specifying the qualities of their egg or sperm donor – such as sportiness, musicality or physical attractiveness. One sperm bank in the US holds the sperm of Nobel Prize winners, Olympic athletes and outstanding sportsmen. Being human has been finally detached from the biological, and perfection appears a real possibility. The ideal image has influenced the construction of flesh-and-blood babies.

Making babies: birth

If the fantasy of a peaceful life in the womb has not been unduly disturbed by the technologisation of conception, it is most definitely broken by the violent imagery of birth. Birth has long been a taboo subject for pictorial presentation, since it must deal with the private parts of the female body, associated with horror and disgust as well as the fascination of the forbidden. Representations of birth have traditionally been hedged around with warnings and explanations.

In 1991, when the garment manufacturer Benetton used public hoardings for a poster campaign showing a baby at the moment of birth, there was a sense that public decency had been breached. The baby's face was crumpled, the umbilical cord still attached, and the body streaked with blood and messy substances. The image spoke of pain and distress. The Advertising Standards Authority received 800 complaints – an unusually high number. Benetton's advertisements at the time were designed by the charismatic Oliviero Toscani, who specialised in the outrageous. This was one of a series of advertisements based on 'found images' which showed traumatic moments in human life, including an equally notorious photograph of a man dying of AIDS. The public unease came not only from the prominence of taboo images, but from the double function of the posters – to shock, and to advertise cheap-and-cheerful clothing. Private moments were wrenched from their context and thrust into public spaces, so that passers-by were forced to contemplate mortality and bodily pain while lightly making their consumer choices. However, a new-born, complete with umbilical cord, was by no means new to advertising imagery. In 1989 Yorkshire Television had offered no fewer than four full-colour births on a single poster. The image of a baby as it first leaves the womb, which had once been considered for professional eyes only, had already become public currency as a symbol of a hopeful beginning. But, like the Toscani poster with its glistening bodily fluids, these pictures distanced themselves from the terrifying and messily feminine processes of birth itself by excluding the woman whose labour this was.

Just as the foetal image has directed visual empathy away from the woman towards the unborn child, the imagery of birth has played down the experience of the mother to focus on the new-born. In 1956, Grace Robertson – one of the few women documentary photographers working at the time – shot a sequence of pictures following a birth for the prestigious news magazine *Picture Post*. But the magazine 'feared the realistic shots of a young woman in labour would alarm too many readers!' and the sequence was not used. By contrast, Frederick Leboyer used photographs to demonstrate the trauma of birth from a baby's perspective. In a powerful image, a doctor triumphantly holds up a screaming child by its legs, like a fisherman's catch. In the picture, the agonised face of the new-born is ignored by the celebrating adults. By isolating the face of the child in another

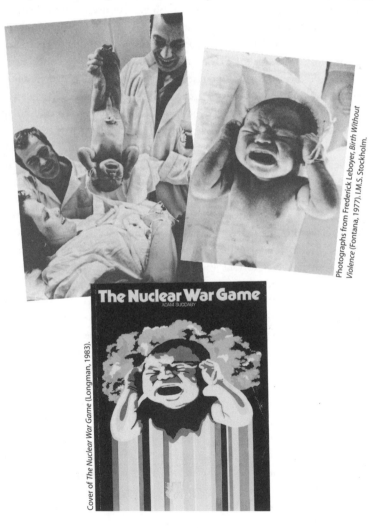

Photographs from Frederick Leboyer, *Birth Without Violence* (Fontana, 1977). I.M.S. Stockholm.

Cover of *The Nuclear War Game* (Longman, 1983).

frame, and reversing the image so that it is no longer upside down, Leboyer forces the baby's distress onto the attention of his reader. Instead of a doctor's trophy, we now see a small human. (The British peace movement took up the image and adapted the crumpled face and helpless arms of the baby into the mushroom cloud of a nuclear explosion, a symbol of the ultimate in human vulnerability. It became a giant backdrop to a rally in Trafalgar Square in 1980, and appeared on a book cover in 1983.) The image of the tortured face of this new-born infant was the antithesis of the beatific foetus, but Leboyer demonstrated the possibility of a continuing foetus-like peace, through another visual comparison – juxtaposing the face of a baby who had experienced a peaceful birth with the serene face of the Buddha. Leboyer's work was highly influential in the move to make child-birth techniques gentler and less technological, but once more the humanising of the child had problematised the position of the mother. This time she was not a 'convenient roof' but some kind of monstrous machine which crushed and pushed the baby unwillingly into the world.

In 1976, *Parents* magazine published another landmark documentary sequence, a second-by-second series of photographs showing the bloodstained head of a baby as it emerged. These pictures showed sex organs and pubic hair, but the viewing public were protected from the mother's agonised effort. In the final picture she lies comfortably against the pillows as the midwife hands her the infant. The medical context, the clinical observation, the empiricism and rational sequencing of the series has the effect of demythologising and normalising the moment of childbirth. In the late 1970s *Parents* had been relaunched and was realigning its audience from a rather patronising advice culture, appropriate to the post-war era, to a late-twentieth-century promotional one, with much more colour and a glossy format. The new magazine was based on a German model and used many pictures from European sources. Unlike its rivals, it took its visuals seriously. In the context of feminist campaigns, the magazine faced the taboos head on and sought out images that would show childbirth under women's control. Amongst its full-colour features there was a 'do-it-yourself' birth in which the mother had no assistance, and a 'primitive' birth in which a French model chose to have her baby in the 'traditional' way amongst a nomadic tribe in North Africa. More conventional variations ranged from caesareans to high-tech births with epidural and forceps. With its frank discussions of children's sexuality, together with a relaxed celebration of nakedness, the magazine was seen by conservative critics as part of the unwelcome counter-culture of the hippy 1970s.

The twenty years which separated the photographic sequences in *Picture Post* and *Parents* had seen the coming of high-quality colour printing in magazines and the launch of colour supplements to Sunday newspapers, which balanced powerful photojournalism with increasingly sophisticated advertising. The proliferating consumer publications were precisely targeted at specific audiences, their visual style set by the advertisements which occupied a high percentage of their pages. There has been a growing market for baby-care advice (but not, interestingly enough, for advice on bringing up older children). By the late 1980s there were nine paid-for baby magazines, most of them printed in lush colours on quality paper. By the year 2000 that number had increased to 15, (and the magazines have been joined by publications sponsored by supermarkets, such as Tesco's *Baby Club* and Sainsbury's *Little Ones*). This all-powerful consumer context has, to a certain extent, succeeded in calming the unwelcome irruption of painful reality. The dominant imagery of giving birth and caring for a baby is now placed firmly against a supportive background of purchasing and consumerism. Advice and promotion imperceptibly interweave, and interchangeable pictures of happy, healthy babies illustrate them both – pictures which attempt to incorporate sufficient realism into a fantasy of perfection.

Birth does not easily lend itself to hedonistic imagery, but in the pages of *Practical Parenting, Mother and Baby* and the rest, pain and problems have come to sit easily beside advertisements for soya milk, bootees and Baby Gap. At the same time, the magazines remain a contemporary forum for gossip and the exchange of experience, including childbirth stories. *Practical Parenting* has an 'Ask our midwife' letters page; *Mother and Baby* investigates '10 top birth secrets'. In the spirit of consumer choice, features compare hospitals and birth styles. The tone is intimate and informal, and pictures are often those sent in by readers. These tend to show the moment *after* the birth when the baby rests comfortably on the mother's body. Ultimately, this is the desired image, in which the feared crisis of birth is transformed into an image of calm, and turbulence is pacified. The spirit of kitsch overcomes the dangers of taboo.

Mother, breast and bottle

I once risked the remark 'there's no such thing as a baby', meaning that if you set out to describe a baby you are describing a baby and someone. A baby cannot exist alone but is essentially part of a relationship.

D.W. Winnicott

When a new baby makes its first public appearance, it is in the arms of the woman who bore it. Midwives, doctors and professional helpers are no longer needed, and the faces of woman and baby can now be shown in mutual satisfaction. Mothers on the covers of 1970s magazines (Princess Anne, Esther Rantzen) took up the traditional posture, cradling the infant in their arms. By the 1990s they were more likely to turn towards the camera, displaying the little creature (Duchess of York with Princess Eugenie). The early 2000s found Mandy Smith on the cover of *Hello!* bent over the naked body of her baby in a more artful pose. The key image of mother and infant, 'a baby and someone' in Winnicott's words, remains secure, and the celebrity baby remains a staple of engaging babyhood.

Although there is a baby at the centre of each of these presentations, in this pictured moment the imagery is working on the meaning of 'woman' in order to ensure a convincing transformation into 'mother'. In the 2000s, the visual possibilities for 'motherhood' are wide and varied, but, despite cynicism and doubts, the presence of a baby continues to change the nature of the woman whose arms encircle it. In her study of the myth and cult of the Virgin Mary, Marina Warner describes the fourteenth-century transformation of Mary from a transcendent queen into the ideal of feminine humility and submission, brought about when she was regarded above all as a mother: 'In motherhood Mary was glorified, and through her position before her child became more glorious for her humility'. Outside the Roman Catholic Church, thousands who would otherwise take no part in the cult of Mary as Madonna continue to circulate her picture. In a familiar Christmas-card image, mother and baby are placed beyond the everyday world, sanctified with a halo, associated with the solemn, if childlike, aspects of Christmas and the hushed intensity of the art gallery. The holiness of the couple is secured by their freedom from worldliness and sexuality. They have aesthetic as well as exemplary value. The private relationship of mother and baby gains a public dimension which places it firmly in the context of culture, and puts a tangible pressure on women who live out the social reality of motherhood.

Christmas cards from the 1970s to the 2000s.

In an intimate image, more frequently exemplified by anonymous mothers, the crook of the woman's arm, instead of serving to display the baby to the gaze of the onlookers, draws the child inwards, supporting it in the act of suckling. This resonant image tends to be shaped by the curve of the woman's arm and the downward tilt of her head, so that her gaze is totally concentrated on the baby. The image creates an exclusive couple, as if unaware that they are the objects of contemplation. The egg-shaped logo of the National Childbirth Trust fuses them into one. An advertisement from 1991 and a medical expert from 1981 are amongst many who emphasise the point: 'A mother and her baby. Two people who, for the next few years of their lives, will be inseparable. Emotionally. Physically'; 'You will find yourself completely preoccupied by him. You and your baby are not yet wholly separate people, and in some ways you never will be.' Pictures of active mothers and babies refusing to be shaped by the curve of the image can be read as a resistance to the pull of these powerful pressures.

But while the effect of such imagery is to shrink the possible meanings of 'woman' to those associated with 'mother', at the same time it encourages an infinite expansion of the possible meanings of 'baby'. When you hold a baby, 'you've got the whole world in your hands,' warns an advertisement for Infa-care bath products. The baby represents the potential of all humanity. In contemporary baby magazines the child is almost as likely to be a 'she' as a 'he' (Tesco's *Baby Club* notes 'for consistency we use "she" to refer to baby throughout the magazine, but all information applies equally to boys!'), but until very recently writers have found it difficult to reconcile the expansive universality associated with babyhood with the feminine pronoun. 'It is tedious to put "he and she" and it also saves confusion when "she" is the mother,' the BMA told their readers tetchily in their 1976 leaflet for mothers. In a 1991 pamphlet, the Child Accident Prevention Trust put the explanation at its starkest: 'This booklet refers to all babies as "he" or "him" to make for easier reading'. This universal 'he' who makes for easier reading and must be defined in antithesis to 'she', the mother, is not the 'he' of a potent and active masculinity but seems to represent a more generalised 'he', a god-like manifestation of humanity itself who, merely by existing, can command service and nurture from 'she'. At this point 'she' seems little more than an encircling and protecting environment, Mother Nature, the providing earth.

At the centre of this set of pictures is that highly charged object, a woman's breast. Pictures of breastfeeding mothers show a three-way relationship – not just between woman and baby but between woman, baby and breast. That part of a women's body which is overlaid with innumerable taboos and fascinations must here be seen as chaste and desexualised. The breast poses a problem for the image, just as it poses a practical problem for women who want to feed their babies on a day trip or a shopping expedition. We are assured, however, that this breast is quite different from the provocative breasts of the topless sunbathers, joke-shop falsies, the partygoers who allow them to 'pop out', or the top shelf at the local newsagent. Unlike the arrogant breasts on page three, these visible breasts are not an assertive element of female display. Indeed, 'as she prepares to feed him ... her breasts change in appearance in a subtle and beautiful way,' the BMA informed new mothers. (The pamphlet was anonymous, but the sentence has an almost prurient feel, if for a male observer.) The imagery must struggle to retain 'mother' as an asexual category, despite – and partly because of – the exposure of her breast. This struggle over meanings centres on the visible contact with the baby. Although writers such as Sheila Kitzinger have discussed the sexual component of the experience of breastfeeding, the cultural expect-ation is that the visible touch between this 'he' and this 'she' will repress the sexual implications of that antithesis. The baby (a person) is presented as the object of 'her' love and concern, but the breast (part of a person) is the object of 'his' desire. Their relationship is not reciprocal. In the psychoanalysis of Melanie Klein, the breast appears as a separate entity with which the baby builds a relationship before becoming aware of the mother as an individual.

In a famous passage from his *Three Essays on Sexuality*, Sigmund Freud wrote, 'No-one who has seen a baby sinking back satiated from the breast and falling asleep with flushed cheeks and blissful smile can escape the reflection that this picture persists as a prototype of the expression of sexual satisfaction later in life'. Although the analogy between mother and lover is disguised by an array of taboos and prohibitions, it emerges in the sense of nervous impropriety behind a headline such as 'How could I know it was the wrong baby at my breast?' and the saucy joke behind a 1991 advertisement for Triumph nursing bras: 'There are times when you can allow the man in your life to choose your bra'. A 1984 advertisement for Cow and Gate baby foods, which shockingly showed the breast as nothing but food – 'May we suggest the liver and bacon to follow?' – won advertising industry awards for both effectiveness and creativity. In these ways the sensuous touching between lips and breast has been carefully negotiated. The baby is allowed full flow of 'his' emotions, but the mother must temper hers in the knowledge of her responsibility and service. Viewers of these presentations are expected to appreciate the satisfactions experienced by the baby and disavow their own erotic response. Perhaps for this reason, the woman's presence in the image is, once more, a precarious one. While seeking to present the satisfaction of the nursing couple, the picture of the suckling baby is frequently cropped, so that only baby and breast are included. The woman's face remains outside the frame and her ambivalent emotions invisible.

The bottle enters the popular imagery of babyhood very much as second best, usually in advertisements for formula baby food or the paraphernalia which accompanies bottle feeding. In an advertisement for Babysafe products, the artificial nipple intrudes into the image of breast and baby, accompanied by text which admits that 'breast is best' while it offers itself as a humble but adequate substitute. As breastfeeding declined in Britain throughout the 1980s, campaigners from organisations such as Baby Milk Action pointed to pressure from the powdered-milk manufacturers and to 'glossy little brochures featuring smiling babies and baby milk brands which are placed on maternity ward bedside tables'. Such promotion is specifically forbidden under the World Health Organisation code established in 1981 after the exposure of methods used by Nestlé to sell formula baby milk to mothers in poorer parts of the Third World. (In July 2001 a group of actors and comedians boycotted the prestigious Perrier awards at the Edinburgh Festival Fringe because Perrier is produced by Nestlé.) In 1989 the *Health Visitor* journal rejected an advertisement for Farley's Ostermilk which showed two tins placed in the two cups of a bra because, they said, it associated formula too closely with breast milk. Throughout this debate, the breast remains a protected value, defended against its sexual connotations, forming a secure link between mother and baby.

Nature, science and magic

The rival claims of breast milk and formula throw into relief a long-running tension between those two props of modernist thought, the 'natural' and the 'scientific'. Yet these two discourses of modernity have both been tempered by references to an older, and possibly more reassuring, appeal – to magic, religion and the supernatural. 'It is a gift bestowed by nature. That special something which bonds mother and baby. That magic touch that brings comfort to the distressed child.' So wrote Edward Vale on the occasion of Prince William's christening on 5 August 1982, addressing the *Daily Mirror*'s three million readers of assorted ages and sexes. At about the same time, 'a professor of obstetrics and gynaecology' addressed the much more specific audience of women who were about to become mothers in an advice leaflet. 'Having a baby is a recurring miracle and still the biggest event in a woman's life,' he reassured them, 'don't worry if you do not feel a great surge of mother love. This unique bond between mother and child takes a little time to develop.' Both writers managed to hold together references to the supernatural – 'that magic touch', 'a recurring miracle' – with the natural – 'a gift bestowed by nature' a 'unique bond' and with science.

'Bonding' became the buzzword of the 1980s, based on an influential book by two Australian paediatricians. Penelope Leach described how the bond between mother and child depends on an exchange of looks: 'His responses create a self-sustaining circle, his smiles leading to your smiles and yours to more from him'. 'Failure to bond' was to become a convenient explanation for all sorts of problems between parents and children. Research reported in the British press in 1977, accompanied by diagrams, claimed that only some babies fulfil the criteria for bonding, with dire consequences for those who do not conform. According to the researchers, small chins and wide eyes make a more effective 'trigger' for mother love. 'We ought to consider the possibility that if their baby has a face that does not trigger the benevolent instinct, the brutal behaviour of their parents (that is child-batterers) would then be cruel and appalling, but in the precise sense of the word, natural.' The fear that without the 'trigger' to secure the 'bond' – natural, yet confirmed by science – women may escape the duties of motherhood, was reiterated by the hospital which provided photographs of babies in intensive care for their mothers to keep with them, to assist the bonding process: 'If the bond is loosened, a demanding baby can be too much for a mother to tolerate'.

Thus the faces which gurgle from Junior Disprol packets, Fisher Price advertisements and the magazine shelves at W.H. Smith are the faces of *beautiful* babies, their beauty judged by their rounded symmetrical faces, their small chins, their sparkling eyes and their appealing expressions. 'Because the agency insists that the babies in the ads have to be just right, casting is a tricky business,' wrote Gail Kemp in the advertisers' journal, *Campaign*. Yet the image of a baby's face, smiling wide-eyed directly out of the picture, is an image which seeks to bond with *all* viewers, placing us all, for that particular moment, in the position of mother. Paradoxically, this resonant image, with its carefully researched 'trigger' for mother love, has effectively broken the uniqueness of the bond, since its magic is re-created for *all* potential consumers. When D.W. Winnicott wrote of a 'baby and someone', he had mother or carer in mind. In the consumer world, that 'someone' may be the purchaser of the magazine, or of the perfect babyfood or of the financial Baby Bond.

By the 1990s, the 'fashion' for voguish parenthood meant that the image of a baby was promoting a wide variety of products, from lambswool jumpers to perfume and high-performance cars, aimed at men as well as women. Concern was expressed that the practice was an exploitation – not only of the pictured babies, but also by causing an unfair arousal of parental emotion. The advertisers' professional magazine *Campaign* invited comments from its readers on the issue. The not-so-serious replies it received were summed up by the 'baby' who wrote, 'Some people are simply jealous of our success and glamorous lifestyles'.

Magazine cover, London, 1998, courtesy of *Time Out*.

Agencies continue to produce catalogues with ranks of aspirant baby models, and advertisers vie with each other for the most gorgeous baby face – but the symmetrical faces, the wide sparkling eyes and the appealing expressions remain remarkably repetitive. 'Just right' also turns out to mean that the babies are of an incredible whiteness; the eyes are usually blue and the faces the softest of pinks. It was not until the end of the 1980s that the occasional black baby began to appear in advertising and in the editorial pages, and things have hardly changed in the early 2000s.

Any baby can easily be spoilt

Although the perfect baby smiles the delighted smile that mothers long to see, even advertisers with plenty of resources and cash know that this image can only be achieved through hard work and at the expense of many tears and tantrums. The perfect image can all too easily be spoiled. Truby King, the austere mentor of an earlier generation of childcare experts, was obsessed with the possibility of 'spoiling'. 'Any baby can easily be spoiled and made a cross, fretful and exacting little tyrant,' he wrote in 1912. Pictures of babies in their fretful and tyrannical moods are less frequently visible and are rarely allowed to dominate a page. A bawling baby may bring disruption so awful that it is best dealt with by resorting to comedy, and desperate babies become a handy metaphor. 'Only reality looks more real,' claims a 2001 advertisement for Hewlett Packard inkjet printers, promoting a technology which produces 'outstanding photographic images', including the comic realism of a bawling child. 'Take cover now,' cries a leaflet for Cornhill life insurance, under a cartoon image of a cavernous mouth, vibrating tonsils and food flying in all directions. The peaceful image may be restored either by one of innumerable branded products – Anebesol, Dinnefords, Colic Drops – as well as life insurance, health care and the advice of experts. The situation is made light of and things are soon put right.

The imagery continues to imply that it is up to the mother to maintain harmony within the domestic setting. Yet, in the advertisements, such as one for Asilone soothing medicine, she is turning her gaze out of the frame towards the viewer, looking beyond the self-sufficiency of the nursing couple. The baby also looks beyond its mother, as if it too is appealing to the world beyond. When 'Mum needs help'; when she lacks the expertise and equipment; when 'a cuddle isn't enough', another character in the story, although not always a visible one, is called on to restore order. In advice literature, a doctor, nurse or health visitor puts in a helpful appearance; in consumer imagery this role is played by the product. Either way, the autonomy of motherhood is once more thrown into question.

When the imagery is dominated by its welfare aspects – for example in advertising for medicines, toiletries and other products concerned with health and hygiene – a clinical eye supervises the parental eye. The normative regime of science enters the home – and the imagery – in the guise of professional advice. Professional scrutiny sets standards as growth and development are measured, monitored and assessed. 'You and Your Baby will help you because it is written by experts who will tell you what is normal and what is not,' was the confident assertion which began a late-1970s BMA booklet. In *Parents* magazine of the 1940s, the professional was an SRN (State Registered Nurse) or a doctor, usually uniformed. The white coat and the stethoscope have had a long life as guarantors of health and hygiene. By the 2000s, the advice is cosier, the gap between medical expert and 'patient' has closed, and the professionals present themselves as friends rather than harsh teachers. Nevertheless, the baby never totally leaves the discursive space of medicine and welfare, where close observation and the measurement of change are all-important. The repertoire of the baby magazines includes checklists of the expected stages of development, offered both as yardstick and as reassurance. Each expected change has its own appropriate visual representation. The editors of the Time-Life book *Photographing Children* long ago alerted amateur photographers to the opportunities: 'A general itinerary of his [sic] rapid journey from infancy and babyhood into childhood has been plotted by the Yale University Clinic of Child Development after close observation of thousands of children. Each of these stages of development provides valuable insights as to what to look for as photographic behaviour.' In the contemporary resonant image of babyhood, such is the interplay between a normative medical discourse and a sensuous pleasurable one, that the distinction between them has all but disappeared.

Fathers and the reconstruction of parenthood

Winnicott's observation that 'there's no such thing as a baby' has gained a new set of meanings as the image of parents and their babies has moved through a series of transformations in recent decades. As with all images of children, the resonant meanings of babyhood carried by the changing image only make sense in the context of the changing relationships around it – albeit pulled in different directions as several different trends run in parallel. Perhaps the most striking change has been the arrival of fathers as an expected part of baby imagery, and men's very public desire to be seen sharing the pleasures – if not always the stresses – of the early years of parenthood. Even so, as we have seen, the actual presence of the mother and her servicing role remains taken for granted to the extent that her visual representation is frequently unnecessary. Images of the foetus render transparent the woman who carries it; images of childbirth and of breast-feeding focus on the baby rather than the mother; consumer imagery shows babies gazing out of the frame towards a space assumed to be occupied by a loving, purchasing mother. These resonant images may centre on babies, but they are laden with implicit information about mothers and their duties. Yet in parallel with a renewed acceptance of a traditional, biological role, motherhood has undergone intensive social restructuring. One powerful theme from the 1990s celebrates the successful working mother. She is the soldier kissing her baby goodbye as she leaves for the Gulf War; she is high-flying business executive Nicola Horlick with her numerous children; she is the fashionable woman who wants to carry on wearing the kind of clothes she wore before she was pregnant; and she is the target readership of *She*. At that magazine's relaunch in May 1990, it told its advertisers that a 'massive, growing, attractive and affluent market' is made up of women who 'juggle their lives', balancing committed motherhood with work and an active social life: 'You need the juggler and we've got her'. By the 2000s the desirability of such a pressured lifestyle had been questioned, and 'downshifting' was recommended. Rather than kissing your baby goodbye, or balancing it on your hip with the phone tucked under your chin, the preferred image for media-conscious mothers was now to be seen out and about with their babies in tow. The daily business of being a mother became part of an energetic discussion in the broadsheet press as a new generation of high-profile women writers shared their experiences of motherhood with the public at large. ('I feverishly take photographs of us doing things together so I can say, "There we were"', wrote BBC arts correspondent Rosie Millard.) One consequence of these changes in attitude was that the visual interest could be drained away from the baby to the confident, smiling, attractive mother pushing the buggy.

Of course, these very visible mothers continue to represent the 'affluent market'. Poorer women, who have always worked, and not always from choice, are not seen to share in this new, publicly expressive motherhood, and we are almost never shown babies in the care of the nannies or childminders who so often make the image possible. These other workers only become publicly visible in the recruitment literature, or when inadequate or abusive carers hit the headlines. An imagery based on consumerism finds little space for low-paid, working women – however important their role.

However, plenty of space is made for the new fathers. Until relatively recently, male medical advisers appeared in advertisements and advice literature rather more frequently than fathers, but it is no longer surprising to see a man as the adult half of a baby/parent couple. In the mid-1980s, *Mother* – the oldest of the baby magazines – ran a regular column by 'role-reversing father' Stephen Lugg, coyly pictured at his typewriter in a frilly apron. But the newly emerging image of fatherhood was a rather more sensuous affair. In 1986 one of the most successful posters sold by Athena was 'L'enfant', a dramatically lit black-and-white photograph showing a muscly young man with stylishly tousled hair cradling a baby, whose look is of pure amazement. 'Alienated, self-absorbed manhood is becoming redundant as a marketing tool,' stated John Hegarty of advertising agency Bartle, Bogle, Hegarty. Advertisers identified a 'thirtysomething' culture, 'a slackening of the fierce ambitions that gripped the '80s', a more home-centred and relaxed approach, seeking pleasure with the children. Fathers were almost ousting mothers in their anxiety to be a nurturing parent and to play a caring role. Some pictured fathers clung on to their besuited yuppie style (as in the Lanvin advertisement), but when in 1990 the *Times* announced its 'new baby' – its Saturday magazine – it was a man naked from the waist up who caressed the infant on its posters. In 1991 the Body Shop promoted a 'labour day pack' with

Advertisement, 1997.

photographs in sculptural black-and-white in which the arms encircling the wriggling infant were unmistakably male. Babyhood legitimises nakedness, and this new-age, neo-Romantic vision allowed men too to share the pleasurable touch.

But while parenthood continues to be asserted as a choice, and young and articulate celebrities – women and men – are pictured with their babies in a newly confident way, commerce is already working to direct the baby's gaze beyond its parents towards the world of consumer goods. The hedonistic image of babyhood is increasingly confined to a purchasing context. These delightfully smiling faces, appealingly naked bodies, and the romping, tumbling, wriggling, playful pictures which have made the imagery richer than ever before, are presented within this limited social framework. In Western economies, babyhood is part of commodity culture. Even more alarmingly, babies themselves are on the brink of becoming commodified. Medical intervention into the processes of conception and birth means that, for a price, babies can be constructed out of minute elements of genetic material almost as a digital image is put together out of tiny, discrete elements. A computer-generated baby – self-absorbed in a strange and ghostly dance – became a late-1990s hit on the television show *Ally McBeal*. This uncanny and rather threatening fantasy, which haunted a working woman who dreamt of motherhood but shied away from it, was in many different ways a significant sign of the times.

Notes on Chapter 1

p. 25   **There's no such thing as a baby**: quoted from R.W. Winnicott (1964) *The Child, the Family and the Outside World*, Harmondsworth: Pelican, p. 88.

Anne Geddes: quoted from the documentary series *Myths of Childhood*, Producer: Anna Grieve, Film Australia, 1997. In an interesting reflection on the ways in which the circulation of pictures is controlled and licensed in the contemporary world, the Anne Geddes company would not give permission for any of her greetings cards to be reproduced in this book. 'Anne's images can only appear in material related to her, her work, and the Anne Geddes brand,' wrote her New York representative.

p. 26   **Richard Dadd**: (1817–86) painter of immensely detailed and complex fairy scenes. See Susan P. Casteras (2002) 'Winged fantasies: constructions of childhood, innocence, adolescence, and sexuality in Victorian fairy painting', in Marylin R. Brown (ed.) (2002) *Picturing Children: Constructions of Childhood between Rousseau and Freud*, Aldershot: Ashgate.

Arthur Rackham: (1867–1939) watercolourist and illustrator, including J.M. Barrie's *Peter Pan in Kensington Gardens*, 1906.

Goblin Market: published in 1863.

Mediterranean holiday: contemplating Della Robbia's 'divine babies' which decorate the fifteenth-century building which now houses the UNICEF Innocenti Research Centre in Florence, Judith Ennew made a link to the history of children's rights. 'It is believed that these babies gave Eglantyne Jebb the idea for the emblem of the first five-point declaration on the rights of the child', in Bob Franklin (ed.) (2002) *The New Handbook of Children's Rights*, London: Routledge, p.388. See also Chapter 6.

'ornamental nudity': Phillipe Aries (1960/1973) *Centuries of Childhood*, Harmondsworth: Penguin, p.42.

p.27 **Sistine Madonna**: Anne Higonnet (1998) *Pictures of Innocence: the History and Crisis of Ideal Childhood*, London: Thames and Hudson, pp.44, 72.

howling mouths and scrunched-up eyes: Oscar Rejlander's photograph of a crying infant, nicknamed 'Ginx's baby', sold sixty thousand prints and a quarter of a million photographic cards. Lindsay Smith (1998) *The Politics of Focus: Women, Children and Nineteenth Century Photography*, Manchester: Manchester University Press, pp.86–87. See also Higonnet (1998) above, especially Chapter 3.

Douglas Tempest: designed the 'Kiddy' series of comic postcards for Bamforth and Co. during the 1920s. The company was founded in 1870, the same year that the postcard was launched, and became notorious for its saucy seaside jokes.

kewpie: Caroline G. Goodfellow (1998) *Dolls*, Princes Risborough, Buckinghamshire: Shire Publications, p.17. Caroline Goodfellow is the curator of dolls and toys at the Bethnal Green Museum of Childhood.

photography both as a record and a campaigning tool: Val Williams (1986) discusses the work of photographer and Suffragette organiser Nora Smyth in *Women Photographers: the Other Observers 1900 to the Present*, London: Virago, pp.40–46.

campaigns around mother and infant welfare: on concerns with infant welfare in the early part of the twentieth century see Anna Davin's classic article 'Imperialism and motherhood', *History Workshop Journal*, Vol.5, 1978, pp.9–65.

p.28 **Lennart Nilsson's**: in *Pregnant Pictures*, London: Routledge, 2000, Sandra Matthews and Laura Wexler discuss the breakthrough in foetal photography and the production of the 'foetal spaceman' by Lennart Nilsson (*A Child is Born*, 1965), and Geraldine Lux Flanagan (*The First Nine Months of Life*, 1962). They refer to Rosalind Petchesky (1987) 'Fetal images, the power of visual culture in the politics of reproduction', which discusses the apparent autonomy of the foetus and the absence of the woman in these images, pp.11, 195–99.

p.29 **Feminists of the 1970s**: see Lynne Segal (1987) *Is the Future Female?* London: Virago, for an account of the various trends of feminist thought, especially pp.64 and 82–83 for the National Abortion Campaign and the Reproductive Rights Campaign.

p.30 **A foetus is a baby**: leaflet published by the Society for the Protection of Unborn Children, 1970s.

ProLife Alliance: the party political broadcast was transmitted in Wales, 6 June 2001. *Daily Telegraph*, 15 March 2002. ProLife Alliance: www.prolife.org.uk.

Aminatta Forma: (1998a) *Mother of All Myths*, London: Harper Collins. Also 'Wanted the perfect baby', *Independent on Sunday*, 19 July 1998b.

headlines predict a future: 'Couples pick sex of baby for "ideal family"', *Daily Telegraph*, 5 July 2001; 'End Test Tube Chaos. In Britain today it is harder to rent a video than to get fertility treatment', *Daily Express*, 22 January 1998. The accompanying picture of a baby born to a 60-year-old mother was captioned 'The innocent'.

p.31 **One sperm bank in the US**: quoted by Forma (1998b) above.

horror and disgust: Julia Kristeva (1982) *Powers of Horror: an Essay on Abjection*, New York: Columbia University Press. Barbara Creed (1993) expanded on the idea of women's bodies as a source of horror in cinema in *The Monstrous-Feminine: Film, Feminism and Psychoanalysis*, London: Routledge.

The Advertising Standards Authority received 800 complaints: the authority upheld the complaints and the advertisers agreed to withdraw the poster. For other comments on Benetton advertising see Les Back and Vibeke Quaade (1993) 'Dream Utopias, nightmare realities: imaging race and culture within the world of Benetton advertising', *Third Text*, no 22; Anandi Ramamurthy (2nd edition 2000) 'Constructions of illusion: photography and commodity culture', in Liz Wells (ed.) *Photography: a Critical Introduction*, London: Routledge.

p. 32   **Grace Robertson:** quoted by Val Williams (1986) in *Women Photographers: the Other Observers 1900 to the Present*, London: Virago, p.138. Two of Robertson's birth photographs are reproduced on p.141 of that book.

Frederick Leboyer: (1974/1991) *Birth Without Violence*, London: Mandarin.

p. 33   **British peace movement:** on the cover of Adam Suddaby (1983) *The Nuclear War Game*, London: Longman.

monstrous machine: see Creed (1993) above, Chapter 4, on 'Woman as monstrous womb'.

another landmark documentary sequence: April 1976. I am grateful to Isobel McKenzie-Price, editor in the 1990s, for allowing me to look through the collection of back issues of *Parents*, and to Máire Messenger Davies for discussing her time working on the magazine.

'do-it-yourself' birth: 'Birth without help', May 1976; 'Primitive childbirth', January 1977. It may be relevant to note that a United Nations Development Programme report published in 2002 stated that death during childbirth in the Arab countries is double that of Latin America and four times that of east Asia. Ziauddin Sardar, 'Self-assessment, warts and all', *New Statesman*, 15 July 2002, pp.15–16.

frank discussions of children's sexuality: for example, 'Talking to children about sex', May 1976; 'The sensual child', October 1976; 'How a child develops sexuality' and 'When girls masturbate', November 1976.

p. 34   **sufficient realism:** Isobel McKenzie-Price described her aim as steering a careful course which avoids both pictures of children which are so perfect that parents would be intimidated by them, and the sort of gritty realism that readers might find depressing (interview with Patricia Holland, 1992).

I once risked the remark: Winnicott (1964) above.

Princess Anne: on the cover of *Woman*, 4 February 1978.

Esther Rantzen: on the cover of *Woman's Own*, 29 April 1978.

p. 35   **Duchess of York:** on the cover of *Tatler*, September 1990.

Mandy Smith: on the cover of *Hello!*, No 666, 12 June 2001.

Marina Warner: (1985) *Alone of All Her Sex*, London: Picador, p.183.

p. 36   **'completely preoccupied by him':** British Medical Association (1981) *You and Your Baby*, p.5. Working as a journalist on baby magazines in the 1970s and 1980s, Máire Messenger Davies posed feeding one of her younger children with her husband and the older children as part of the image. A male expert used the picture in a lecture she attended and, without knowing she was its subject, criticised the picture because it lacked that total absorption between mother and infant (personal communication).

advertisement for Infa-care: baby bath, *Woman's Own*, 1970s.

'It is tedious to put': Dr Shelagh Tyrrell (1976) *You and Your Baby*, London: British Medical Association.

p. 37   **page three:** Patricia Holland (1983) 'The Page Three Girl speaks to women, too',
        Screen, 24, No3 May/June, reprinted in Paul Marris and Sue Thornham (eds)
        (1996) *Media Studies: a Reader*, Edinburgh: Edinburgh University Press.
        Sheila Kitzinger: (1984) 'The Psychology of Breastfeeding', in B*reastfeeding: a
        Challenge for Midwives*, Melbourne, International Council of Midwives. See
        also her influential *Experience of Childbirth*, London: Gollancz, 1962.
        Melanie Klein: Hannah Segal, 'Introduction' to Melanie Klein (1987) *Love, Guilt
        and Reparation and other Works 1921–1945*, London: Virago, p.ix.
        Three Essays on Sexuality: Sigmund Freud (1905), quoted by Adam Phillips
        (1998) *The Beast in the Nursery*, London: Faber and Faber, p.45.
        'the wrong baby at my breast?': *Today*, 11 August 1990.
        Cow and Gate baby foods: advertisements by Abbott Mead. *Campaign*, 19 May
        1989.

p. 38   **The bottle enters:** see Christina Hardyment (1993) *Dream Babies: Childcare from
        Locke to Spock*, London: Jonathan Cape, for a history of changing fashions in
        relation to bottle and breast feeding.
        World Health Organisation code: Rebecca Eliahoo, 'WHO battles for breast
        feeding', *Marketing Week*, 6 March 1981.
        boycotted the prestigious Perrier awards: *Independent*, 31 July 2001.
        ***Health Visitor* journal:** quoted by Dinah Hall, 'When milking profits breast isn't
        best', *Sunday Correspondent*, 26 November 1989.

p. 39   **'a professor of obstetrics':** (1980) *The Baby Book*, London: Charing Cross
        Hospital Obstetrics Department.
        an influential book: John Kennell and Marshall Klaus (1976) *Maternal Infant
        Bonding*, see Aminatta Forma 'The baby bonding myth', *Independent on Sunday*,
        12 July 1998.
        Penelope Leach: (1979) *Baby and Child*, Harmondsworth: Penguin, p.16. (Penelope
        Leach was less emphatic in the 1997 update of the book.)
        We ought to consider: research from the American journal *Animal Behaviour*, on
        which facial characteristics of an infant were considered most attractive. 'Nearly
        700 psychology students were asked to rank a collection of drawings of babies
        in order of "cuteness".' Quoted by Tony Osman, 'Survival of the cutest', *Sunday
        Times*, 21 August 1977.
        If the bond is loosened: 'Image of Love', *Mother*, No 496, July 1978.
        Because the agency insists: Gail Kemp, 'Shock tactics that produce great ads',
        Campaign, 25 March 1988.

p. 40   **Baby Bond:** offered by the Tunbridge Wells Equitable Friendly Society as a tax-
        free savings plan exclusively for children in 2001.
        'Some people are simply jealous': Kevin Pilley, 'Ad world gives birth to baby
        power', *Campaign*, 6 January 1990.

p. 41   **Truby King:** quoted by Sheila Kitzinger, *Independent* 'Magazine', 5 May 1990. His
        influential *Feeding and Care of Baby* was first published in New Zealand in 1913,
        and in many subsequent editions up to 1945. See Hardyment (1993) above, p.176.
        'a cuddle isn't enough': advertisement for Dinnefords, 1974.

p. 42   **checklists of the expected stages:** Hardyment (1993) above, p.162.
        Time-Life: (1971) *Photographing Children*, Netherlands: Time-Life International,
        pp.92–93.
        if not always the stresses: Ben Summerskill, 'Why new dads have all the fun',
        Observer, 2 June 2002 quotes a survey carried out by the Future Foundation
        which tracked parents across Britain over 10 years. 'Having children involves
        much smaller changes for men, but they still derive almost all the benefits.'

p. 43   **Images of the foetus:** Matthews and Wexler (2000) above, p.198.

    as she leaves for the Gulf War: 'Mum's off to battle', *Today*, 25 August 1990.

    the kind of clothes she wore: 'We started the company in 1983 when we couldn't find fashionable maternity wear in the shops', wrote Vivienne Pringel and Judy Lever of the Blooming Marvellous catalogue. www.bloomingmarvellous.co.uk.

    'You need the juggler': the new editor Linda Kelsey wrote that she and the Creative Director, Nadia Marks, 'in common with many of *She*'s staff and contributors, are nothing if not jugglers. And I believe we can make *She* even more relevant as the magazine for women of the '90s who juggle their lives', *She*, May 1990.

    high-profile women writers: amongst them Rachel Cusk, *A Life's Work: on Becoming a Mother*, Fourth Estate, 2001; Naomi Woolf, *Misconceptions*, Chatto and Windus, 2001.

    Rosie Millard: *Evening Standard*, 19 June 2002.

p. 44   *Mother:* finally closed in 1990.

    'L'enfant': photograph: Spencer Rowell. Lindsay Baker, *Guardian* 'Weekend', 10 November 2001.

    John Hegarty: quoted by Sarah Mower, 'Macho man gives way to caring father', *Independent*, 6 November 1989.

p. 45   *Ally McBeal:* the computer-generated dancing baby was developed by a computer animation company, Kinetix, as a screensaver, then used in the popular American TV drama series. Jonathan Margolis, 'Dancing Baby', *Daily Mail* 'Night and Day', 20 September 1998.

WE'LL
LOOK AFTER
YOU AND YOUR
HOME

British Gas

Brochure, 2001.

2

Superbrats in the charmed circle of home

PART 1: CREATING A CHILD-SHAPED SPACE

From cereal packets to jigsaws

Of those contemporary Western social institutions which place and contain children, families are at once the most private and the most public. A family is inward-turning, a site of closeness, intimacy and emotional intensity amongst its members (hatred as well as love). But families are also shaped by legislation and social policies (child benefit, inheritance laws, measures to encourage single parents back to work, the availability of health care, to mention some diverse examples). They are subject to ideological pressures from politicians and reformers – especially those for whom 'preserving family values' is at the heart of a moral society, and they are the focus of a barrage of persuasion, information and seduction from advertisers of all sorts. The public imagery of children in a family setting reflects these varied pressures, which sometimes pull together, and sometimes act against each other. Meanwhile, the image of the child within a family is pulled between willing acquiescence and rebellious independence.

The idea of what it means to be a 'family' is highly unstable. Families come in many forms, including multi-generational families, single-parent families (with parents of both sexes), gay parents, reconstructed families of divorced couples (identified by a 2002 survey as 'jigsaw families'), adoptive families and many others. Even the biological limits have been challenged by the technologies of conception discussed in Chapter 1. Nonetheless, the available imagery continues to provide an immediately recognisable visual statement which has remained remarkably consistent over the years. What has been described as the 'cereal-packet family' can be found in advice brochures, in advertisements for cars, holidays and household goods, and in features on insurance and other money matters. It appears in news items and illustrates magazine articles. It sometimes shows a 'real' family, but the classic presentation tends to be posed by a group of models, each of whom can be carefully selected to fit the pattern. In this image a small group of people of assorted ages and genders touch and clutch each other, sometimes smiling at each other, sometimes at the camera. Presented as a single unit, they are linked together by glance or touch. Such pictures are like diagrams, and may indeed be simplified to a line-drawing or a silhouette. They indicate possible relationships between basic family positions, with children at their centre (see pages 58 and 62).

A pared-down version of this image contains four carefully differentiated positions. Alignments tend to be within the genders. Older boys line up with the man; younger children, girls and babies with the woman, so that the male half of the image tends to be larger than the female, and the oedipal implications of cross-gender relations are suppressed. Whether the participants are 'real' families or models, there is always a sense of staging or self-conscious re-enactment. Each individual performs an allocated role, and it is essential to the singularity of the unit that each member plays a *different* role. Sexes and ages are clearly differentiated by clothing, length of hair and sometimes props (the girl clutches a doll, the boy has a ball tucked under his arm). Examples which might spoil the map or add ambiguity – such as teenagers who may be taller than their parents – tend to be excluded, so that the visual differences in themselves produce the expected relations of power and subordination. Frequently, the hands of the adults touch and restrain the children, who offer no resistance to their positioning. In a classic version of this image, each person directs their separate smile at the viewer, as if admiring their own reflection in a mirror or creating a picture for a notional family album (see page 58). The smiles confirm the group as a centre of pleasure which, it seems, is contingent not on personal character or behaviour, but on the satisfactory composition of the family itself. The relaxed expressions demonstrate that these people *want* to be photographed in this way, and to be recorded in precisely *this* relation to each of the others. This is an image of harmony in which the children's acquiescence is pivotal. It is only when this presentation is read against the full range of imagery that a shadow of doubt is thrown across their willing acceptance.

The power of such an image lies in its ability to call up an abstract concept of 'family', even though social and historical research, as well as commonsense observation, has shown such an ideal to be rare in everyday living. Its simplified and satisfactory presentation is a shorthand convenience, trailing a cluster of ideas which determine what we say before we begin to say it. *This* kind of family arranged in *this* way continues to dominate attempts to think of alternatives. The image invites viewers to become complicit in its definitions and to bring their own personal meanings to it. We may not be able to *name* the members of the group, but can instantly *label* them as Father, Mother, Son and Daughter. Making such a recognition is more than giving consent to a set of social arrangements; it means taking an active part in renewing a particular, limited, concept of 'family'. The image becomes not just a picture of an ideal family, but the very meaning of 'family' itself. Its power persists despite its familiar construction as an image, despite the visibility of performance, and despite the fact that we know perfectly well that the individuals in the pictures could easily be a 'jigsaw' family or an unrelated group of models. Yet how could any viewer deny the appeal of those confident smiles? They defy us to spoil their enjoyment. They challenge us to share their happiness and to echo their visible security within our own, most probably less than perfect, group.

The configuration has withstood time. It stands as a quick reference for politicians of both parties and for all who argue for a 'return' to family values. But in the face of multiple critiques, presentations have become more fluid in their arrangement and less assertive. In recent years it occasionally falls to the man to hold the baby; older generations may be introduced and there may be a varying number of children. Nevertheless, at the heart of this image remains a child-shaped space. A child creates a 'family', and it falls to the pictured children to bring about the warmth and mutual pleasures the imagery seeks to evoke. We can trace several influences on this resonant image, each of which creates a space for children to occupy within the family grouping. In each of them the image of a child is offered as a secure value, and in each of them a nostalgic trace of remembered childhood is filtered through the image. We will consider family snaps, the evocation of tradition, and the concept of home.

Family snaps

The classic family image has a specific and emotive source. It refers directly to those valued collections of photographs – including holiday snapshots, studio portraits, wedding pictures and records of baby's first year – which sustain a bond even between relatives who are not on speaking terms. Family pictures are part of the ritual of family life, and contribute to a sense of continuity and personal identity. They are collected and preserved to revive warm memories about a past that is part reality, part fantasy. They are, above all, *desired* pictures, which someone has chosen to make and to preserve, and in which the subjects present themselves as they want to be seen.

Family pictures gain their power because they are stitched into the fabric of personal history. Leafing through a collection of snapshots, whether it is this year's full gloss and saturated colour or the fading black-and-white of earlier decades, we can recall pleasures we have lived, people we have loved and, most poignantly of all, our earlier selves. Family pictures are intensely private, which means that other people's pictures seem thin and insignificant. Who is this woman standing by the Eiffel Tower in 1950s dress? She could be one of many hundreds of mothers, wives, girlfriends who posed in just this way. Who are these children whose features you can hardly discern, building sandcastles in a tiny black-and-white picture with crinkled edges? Who cares? The children of the woman on holiday in France and the adults who were once those children on the beach – *they* care. These pictures depend for their meaning on recognition from those who know, or know of, their subjects. And they are used in complex ways. Enjoying them or merely sorting them through may be a social activity or an intensely private one. It may involve reconstructing memory or arriving at new understandings. It can cement or question relationships, and it can play an important role in confirming or re-thinking personal identity. Over its hundred-odd-year history, Kodak has encouraged millions of home photographers to domesticate their imaginations and use their frozen memories to reaffirm a family setting. Cameras have become increasingly cheap, easy to use and a regular part of holiday baggage. High-speed film or digital disc gives reliable results in rich and gratifying colour. The technology of domestic photography – a medium lens, automatic focus – itself disposes users to produce pictures that will suit the intimate family group. In this context, childhood is always personal.

When a public image, such as an advertisement, uses the snapshot style, it borrows the warmth that belongs to familiar faces. It invites its viewers to act as if they were looking at their own family pictures, to undertake the same imaginative work and to invest these anonymous public figures with something of the same emotional charge. In a reciprocal move, personal pictures are enhanced by public imagery, since advertisements, particularly those for photographic products, offer a repertoire of possible images for family use, and situations which may be staged in order to be photographed, in what Jo Spence described as 'precious moments'. Jennifer Ransome Carter, advertising photographer for Kodak between 1970 and 1984, says she 'tried to get pictures that were as close as possible to those that people would have liked to take for themselves'. She described them as the 'supersnap in Kodaland'.

Despite the interplay between them, private pictures remain radically different from public imagery. As usual, the difference depends on use and context, rather than style and content. Private pictures notoriously recall complex emotions, and the individuals in a family photograph may have memories which are utterly at odds with each other. Many writers have recalled the trauma behind apparently cheerful pictures of themselves as children. In private imagery a picture is never quite what it seems. Its depths can only be explored with knowledge brought to the picture from unrecorded events beyond the frame. Commercial pictures, on the other hand, make instant sense. After all, if the supersnap is *not* exactly what it seems, its makers have wasted their time and money. Such pictures *are* their surface. There is nothing more to them; nothing beyond the frame but the paraphernalia of a professional shoot. We should understand them by looking for their wider rather than their deeper meanings. They make best sense when they are explored horizontally within the broad network of contemporary media. *Private* imagery remains expressive imagery, only fully revealing itself to those who are part of its own private circle. *Public* imagery greedily appropriates those expressive values, but the richness of its promises can never be fulfilled.

Inheritance, biology and the invention of tradition

Celebrity photography transforms family imagery for a wider audience. Pictures of the children of the famous are a staple of the tabloid press and consumer magazines, recycling private lives for public consumption. The motherhood and sexuality of Princess Diana obsessed the public for more than a decade, and the royal soap opera continues to absorb the nation as new generations grow up in the public eye. These most privileged of children and their mothers, fathers, grandmothers, aunts and uncles are both very special and reassuringly ordinary. The fascination is not new. Although Queen Victoria at first thought that a photograph of her children playing at dressing up taken by Roger Fenton in 1854 was too private to be published, photographs of the Royals and their families were soon widely circulated in Victorian Britain. Eric Hobsbawm has described the ways in which a variety of nineteenth-century institutions created an instant history for themselves by reviving or inventing traditions which would give them a sense of ancient legitimacy. The monarchy was amongst them. But Victoria and Albert's 'traditions' were not only ceremonial. They established a royal *family*, which effectively reflected the new middle-class domestic ideal and helped transform celebrations such as Christmas into domestic affairs.

A sense of continuity and stability is created by families whose apparent cohesion over the generations is ensured by their wealth and status. It continues to underpin one contemporary concept of 'family' and to imply a special responsibility for the children who are its inheritors. The aristocratic family, with its ancestral portraits, family trees and ownership of stately homes, still appears in popular discourse as a culturally valued protector of history and tradition. A colourful medieval vision of tapestry and heraldic design trails behind it a petty snobbery that can be handily commodified. For a few pounds anyone can trace back their surname or equip themselves with a coat of arms or a parchment scroll as proof of antiquity. A renewed interest in family history, helped by links and exchanges over the Internet, has fuelled this backward glance and linked it to a sense of inheritance and continuity previously thought to be the province of the upper class alone. Intriguing sepia photographs, crumbling at the edges, may signify generational dignity. In this image which looks to the past, the child becomes the focus of a particular vision of the future; not as representing the human race as a whole, but representing the family as a limited and competitive unit.

Since the 1980s home-ownership boom, the idea of inheritance has developed a different face. Increasing numbers of ordinary people in Britain have inherited wealth from their parents – if only in the form of a 1930s semi or a mortgaged ex-council house. A new range of images place children as potential inheritors, and the central figure is, once more, that of the father, as it is he who is expected to pass on his name and his wealth. Advertisements for insurance and investment plans show fathers enjoying the company of attractive and healthy children and urge them to protect the future of 'their' family.

The theme of material inheritance overlaps with that of biological inheritance. An awareness of tradition and social continuity over the generations is paralleled by an acute anxiety over biological origins. In both cases the 'natural' father appears all-important. The 1975 Children Act gave adopted children the right to seek their 'real' identity, and since the late 1980s a regular theme in the popular discourse around childhood has involved a search for biological roots. The discovery that a 'real' father was an anonymous sperm donor has been seen as deeply traumatic. Artificial insemination by donor (AID) was described in the *Sunday Times* as 'sowing the seeds of despair'. Within these debates, childhood is deeply embedded in family structures and has come to stand for forms of continuity which reach beyond personal mortality.

Home: precious moments behind the laurel hedge

The concept of childhood as a time of innocence developed during the nine-teenth century in parallel with the notion of domesticity and the creation of the 'home' as a centre of privacy, order, morality and security. Childhood came to be seen as a stage of life with special needs and values, and the space within which those values could best be secured seemed to be the domestic environment – ultimately one exclusive to a two generation, structured nuclear family, as reflected in the key image. 'Home' appeared as a refuge from the world of commerce and work, and childhood, with its special qualities of warmth and spontaneity, enhanced the sense of well-being found within its walls. The image of 'home' was epitomised by the family gathered around the hearth.

By the mid-nineteenth century the 'respectable' middle classes were moving away from the chaos and corruption of the urban centres and developing their private lives protected by high laurel hedges in the outlying parts of the cities. As childhood was increasingly required to be an age of innocence, the suburb became a place where girls, especially, could be protected. The separation between economic activity and domesticity was a supremely modern development, yet the imagery that accompanied it harked back to a nostalgic, pre-modern, pre-industrial past. Nostalgia is intimately connected with the idea of home and with one's own lost past. Bryan Turner describes it as a 'sense of historical decline and loss, involving a departure from some golden age of "homefulness"'. The desire to recreate a 'golden age' is reflected in the architectural design of many English suburbs as a fantasised medieval idyll became an aspiration for philanthropists, city planners and municipal authorities in the late nineteenth and early twentieth centuries. The Cadbury family at Bournville near Birmingham and the Lever family at Port Sunlight near Liverpool built model villages for their workers, designed to be more healthy and child-friendly than the Dickensian slums and overcrowded back streets which provided the living conditions for most of the nineteenth-century working class (and, incidentally, to ensure a more satisfied and docile work-force). Their timbered cottages, rustic bridges and picturesque village greens were a three-dimensional, fully inhabitable complement to the popular drawings of children dancing and playing in a rural setting drawn by Kate Greenaway in the same period. This was the age of a new cult of childhood, of *Peter Pan* and *Christopher Robin*, reassuring, nostalgic, and relishing kitsch.

I want to argue that this nostalgic formation was not merely backward-looking, but a dynamic force, since it deployed a set of concepts that had some purchase on social necessity. It was clear that the rural image could express

aspiration as well as conservatism, social aspiration as well as relaxation. The sensibilities it brought with it were an important strand in changing attitudes which eventually achieved a vast improvement in the experience of most working-class children. By the 1930s, the new suburbs for the rising lower-middle classes incorporated similar ideals. (Publicity for the Boots estate at Hayes in Kent, where I was brought up, described itself as housing of which 'thousands had only dreamed'.) This child-friendly image was the antithesis of the 1960s estates and tower blocks built in a forward-looking modernist style. They were intended to reflect functionality and practicality, but they came to be seen as the harbourers of delinquency, violence and uncared-for children; places from which there was no escape and no upward mobility. The twenty-first-century imagery of childhood has done its best to shake itself free from the chocolate-box legacy, but the yearning for the countryside as a natural place for children remains in frequent visual references to simpler, more rural times and in arguments that children need fresh air and green spaces. The pre-industrial image still defines the dream home. An advertisement for Hovis bread in 1984, bathed in a nostalgic sepia tone showed a family at tea and claimed 'it's the little things that make it home'.

Creating a sense of a home-centred family, one set of advertisements uses a constructed documentary style as if to capture family groups absorbed in their daily lives. Making a snapshot is a collective activity with collaborative interaction between the person taking the picture and those who are in it; making a documentary picture usually means photographing others without their knowledge. A snapshot is intended to remind its viewers of events and people they know; a documentary usually offers information about those who are unknown. The snapshot depends on our memory; the documentary claims to be complete in itself. It seeks out the unguarded moment, peers into forbidden places and does not hesitate to uncover truths the participants may prefer to conceal. Documentary photography prefers harsh realism. But when advertising presentations imitate the documentary mode, far from revealing scandal and chaos behind the family image, they show us – perfection. Anne McLintock has pointed out that nineteenth-century advertising developed in parallel with the idea of private domesticity, and was already bringing the 'intimate signs of domesticity (children bathing, men shaving, women laced into corsets, maids delivering nightcaps) into the public realm'. By the late twentieth century this was being done by advertisers to glimpse happiness, laughter and relaxation, with the coherence of the family secured by the joyful presence of the children. Presentations show affluence and abundance either in well-furnished homes or in some family playground – a beach, a country lane or a holiday trip. The car is a recurring feature, a sort of mobile home which transports the family between its two locations. The wholeness of the group is confirmed by the presence of all the members – often a dog too – and gilded by a ubiquitous family smile. No one withholds their commitment nor the intensity of their enjoyment. An advertisement for Pakistan International Airlines shows a (white) family picnicking on an archetypal village green beside a cricket match. 'You know the feeling,' it reminded its viewers. 'It's a warm smile. A relaxed atmosphere. A lot of caring. You can be yourself.' The codes of documentary naturalism mean that people have their backs to the camera, are frozen in the middle of activity or appear awkward or ungainly, giving a particular sense of authenticity. On display is that moment of perfect satisfaction we feared we could never attain.

A harmonious image of domestic life takes many seductive forms. It tends to involve children well below adolescence, and to express the 'simplicity, personal authenticity and emotional spontaneity' on which nostalgia feeds. As we will see, much of the other available imagery of the family works to undermine such blissful harmony. Yet the disturbances which threaten from within – the fear of violence, of inappropriate sexuality, of children who are uncontrollable, sullen or destructive, or who simply do not fit the picture of what children 'should' be like

– all these possibilities leave traces which contribute in a paradoxical way to the pleasure of presentations designed, above all, to please. Their very distance from lived experience enhances their comfort and reassurance.

Breaking the image: men and money

However, looked at another way, the perfection of the family image holds the seeds of its own destruction. The first step in the construction of the key image of a 'family' is when the father invades the imagery of babyhood, so that the inward-turned oval of mother and baby becomes a sharper triangle, with the man at its peak. In one powerful contemporary theme, the man attempts to imitate the perfection of the nursing couple. (Photographs of Prime Minister Tony Blair with his fourth child Leo were described as 'sultry', his vulnerability visible, while his wife, barrister Cherie Booth, greeted the camera with make-up in place and a practised smile; television presenters Davina McCall and Matthew Robertson posed for their baby picture with Matthew bare-chested, cradling the baby, while Davina is fully clothed. Psychologist Andrew G. Marshall, writing in the *Daily Mail*, described this picture as 'extraordinary'.) But the roles can never be completely reversed, despite the softening of the masculine persona. All the other photographs analysed by Marshall in the *Daily Mail* spread showed the man as an admiring and protective third party – and even Davina leans her head on Matthew's shoulder, so that her head is lower than his, and the outlined shape within the frame conforms to the new, three-point harmony.

When the family achieves the key image discussed at the beginning of this chapter, it has developed beyond this baby-centred triangle, to include four positions – two parents and two young children. But this larger group still retains a triangular shape with the man at its apex. In the classic presentation, his encircling arms mark its boundaries and separate it from the outside world. The direction of the touch is from him, towards them. He is the only one who remains unenclosed, so that his body marks the transition between an exterior, public world and the interior, private one associated with the concept of 'home'. He asserts his power to define a space and to limit the ways in which others may be present in it. He draws from its members their individual expressions of pleasure and affirmation. His touch confirms the physicality of their pleasure but prevents the uncontrollable chaos of the erotic from emerging. He literally holds the group in place. As well as being pictures of a *family*, the classic image pictures a *man*. They reflect *his* fantasy. ('Now all you need is wife and kids', an advertisement in a lifestyle supplement tells a man looking longingly at a good-sized Volvo.) Yet, paradoxically, this defining position allows the man to absent himself from the group and become invisible. He can be outside the picture and yet retain control when it is he who, as seems so natural, 'takes' the snap. A family picture may be a proud image of *his* possessions, *his* people. Within the frame he encloses the family with his arms, but when he is outside it, he claims the right to create the frame itself and to enclose the family members with his directing eye.

There is another, more practical, reason for his reduction in visibility. His absence may be necessary to achieve the all-important *presence* of the consumer goods he has provided. An advertisement for de Beers from the 1970s could hardly put it more clearly. A family trio are sitting on a lawn. The father is reclining, his back to the viewer, his visible status diminished. The text declares, 'He'd been in Bombay on her birthday. In Istanbul on his daughter's first day at school. And in Tokyo on their wedding anniversary. When he got back from his last trip he gave her a diamond eternity ring. "I know I'm a rotten letter writer," he said, "but I'm always thinking about you"'. Routine departures for a daily job can be compensated for with routine goods, but an extreme absence in Tokyo or Bombay requires something more dramatic. In more recent years, such a history of absence is at odds with the image of the new family man. But within the narratives of perfection, the father's position remains one that cannot be *delegated* (to another person), but must be *replaced*, either symbolically (a diamond ring might just do) or effectively. Insurance advertisements frequently remind a man that his most satisfactory replacement is money. In the symbolic system evoked by commercial imagery, the power of the father and the power of money are frequently interchangeable.

Thus, a closer look at the imagery makes it clear that even the apparently perfect family group is not so perfect after all. It creates a lack by its very existence. 'Families need…' is a recurring phrase in the language of advertising. To keep the smiles in place, families need money and they need goods – houses and mortgages, holidays, furniture, whiteware and kitchen utensils, cars, clothes and toys for the children. To achieve these necessities, we have seen how the image will need to be broken by the absence of an adult – most often the father. But the whole family image may be undermined when it is not sustained by the necessary funds. This is strikingly demonstrated by two presentations from the late 1970s – a leaflet advertising Barclays' insurance and one issued by the Department of Health and Social Security to publicise Family Income Supplement. In the Barclays' presentation a photograph in saturated colour reveals the detail of the fashionable clothes worn by all four family members. Behind them is a comfortable home with creepers over the porch. They pose beside an expensive car into which they are about to load a picnic basket and golfing clubs. The point is made to excess. They are well supplied with everything – home, car, food, clothes and leisure equipment. By contrast the family who need to draw Family Income Supplement is virtually simplified out of existence. The family members pictured on the leaflet are nothing but empty shapes. Not only are there no smiles, there are no faces. The four family positions of the diagrammatic key image are present, but they are represented by mere geometric shapes. The figures have triangular bodies, like a child's drawing, and circles for heads. They have no features, no possessions and no individuality.

The difference in the two presentations reflects the difference in the funds available to produce a costly advertising image and a welfare leaflet. Even so, this bizarre contrast points to the potential instability in the image of the apparently perfect family group. A stark distinction between consumer plenitude and welfare austerity has, if anything, increased over the years as available imagery finds new ways of celebrating family pleasure based almost exclusively on domestic consumerism. Advertising imagery has no space for families which fail, and little space for those which do not conform. The pleasure of consumption within the family and the home is always tempered by the fear of losing face – like those

Leaflet for DHSS Family Income Supplement, November 1978. Leaflet for Barclays Insurance Services, mid-1970s.

who live on Family Income Supplement and its contemporary equivalents. The absence of an image of civic well-being, outside the operations of the market, means that poorer families have become more difficult to imagine in a positive light.

New realism: problem families and family problems

The richness and diversity of family structures in contemporary Britain is well documented, and many photographers have set out to record that diversity. Richard and Sally Greenhill pictured every mundane detail of their own family life from the birth of their children in the early 1970s; Brenda Prince photographed lesbian mothers and their children in the 1980s; Donovan Wylie documented a community of travellers in the 1990s – to mention only a few whose work have featured children's family lives. Such work is occasionally featured in the broadsheet press, whose project includes reflecting the diversity of society to itself; it appears in photographic books and catalogues and is increasingly available online. Even so, the key image continues to hover in the background as an ever-present undertow to documentary realism. It remains available for those who have sought to affirm 'traditional' family values in the face of a complex reality. While historical and sociological investigations demonstrate the multitude of different ways in which adults and children have long coped with the contingencies of life, news stories, in thrall to the dominant image, are all too eager to describe diversity as breakdown and the variety of possible family groupings as perversely inappropriate. ('Lesbians stole my baby girl' is the sort of headline relished by the *Sun*).

However, there is a recent self-consciousness in image-making which expresses a deep concern about family life – not only 'abnormal' families but also the most conventional. Photographs in the new realist mode illustrate articles on the troubled relation between parents and children, uncertainty about parental discipline and control, and efforts to protect 'childhood' against the pressures of modern life. A burgeoning genre of domestic documentary sets out to expose the cracks in the perfect surface and to pull into public view emotions that have been kept firmly behind the metaphorical laurel hedge which separates family life from the rest of the world. By seeking out the awkward glance, the scowl on the face of the truculent child, the uncontrollable tantrum, this genre of documentary photography reminds viewers of the difficult underside of family relationships – without pushing the debate over the edge and into the realm of abuse and family collapse. In contrast to those advertisements which use a

constructed documentary style, the intention here is to peel away the smooth-
ness of the ideal image. It is part of a wider discourse on family problems – an
uneasy undertow in all family pictures – which includes a fear of troublesome
children and of parents who can't cope, and deal with negotiations over the
balance of power within families. In this set of images, children's energy may
become uncontrollability which breaks rather than confirms family cohesion.

The sober moralism of classic documentary observation is continuously
challenged within a visual regime powerfully influenced by advertising and fashion
styles. A more self-conscious documentary mode has taken these influences on
board and has sought to create a heightened, post-modern neo-realism, usually
in colour, in which patronising morality is thrown aside and 'dysfunctional'
families play a more active role in creating their own image. Such pictures do
indeed seek out disorderly homes, messy clothing and crying children, but they
may potentially deal with stresses and conflicts in a more indulgent way. Jillian
Edelstein's photographs of single parents for Yvonne Richards's article 'Holding
the baby' use collaboration and performance as the participants confront the
camera with a refusal to be pigeon-holed or pitied.

PART 2: THE CONSUMING CHILD

Euphoric values

Within the family context, children are largely defined by negative values. They
do not do productive work; they have no responsibility and they are dependent
on adults. The imagery of children together with their parents largely works
to reinforce these prohibitions. In the ideal family image, children retain their
childishness. Their tendency to excess, their instability and their vulnerability
reassuringly justify the protective shell of the nuclear family. However, negative
definitions are counterbalanced by the positive pleasures of childhood play.
Play is the opposite of work; it turns irresponsibility into pleasure; and it is
legitimised by childish dependence. Play is an expression of euphoric values – of
freedom, authenticity, purposelessness, creativity, and above all of enjoyment and
fun. These, too, are qualities that are seen as essential to children's childhood.
During the twentieth century, as children's play became increasingly domesticated,
the image of playful activity became a resonant public image.

The values of play are at the heart of family life and of contemporary
constructions of childishness, yet they bring their own subversive influence.
Playfulness and expressiveness all too easily lead to uncontrollable children,

Catalogue, 2002.

while hedonistic values may well disrupt socially cohesive family structures. Play is licensed within the family but is constantly pushing at the edges of the tolerable and threatening to shatter the harmony. 'The arrival of a child can turn your once beautiful house into a playground' was the heading of an article in the *Guardian* accompanied by a very blurry picture of a child leaping on a bouncy castle. Uncontained play can all too easily topple into chaos, and ruin more than your once beautiful house.

In recent years children's actual mobility has been increasingly limited for fear of dangers outside the home, yet bodily freedom and movement has become essential to the playful image. Separated from their family context, pictured children romp through the advertisements, catalogues and fashion features of the new century, often loosely arranged against neutral backgrounds. No fake documentary realism here, just an intensity of movement condensed into small, energetic bodies. As expenditure on children has increased, so has the frenzy of the image. Play is presented as an autonomous value, as the ultimate justification for the sustenance of the family itself. Playing with the children is now an important part of what adults – aunts, uncles, grandparents and friends as well as parents

– do with their leisure time. It remains an apparent guarantor of authenticity, and of values which adults envy and greedily want to reclaim for themselves.

But playful values are posing another challenge to family self-sufficiency, for these mobile childish bodies have become a sign of political and economic change. Children are now at the cutting edge of market expansion, heralding a social regime which pays less respect to traditional structures. At the end of the nineteenth century, children were excluded from economic activity when they were forbidden to engage in paid employment. By the end of the twentieth, they have decisively re-entered the economy in their role as consumers, and those precious qualities which characterise protected childhood have been re-appropriated for economic use. The antithesis between childhood and economy has been thrown into confusion; play has been transformed into a form of consumption. In the promotional image, children appear to have leapt beyond familial constraints. Surrounded by prices and product information, the context of this playful child appears to be provided by commerce alone. The parents or other adults who are expected to pay for the goods are invisible, taken for granted, replaced by financial symbols. In this commercial image, where euphoric values have a practical significance, it is easy to overlook the financial exchange which makes such exuberant playfulness possible.

Becoming a market segment

'Children's pocket money is much in demand,' the advertisers' journal *Campaign* told those of its readers who were interested in the bubble gum and cheap confectionery market. Items which stretch beyond the pocket money level must appeal to both children and to the adults who pay out on their behalf. This means that goods must convey something of the way children see themselves *and* something of the way parents see them. There remains a striking difference between the fangs, blood, skulls and lavatorial humour of items designed for children to buy, and the educational toys and tasteful clothing targeted at their parents. As Stephen Kline wrote,

> The merchants and marketers of children's goods have always paid more diligent attention than educationists to children's active imaginations and incidental cultural interests. These researchers don't bother to observe comatose children in the classroom being battered with literacy; they study them at play, at home watching television or in groups in the streets and shops. They have talked to kids about why they like playing Nintendo or trading sports cards...Marketing's ethnography of childhood has validated children's emotional and fantasy experience, which the educational researchers have by and large avoided and derided.

In 1989 the Royal Society for the Prevention of Accidents estimated that each of Britain's ten million children under 14 receives on average 20 new toys each year. The *Mail on Sunday* displayed under-fives surrounded by their possessions – toys totalling between £1000 and £2000 in value when new. In 1999 it was estimated that the average child received presents totalling £250 at Christmas. Equipment for children – to call many of these sophisticated objects 'toys' seems, in itself, rather archaic – is more complex and more varied than ever before. Famous toy shops, such as Hamleys in London, and big chains such as Toys R Us, are stacked with everything from traditional dolls to electronic equipment and the latest fad to sweep the playgrounds. In the run-up to Christmas 1994, such was the competition for Power Rangers dolls that there were all-night queues outside Hamleys. The shop rationed its sales to one per customer and fathers came to blows as supplies ran out. In 1997 Teletubbies topped the sales, and in 2001 the UK Toy and Game Council named Nintendo's Game Boy Advance, closely followed by Lego's Harry Potter. Children pressurise their parents to buy the essential toy of the year, and advertisers exploit that 'pester power'. 'Kids ... are marvellous manipulators of parental pockets', wrote a reporter for the television trade magazine *Broadcast*, 'a fact that is becoming increasingly clear to the television industry'.

The increasing consumer sophistication of children has been deplored as a loss of innocence. Children are said to be, in the title of a television programme, 'getting older younger'. Indeed, consumerism has, in the view of many critics, brought about the death of childhood itself. However, although they may be acquiring the sophisticated adult skills of consumer choice, the commodities targeted at them go directly for childish tastes. Children's preferences are intensively researched, through focus groups, interviews and observation in order to produce precisely that product which will tempt and gratify them.

> The marketers didn't have to assume that children's day dreams, hero worship, absurdist humour and keen sense of group identity were meaningless distractions or artefacts of immaturity. Rather they recognised that these attributes were the deep roots of children's culture, which could be employed as effective tools for communicating with them. Identifying the basis of children's daily experience provided the means of transforming them into a market segment.

As children change their social positioning, with their new economic importance, new child-shaped spaces have developed – including the toy shop, with its towering piles of goods on offer, and the children's bedroom, which is now not simply a place to sleep but an amply provided play environment. The catalogues of Argos and Toys R Us, advertisements and parents' magazines illustrate children's rooms in which youngsters are surrounded by their possessions. In contrast to the image of euphoric activity, this displays calm satisfaction, in which the presence of the children is subordinated to that of the goods on display. It seems that the limits of childish identity are no longer defined by their physical bodies, but are dispersed into those childish objects which surround them from the youngest age. Soft building blocks, toy trucks, a whole menagerie of anthropo-morphised animals, activity centres, Lego, Fisher Price plastic learning toys, curtains and duvet covers illustrated with popular characters, mobiles hanging from the ceiling, posters on the walls – contemporary children in their homes have access to a world peculiar to them. In its own way it reflects the outside world, but it is more colourful, miniaturised, sanitised and fantasised. Children's presence and identity have become externalised into a cast of characters which reflect childish qualities. Some have long histories, such as Pooh Bear, Noddy, Postman Pat and Barbie (who recently celebrated her fortieth birthday); others are more recent and may be shortlived – Tweenies, Teletubbies, Power Rangers, He-men, Spice Girls, Bob the Builder.

Contemporary consumer capitalism prioritises economic values above all others. Speaking directly to children, its cultural images of childhood may be in tune with family structures or may bypass them altogether – bypassing at the same time traditional morality and values. Underlying the image of the child surrounded by possessions is an intense negotiation between the moral limits of childhood, painfully established over the nineteenth century, and a much newer set of economic constraints. Children's inability to defer gratification is welcome to the marketers, but it threatens their parents' purses and often their parents' sense of the proper limits to consumption. However, by the beginning of the new century, well-provided pre-teens – already owners of personal stereos, Playstations and television sets as well as their well-stocked and constantly renewed wardrobes – are in training to be a new kind of adult. As children negotiate their tastes with the parents who buy for them, it is the parents who are learning to defer to children's wishes, recognising in them an accession to adulthood in a market-orientated world (even when the appeal to buy is disguised as 'educational'). The image of children's euphoria is working to harness children's joys and sorrows to their new role as discriminating consumers. Is this an exploit-ation of childhood, as some commentators argue, or is it the triumph of those libidinous values that, until now, children have been required to express on behalf of us all? Within these marketing presentations, if not in real life, children's desires are always satisfied.

The electronic future

In the huge imbalance of power between adults and children, new opportunities for adult fantasy are continuously presenting themselves, and the notion of children's special affinity with new media is the most recent. Online, children may be taken out of their bodies even more effectively. While sitting still, rather than physically running and jumping, they can take part in intricate virtual acrobatics. The advertisers' journal *Campaign* wrote of a 'Subclub site' aimed at 7–15-year-olds in which each child gains an avatar, a virtual personality, and can choose their own character. Significantly, the site includes 'shopping' and 'cashpoint' as well as 'joyzone' and 'my place'...'parents can credit an online account for their children which enables them to shop independently online within the subclub's walled garden of retailers'. Children's bedrooms have changed from secure and cosy environments to network centres from which they communicate way beyond the protective walls of the family home through television sets, computer games, the Internet and text messages on their mobile phones. One eight-year-old, in a study of children's views of what their future bedroom might be like, drew a room filled with enormous screens and a tiny 'virtual Mum' up in one corner.

Nervous press reports suggest that children's facility with these tools of the future have already taken them to realms incomprehensible to their elders. Anxieties range from 'An 11-year-old computer whizzkid from Sunderland ran a £10,000 copying scam from the bedroom of his home...' to 'Computer games can be as addictive as hard drugs for the most besotted children' and 'An intelligent, determined and computer literate child...could...amass a huge collection of startlingly disgusting and realistic pornography'. US President George W. Bush declared, 'a child can walk in and have their heart turn dark as a result of being on the Internet'. At the other extreme a group of (mostly American) utopian writers celebrate the imagined freedom and independence of the digital generation as they take off into the future. 'They have unprecedented mobility. They are shrinking the planet in ways their parents could never imagine.' 'They will bring about "a generational explosion" a "social awakening" that will overthrow traditional hierarchies of knowledge and power.' The rather static image of children in front of a computer screen which tends to accompany such excessive language has difficulty in matching the flights of fantasy. However, an image of a child bathed in an other-worldly glow and gazing beyond adult horizons has long represented a future that is partly unknown. At the moment when some writers see the move to consumerism as one more sign of the death of 'childhood', a new form of 'childhood' is re-born, in which the glow comes from a computer screen. This 'childhood' is transformed by digital technology and is leading the adult world into a future based in cyberspace.

NOTES ON CHAPTER 2

p.51   **charmed circle of home**: a reference to Leonore Davidoff and Catherine Hall (1976) 'The charmed circle of home', in J. Mitchell and A. Oakley (eds) *The Rights and Wrongs of Women*, Harmondsworth: Penguin.
        'jigsaw families': a survey by Virgin One, June 2002, reported by the free London newspaper *Metro*. David Fickling, 'Family life, but not as we know it', 29 May 2002.

p.52   **'cereal-packet family'**: Stephen Kline (1994) *Out of the Garden*, London: Verso, pp.56–61.
        social and historical research: for example Leonore Davidoff, Megan Doolittle, Janet Fink and Katherine Holden (1999) *The Family Story: Blood, Contract and Intimacy 1830–1960*, Harlow: Longman; Historian John Gillis (1997) distinguishes between the 'families we live with' and the 'families we live by', in other words the reality of actual family lives and the mythologies which create a sense of family solidarity, whatever the real experience. 'We would like the two to be the same, but they are not.' *A World of Their Own Making: a History of Myth and Ritual in Family Life*, Oxford: Oxford University Press, p.xv.

p.53   **Family snaps**: Jo Spence and Patricia Holland (eds) (1991) *Family Snaps: the Meanings of Domestic Photography*, London: Virago; Patricia Holland (2nd edition 2000) '"Sweet it is to scan"... Personal photographs and popular photography', in Liz Wells (ed.) *Photography: a Critical Introduction*, London: Routledge.

p.54   **one of many hundreds**: the German artist Joachim Schmidt collects snapshots sent to him from all over the world. His project is to display them in new contexts: for example as multiples of images that have an uncanny resemblance to each other, or compared with the work of prestigious photographers.
        confirming or re-thinking personal identity: see for example (from two very different perspectives) M. Csikzentmihalyi and E. Rochberg-Halton (1992) *The Meaning of Things: Domestic Symbols and the Self*, Cambridge: Cambridge University Press; Roland Barthes (1982) *Camera Lucida*, London: Jonathan Cape.
        Kodak has encouraged millions: Nancy Martha West (2000) *Kodak and the Lens of Nostalgia*, Charlottesville and London: University of Virginia Press; Don Slater (1995) 'Photography and modern vision: the spectacle of "natural magic"', in Chris Jenks (ed.) *Visual Culture*, London: Routledge.
        Jennifer Ransome Carter: interviewed by Patricia Holland, 1996.

p.55   **cheerful pictures of themselves as children**: Annette Kuhn (1995) *Family Secrets: Acts of Memory and Imagination*, London: Verso; Valerie Walkerdine, 'Behind the painted smile' and Simon Watney, 'Ordinary boys', both in J. Spence and P. Holland (eds) (1991) above.
        the invention of tradition: a reference to Eric Hobsbawm and Terence Ranger (eds) (1983/1992) *The Invention of Tradition*, Cambridge: Canto.
        Roger Fenton: Time-Life (1973) *Photographing Children*, New York: Time Inc., pp.37–38.
        Christmas: Gillis (1997) above, pp.101–4.

p.56   'sowing the seeds of despair': Lesley Garner and Ivor Davis, 'The proxy fathers: sowing the seeds of despair?' *Sunday Times* 'Magazine', March 1982.

p.57   **parallel with the notion of domesticity**: Anna Davin (1999) 'What is a child', in Anthony Fletcher and Stephen Hussey (eds) *Childhood in Question: Children, Parents and the State*, Manchester: Manchester University Press; Hugh Cunningham (1995) *Children and Childhood in Western Society since 1500*, London: Longman; Catherine Hall (1992) 'The early formation of Victorian domestic ideology', in *White, Male and Middle Class: Explorations in Feminism and History*, Cambridge: Polity.

the creation of the 'home': Witold Rybczynski (1986) *Home, a Short History of an Idea*, London: Penguin. Rybczynski points to the influence of women in designing child-friendly homes. Lillian Gilbreth, whose books on household management had considerable influence in the US, named one of them *Living with our Children* (1928). Rybczynski, p.190.

Bryan Turner: (1987) 'A note on nostalgia', *Theory, Culture and Society*, vol.4, pp.150–51.

architectural design of many English suburbs: see also Ebenezer Howard's designs for a 'social city' and his 'garden city' layouts at Letchworth and Welwyn. Patrick Wright (1985) *On Living in an Old Country*, London: Verso, especially Chapter 1, 'Everyday life, nostalgia and the national past'.

Bournville Village: built in 1879 by George Cadbury to house workers in the Cadbury Bournville factory and others. From 1900 it was run by the Bournville Village Trust. *Cadburys at Bournville 1879–1979*, Bournville Publications Department, 1979. Thanks to Arthur Lockwood for the loan of materials from his collection. The celebrated photographer Bill Brandt made a rarely seen series of pictures in 1943, showing life in the 'village', owned by the Bournville Village Trust.

Port Sunlight: built as a 'garden village' in 1888 by William Hesketh Lever, the first Lord Leverhulme. 'In line with his ideas on prosperity-sharing the building and maintenance of the village was subsidised with a portion of the profits from Lever Brothers Limited.' *The Origins of Port Sunlight Village*, Unilever External Affairs Department, 1992.

Kate Greenaway: Anne Higonnet (1998) *Pictures of Innocence: the History and Crisis of Ideal Childhood*, London: Thames and Hudson, pp.51–55.

Peter Pan* and *Christopher Robin: see Peter Coveney (1967) *The Image of Childhood*, Harmondsworth: Peregrine, Chapter 10; Jaqueline Rose (1984) *The Case of Peter Pan, or the Impossibility of Children's Fiction*, London: Macmillan.

p.58   **'thousands had only dreamed'**: see Patricia Holland (1991) 'The old order of things changed', in Spence and Holland (eds) above.

still defines the dream home: *Homes and Gardens*, in August 2001 included an advertisement for old-style English furniture; a feature on the use of lace; a feature on converting a Gloucestershire cottage and another on converting a French farmhouse.

p.59   **Anne McLintock**: (1995) *Imperial Leather: Race, Gender and Sexuality in the Colonial Conquest*, London: Routledge, p.209.

'simplicity, personal authenticity and emotional spontaneity': Turner (1987) above.

p.60   **Tony Blair**: photographs of young Leo Blair with his Prime Minster father and barrister mother, taken by Mary McCartney, daughter of the former Beatle Paul, gave rise to much comment on the softening of Tony Blair's image as well as the changing role of fathers. The *Daily Mail* invited 'experts' to analyse the photographs; it was 'body language expert' Judy James who described Blair as 'surprisingly sultry' (23 May 2000). Victoria Coren in the *Evening Standard* devoted paragraphs to 'the Peter Pan of pop. Sorry, politics', and declared, 'I think we should all take two weeks off, just to look at the pictures' (24 May 2000). The *Sun*'s agony aunt, Deirdre Saunders, captioned a tongue-in-cheek photo-story (posed by look-alikes), showing Tony woken in the small hours and dealing with the affairs of state, baby in one arm (23 May 2000). As well as on the front pages of all the newspapers, the pictures were instantly available on the No 10 website.

Davina McCall: in Andrew G. Marshall, 'Coochie-Coo (So what do those photos REALLY reveal about her, him and darling little diddums?)', *Daily Mail*, 29 September 2001.

'Now all you need is wife and kids': *Independent on Sunday*, 8 November 1998.

p.63   **Brenda Prince:** her sequence of photographs *The Politics of Lesbian Motherhood*, June 1982, is discussed by Val Williams (1986) *Women Photographers: the Other Observers, 1900 to the Present*, London: Virago, pp.176–78.

domestic documentary: the *Independent* and the *Guardian* newspapers, with their critical, educated readerships and their regular features which nag through issues of parenting, relationships and the problems of domestic life, are a prolific source for this kind of imagery.

abuse and family collapse: see Chapters 5 and 6.

p.64   **a heightened, post-modern neo-realism:** the exhibition *Who's Looking at the Family?*, curated by Val Williams at the Barbican Centre in 1994, explored many genres of photography dealing with families and family relationships, including the heightened drama of Nick Waplington's 'Living Room' series. The work of photographers such as Richard Billingham and Nan Goldin, circulated in a fine-art context, have influenced the trend. Jillian Edelstein's pictures appeared in *Sunday Times* 'Magazine', 1995.

Euphoric values: Roland Barthes (1977) 'The Rhetoric of the image', in *Image, Music, Text*, trans. Stephen Heath, London: Fontana.

play became increasingly domesticated: Lisa Jacobsen 'Revitalising the American home: children's leisure and the re-valuation of play 1920–1940', *Journal of Social History*, Winter 1996/Spring 1997, pp.573–97.

p.65   **'turn your once beautiful house into a playground':** *Guardian* 'Weekend', 21 July 2001.

p.66   **guarantor of authenticity:** 'children are the necessary countervailing force to liberal modernity', writes Laurie Taylor, *Prospect*, June 2001. See Chapter 4.

role as consumers: Barrie Gunter and Adrian Furnham (1998) *Children as Consumers: a Psychological Analysis of the Young People's Market*, London: Routledge.

'Children's pocket money is much in demand': Walls Pocket Money Monitor began in 1975. In 1997 pocket money was shown to average £2.33, but children's weekly income, which includes jobs and gifts, averaged £5.14. *Independent*, 7 August 1997.

The merchants and marketers: Kline (1994) above, pp.18–19.

p.67   **Royal Society for the Prevention of Accidents:** quoted by Bryony Coleman and Jenny Cowley, 'What is your little treasure worth?', *Mail on Sunday*, 3 December 1989; *Guardian*, 28 December 1998. See also Gunter and Furnham (1998) above.

UK Toy and Game Council: quoted in *Harrow Times*, 15 November 2001.

marvellous manipulators of parental pockets: *Broadcast*, 2 December 1994.

deplored as a loss of innocence: for example 'The loss of our innocence: the age of computers has robbed children of their fascination with toys', *Independent*, August 1996.

Getting Older Younger: BBC Bristol for BBC2, 1999. The advertising agency Saatchi and Saatchi estimated that the cut-off point for buying toys has been falling by one year every five years.

the death of childhood: see David Buckingham (2000) *After the Death of Childhood: Growing up in the Age of Electronic Media*, Cambridge: Polity, Chapter 2.

The marketers didn't have to assume: Kline (1994) above, p.19.

p. 68   **dispersed into those childish objects:** Alan Prout (ed.) (1997) *The Body, Childhood and Society*, London: Macmillan, pp.2, 11. Prout argues that bodies are 'hybrid entities' inextricably interwoven with artefacts, machines and technologies.

Barbie: manufactured by the American toy company Mattel, and first appeared in 1959. 'We didn't depict Barbie as a doll. We treated her as a real life teenage fashion model.' Quoted by Kline (1994) above pp.169–70.

p. 69   **'Subclub site':** *Campaign*, 9 February 2001.

'virtual Mum': Sonia Livingstone and George Gaskell (1997) 'Children and the television screen, modes of participation in the media environment', in Jo Langham Brown, Sue Ralph and Tim Lees, *Tune In or Buy In*, Luton: John Libbey Media. Also lectures on this research conducted in association with the Broadcasting Standards Council.

'An 11-year-old computer whizzkid': 'Computer buff, 11, ran copying scam', *Guardian*, 27 February 1999.

'Computer games can be as addictive': '"Hard drug" fear for computer children', *Guardian*, 13 March 1995.

'An intelligent, determined and computer literate': 'Doomed', *Independent*, 6 September 1994. See also Patricia Holland (1996) 'I've just seen a hole in the reality barrier! Children, childishness and the media in the ruins of the twentieth century', in Jane Pilcher and Stephen Wagg (eds) *Thatcher's Children? Politics, Childhood and Society in the 1980s and 1990s*, Brighton: Falmer Press.

George W. Bush: *Independent*, 7 June 2001, on a report that parents of the school students massacred by two of their classmates at Columbine High School in 1999 were bringing a law suit against manufacturers and distributors of computer games such as *Tomb Raider*.

'They have unprecedented mobility': Don Tapscott (1998) *Growing Up Digital: the Rise of the Net Generation*, New York: McGraw Hill, quoted by Buckingham (2000) above, p.47. See Buckingham, Chapter 3, for a discussion of the 'electronic utopians'.

Sharpen up with breakfast!

Research studies involving ability tests have shown that children who do not eat breakfast have slower speed and accuracy scores than those who do. Teachers too know the poor standard of achievement reached by improperly nourished, inattentive children. A good nutritious breakfast is provided by Kellogg's Sultana Bran with milk, orange juice or vitamin C enriched drink, toast and a glass of milk. It is a breakfast that is quick, convenient and it will send children off to school with enough energy to see them through to lunch.

Give children a good start in life – give them a Sultana Bran breakfast!

Kellogg's
SULTANA BRAN

Elliott School

making the right choice

"A Good School With Outstanding Features" OFSTED

Elliott is a Foundation school with a dedicated staff that values each child's unique characteristics. We are committed to providing the very best education for each student. We believe that a close relationship between home and school is vital in ensuring a successful, well-ordered school, where children learn effectively and teachers enjoy teaching. Elliott has been recognised by Her Majesty's Chief Inspector of School's as an outstanding school (2000).

3

Ignorant pupils and harmonious nature

In the mind of the child we may perhaps find the key to progress, and, who knows, the beginning of a new civilization.

Maria Montessori

Children are not born good; they have to be disciplined, otherwise they are a threat to the rest of society.

Rhodes Boyson

The key to progress

(Two postcards from my collection: one reproduces a 1930s lithograph by Soviet artist Aleksandr Deineka. It shows a boy and girl wearing red pioneer scarves, against a background of modernist tower blocks. They are hand in hand, unsmiling, with determined expressions. 'We demand universal compulsory education', says the caption. The second is from a sequence of black-and-white photographs by Janine Weidel, documenting British school life in the 1970s. Two bored-looking boys sit aimlessly behind a desk, one picking his fingernails, the other gazing into space. A similar picture was used on a poster made by the National Union of School Students, ironically captioned 'The best years of our lives?')

Pictures of children being educated tend to be constructed to argue a case (in the two examples above either *for* compulsory education or *against* irrelevant schooling) or to quell anxieties. In one of those paradoxes which characterise the imagery of childhood, the desired images of schooling indicate children's incapacities rather than their capabilities. Two key images resonate through the popular media. One is an image of close concentration, with the child's head bent down over a task, usually at a school desk. The other shows a child with hand raised, apparently in eager competition for the teacher's attention. The first is an image of solitary learning, while the 'hands-up' image suggests that such self-absorption is not altogether desirable. This image pulls the child's attention away from his work and towards an adult, a teacher, the representative of the institution, who will scrutinise, criticise and assess. The raised hand places the schoolboy in competition with his classmates (this well-adjusted student striving to succeed is most often male). The teacher is not visible in the image, but the eyes of the eager child gaze towards that potent space in front of the frame where it is assumed a teacher stands, but is, in fact, currently occupied by the viewer. When testing and grading are all-important, it is not learning but the display of learning that counts.

We have seen how the imagery of childhood regularly demonstrates children's lack of adult knowledge. Childish innocence of the world creates the poignancy which pictures exploit. Viewing adults understand all too well the transience of the childish state and the bitterness of real-life experience. We long to preserve a nostalgic image of blissful unknowingness partly to fend off the disillusion that is to come. But the ignorance associated with the image of the schoolchild is of a different sort. Apart from pictures of very young children in nursery or infants classes, viewers are not invited to be sentimentally moved by pictures of a child at school. Instead, the schoolchild's ignorance is shown as a problem to be solved; it is the very rationale for the education system. The face of the child with upraised arm, so eager to please, reflects the anxieties of the whole society. He may well represent a 'key to progress' or even 'the beginning of a new civilization'.

Since the inception of universal state schooling in Britain from the 1870s, the changing image of the schoolchild has reflected shifting political and social ideologies embedded in the school system. Theories of schooling are always related to possible social futures, so whether education is seen as a civic struggle for democracy or as the reproduction and entrenchment of traditional, hierarchical values, this particular image of childhood has carried a strong social resonance. The view which sees childhood as a value in itself does not always fit easily with imagery which contemplates the weighty implications of educational ideologies.

Transition to school

The institutions of family and school put forward competing definitions of childhood, and the conflict can be traced in the imagery. The family is an informal organisation based on sentiment and a network of commitments and ties; the school is a formal structure, subject to legislation and public policy; yet both construct a childhood with no independent validity and little independent existence. In the transition from home to school it is the *quality* of childish dependence that changes. When a child is shown as a pupil, there is a calming of the image, as the disciplines of the institution create a sort of latency period between the euphoria of early childhood and the chaos of youth. The young child's body becomes less mobile. It is encased in special clothing and encumbered with special equipment.

The imagery makes much of the qualities children lack – knowledge, understanding and the competencies of adult life. The job of the professionals of education is to make good these childish lacks, but, in the paradoxical construction of childhood, they must also make sure that children's ignorance and incompetence are preserved and made visible, since the absence of adult skills continues to characterise 'childhood', and to justify the very existence of the institution. Children must not be deprived of their childhood too soon ('The end of childhood? Parents' hopes and fears for the schools revolution' was a headline in the *Guardian* 'Education'). Educational professionals must carry out the double task of dividing childhood from adulthood and of forming a bridge between the two states, but the imagery shows more effort going into enforcing the separation than into enabling the transition from one to the other.

Separation from the adult world involves creating a physical space which is unique to children, within which the meanings of childhood and childishness may be negotiated anew. School buildings are expressive indications of changing views of childhood, from the gothic piles of the first state schools of the 1880s and 1890s to the airily laid out primary schools of the 1930s and the huge, aspirational comprehensives of the 1960s. Each creates its own version of a child-shaped space, where childish impulsiveness can fight it out with school-based discipline.

The image of the schoolchild is modulated according to whether its intended audience is parents or teachers. As children move from the emotional space of the home to the formal space of the school, parents' rights over their children are dramatically curtailed and family relationships must be readjusted in accordance with legal educational requirements. Every September sees 'Back to school' features in shop windows, advertisements and consumer magazines. The

axis of the classic family image is swung around, so that the exchange of smiles
is no longer between family members within the frame, but between the child
who is leaving and the parent-viewer who is left behind. On the cover of *Mother*,
September 1983, in a touching close-up, a little boy who seems much too young
to be encased in his heavy grey uniform, could well be on the edge of tears. A
presentation from *Parents* shows a boy and a girl festooned with the shoes,
crayons, satchels and other paraphernalia needed for 'my first day at school'. In
2002 the supermarket Tesco offered £4 off schoolwear on presentation of a *Daily
Mail* coupon. The promotion showed a group of school-clad model children,
their bodies mobile and energetic, their smiles intended to reassure 'their' mothers
and all viewers of the image who put themselves in the position of 'mother' by
the very act of looking.

The theme of happiness has been part of the discourse of the post-war
primary school, and happiness is evoked to sustain the links between children
and their parents even as they depart through the school gates. It is the parents'
desire which is reflected in these children's faces. 'If he (or she) is happy, then
you're laughing,' *Parents* told its readers. The faces in the image reassure, but the
regime of the school has already laid claim to the children's bodies. The playful
gestures contrast with the dark skirts, stiff blazers, school hats and heavy loads
they carry. Yet it is the parents who must provide the equipment and clothing
which symbolise this contest of definitions. They must purchase those satchels,
pencils, notebooks, sensible shoes, clean shirts, caps and sweatshirts in the school
colours. The well-equipped schoolchild appears as a shiny surface, washed,
polished and brushed, a credit to those who service him or her. To produce a
child in this image is the job of the servicing mother, and in doing so she
services the school itself. The smiles in the picture maintain her relationship
with her children and ensure her support for the school regime.

Since children go to school not to follow their own desires, but to live out
the desires of the whole community, the tentative looks on the faces of these
five-year-olds in their new school clothes express a major social concern. The
weight is on their shoulders. It is up to them to grasp the importance of school
for society and, at the same time, to reconstruct it as the only pathway to their
personal future.

Dangerous coagulation

To realise its promise, the school must enclose this child – and all children – within its boundaries, and the child must be subject to its control. Unlike a family, made up of members of different ages and sexes who may be widely dispersed, schools contain large numbers of the same type of person gathered in a limited and clearly defined space. Pictures which seek to represent 'school' often set out to reflect this multiplicity. Their frames are filled with many children, gregariously bunched together, engaged in similar activities, leading to similar ends. Differences such as those of gender or ethnicity are subordinated to categorisation by age. The children in these school images tend to be unnamed exemplars, each one representing its own generation. On entering school, a child becomes one of a type. One favourite newspaper image to illustrate children in school is a bunch of kids cheerfully waving at the camera in the playground or classroom, in a democratic, undifferentiated mixing.

Such a gathering together of children carries symbolic dangers of its own. School becomes a place where order and disorder constantly confront each other. There is the danger inherent in crowding itself, in promiscuous contact with numerous others ('Is this what they mean by "crammer"?' was the caption to one newspaper photograph of an overcrowded classroom). Assembled together, children may develop autonomous activities which exclude adults. They may egg each other on or form into gangs. Their uproar and mobility are aggravated by their numbers, so that it is difficult to keep track of a single individual at every moment in time. In the imagery of school this tendency is kept at bay by a visual effort to present children as a purposeful group, and to convert the incipient disorder of the crowd into what Michel Foucault classically described as a 'disciplinary society'. For Foucault, 'The principle of "enclosure" is neither constant, nor indispensable, nor sufficient in disciplinary machinery. This machinery works space in a much more flexible and detailed way.' He outlines some of the principles of 'disciplinary space': 'Each individual has his own place and each place its individual. Avoid distributions in groups; break up collective dispositions; analyse confused, massive or transient pluralities. Disciplinary space tends to be divided into as many sections as there are bodies or elements to be distributed.' And any teacher would endorse an effort to 'eliminate the effects of imprecise distributions, the uncontrolled disappearance of individuals, their diffuse circulation, their unstable and dangerous coagulation'.

To achieve an orderly regime, childish spontaneity, which is so highly valued in the family imagery, must take on negative connotations. The restlessness of childhood, its random and purposeless movement, indicates precisely those qualities that school is designed to modify. Spontaneity may be pictured as naughtiness, inattention or downright disobedience. Above all, on entering school, children find their right to undirected play limited to a designated space, the playground, and time, playtime. The playground image itself may be seen as a threat, infested by bullies and children running wild. Play itself is linked to uncontrollability and the fear that children may move beyond the reach of the school's disciplinary regime.

In harmony with the nature of the child

The concept of play is threaded throughout the many definitions of childhood, particularly in the prosperous West. Play is the antithesis of work and of seriousness. It is characterised by expressive values. It is an end in itself. That means there are special problems when children bring playful values to the serious business of education. The imagery of school, and particularly of the primary school, must balance 'play' against the related concepts of 'learning' and 'work'. 'Learning' is the only work permitted to children, since adult, productive work is forbidden to them, and learning becomes suspect if it looks too much like play. On the other hand, play may loose its value if it has too instrumental a purpose. The challenge is to define activities which seem like play as images of learning. The subversive possibility that play may invade the disciplinary space of the school has given rise to acute public anxiety over the last quarter of the twentieth century. On the other hand, the introduction of 'Early Learning Goals' for three- to six-year-olds in 1999 seemed to bring a negation of the essence of childhood at an unacceptably young age.

The desired image of stiff, deskbound, serious-faced pupils which launched the educational initiatives of the late nineteenth century was challenged by a group of child-centred theorists and progressive educationists in the early twentieth. They preferred an image of active bodies and smiling faces, and for them childish play was an inspiration. H. Cauldwell Cook wrote about his 'Play School'; Maria Montessori developed learning equipment which looked very much like toys; Susan Isaacs argued that children should be free to express their playfulness both as expressive exuberance and as intense, pleasurable absorption in an activity. The relation between play and learning became the centre of a dispute which has lasted for more than a century and has both personal and social aspects. In its personal form, a pessimistic definition of childhood in which play is at best wildness, and at worst violent and dangerous, is opposed by an optimistic one in which play expresses a childish freshness. A perceived need to control children and to tame the threat from wildness is opposed by a desire to build on children's playful self-expression. In its social form it is argued on the one hand that society needs well trained and disciplined members who know how to keep play time and work time separate, and on the other that playful values produce well-balanced citizens and a happier community.

In the years following World War II, the campaign to allow playful values into schools was in the ascendant. The Plowden Report, *Children in their Primary Schools*, confirmed what was to become the orthodoxy in classrooms for younger children: 'This distinction between work and play is false, possibly throughout life, certainly in the primary school... Play is the central activity in all nursery schools and many infant schools.'

The report was illustrated with photographs of child-friendly principles, gleaned from the archives of local country councils (and one from toy manufacturer James Galt). A picture of a boy of about eight caught in the midst of an energetic leap was juxtaposed with one showing two boys facing each other in a playground – perhaps playing a chasing game, or perhaps about to launch into a fight – and a group of girls rehearsing a dance. From inside the classroom, photographs showed groups of children, heads down, intent on their activity. They are playing with building bricks, using scientific equipment, making models, painting, working with tools. The pictures echoed those taken at progressive schools, such as Susan Isaacs's Malting House, and provided a model for thirty years of images of primary classrooms.

This is a vision of an education which aims to be, in Plowden's words, 'in harmony with the nature of the child'. In the spirit of harmony, teachers and pupils are presented as collaborators in the enterprise of the school. For Plowden the best teacher was an invisible one, whose values were internalised within the children. The teacher could leave the room and the class would carry on without noticing the absence. Teachers rarely dominate pictures of the progressive classroom. They are either absent from the frame, or their heads rise slightly above the heads of the children. When such pictures do show a teacher – as in advertisements recruiting new teachers – we find them either holding the rapt attention of a group of delighted youngsters, or *behind* the group, encouraging them, initiating and sharing their activity.

But to read these images of the post-Plowden primary classroom as pictures of children doing their own thing is to misinterpret them. Visible or not, the teacher remains the controlling centre. The exchange of looks between teacher and pupil is by no means reciprocal, nor does it display the mutual pleasure seen in looks exchanged between family members. In this image, while teachers watch children in order to control and guide them, children look at teachers only in ways that indicate their status as pupils. They respond when the teacher addresses them directly and pay careful attention when the whole class is being taught. To create a suitable image of child-in-the-progressive-classroom, a pedagogic eye is needed, creating a one-way relationship that has much in common with the structures of documentary photography. The documentary photographer aims to look where the look is not returned and where the subjects of the picture are unaware of the photographic gaze, just as the eyes of the child-centred teacher observes the classroom and its inhabitants. The practice of observation and documentation of children's activities has been a central tenet of progressive pedagogy. At all times children must make themselves available to the professional eye, and must reveal themselves without artifice, forgoing the temptation to adopt what Maria Montessori described as a 'mask of seemliness', or indeed any other mask. To preserve the innocence of the image, they must present themselves without strategies for self-protection.

The Plowden image faces the challenge of play head on and converts it into work through learning. Many books of 1960s and 1970s contained photographs of this sort – a desired image of an energetic child fulfilling their childishness *and* learning at the same time. The imagery seemed to square the circle, to solve the paradox, and to illustrate that learning could be both orderly and 'in harmony with the nature of the child'. The Inner London Education Authority's *Contact*, distributed free to the Authority's teacher employees, was, in the late 1970s, a substantial magazine, printed on glossy paper. In its many pages of colour photographs, concerned teachers are presented with visual confirmation of the value of their work. In a regular feature, *Contact* profiled a London school, using action-documentary-style photography, with children 'captured' in the midst of their activities. Many small frames arranged on a unifying page reflect the diversity of classroom activities. They show cheerful bustle and clutter, each frame filled with the active bodies of children and a rich profusion of objects spread around them – live rabbits, building bricks, paints, plasticine, new technology.

The magazine recognised that the activity of learning was not immediately visible, and instructed its readers on how to interpret the photographs and the classroom itself, so that this image of intricate control would not be confused with forms of childhood play which are completely self-directed. Viewers should not be misled by the apparently unstructured bustle, but should note 'the degree of involvement of the individual child and the work habits acquired', and especially 'the efforts of the teacher to inculcate good habits of orderliness and the necessary persistence to complete a task successfully and learn the correct attitudes of tidiness'. Unstructured play may well put the position of the adult under threat, since a child absorbed in play is not concerned to display the subservience that secures adult power. But in these pictures the movements of the children are organised according to their learning activity, and every object has not only its place but also its label. Working near the borders of discipline, this classroom must be read as a major achievement of discipline. It is designed to challenge and defuse the dangers of disorder and lack of control through an internalisation of the values of structured learning.

A pragmatic social-democratic politics has been associated with both documentary photography and the progressive classroom. They share an aim to create an informed public to participate in a society in which guidance by educated professionals plays an important part. The 'social' eye of the documentarist sets out to provide clear, objective information; the progressive-education movement is committed to improving facilities for the underprivileged and playing down differences in ability and attainment. It was this dual stress on the role of public-service professionals and a commitment to egalitarian politics that brought progressivism increasingly under attack as the political mood changed in the 1980s. Campaigners on behalf of traditional teaching and formal assessment questioned the social-democratic image and demanded who has the right to observe the teachers?

Backlash or promise

From the mid-1970s, the child-centred classroom became an object of scorn from an unsympathetic press, for whom a confusion between work and play was symptomatic of disorder and political subversion. 'Gone are the two-by-two rows of desks. Pupils sit haphazardly grouped at work tables – a doubtful improvement when it comes to a handwriting class in one South London junior school, where, because of the table arrangement, one half of the class were sitting with their backs to the blackboard,' wrote Joanna Patyna in the *London Evening News*, under a Plowden-style photograph. The campaign was on to change the image, to get the teacher back at the front of the class and the desks in orderly lines facing the blackboard. The preferred image of a 'traditional' classroom associated itself with educational standards which must be imposed on children rather than drawn out of them. In this view, children cannot be trusted to internalise disciplinary norms, the nature of the child is far from harmonious, and the appropriate politics are those of competition and market choice.

According to the traditionalists, children need training, clear-cut structures and punishment where necessary. The changing imagery of school illustrates this conflict between internal and external constraint: in the one the body of the child is controlled by the disciplines of the mind; in the other by the disciplines of the regime. Each image deals in its own way with the twin moments of liberation and control. In successive editions of a local paper, published as the contest between the two positions was at its height, the rival images were reflected in different photographic styles. Both presentations set out, in the manner of the local press, to please the readers and to maintain circulation by including as many local names and faces as possible. Both aimed to demonstrate to parents the work of their children's schools. They could hardly be more different.

At St David's we do not see learning in progress. Instead, the children greet the camera, their parents and the outside world, sitting at their desks or grouped around their work. They display the *results* of their learning, holding up certificates and pointing to their paintings. They show their achievements and are themselves achievements. They are the products of the school, presented to the school's customers, their parents. The photographs are formal and static, so that the *processes* of learning are concealed and the work of expressing the values of the school is done by certificates, badges and tidy uniforms. By contrast, in the photographs of Merlin school, we find the familiar documentary image of children absorbed in their activities. Here the process of learning is itself on display in the disposition of the children's bodies and the equipment they are using – weighing machines, cookery equipment, paints and easels. These pictures are directed less at the eye of the notional parent than at the pedagogic eye of the teacher. In this case it is the teacher's eye that is represented by the camera, and composes the pictures.

In the bitter disputes of the 1980s and 1990s, the interests of 'parents' and 'teachers' were frequently presented as incompatible and irreconcilable. 'Parents' were seen as far less threatened by the St David's type of school, and as we look at the two groups of photographs it is not difficult to understand why. At St David's the teachers appear to have accomplished a task. They have worked on their charges and offered them back to their parents/owners, produced, finished and dealt with. The Merlin pictures, by contrast, make considerable demands on the parents who view them. First, they must make an effort to interpret the pictures, which, as we have seen, involves a specialised knowledge that chiefly belongs to teachers. Second, and perhaps more importantly, parents are made irrelevant by the image. The work of this school is shown not as a service to the *parents* but to their *children*. It seems to be encouraging children's independent development and offering them a degree of autonomy. Those mechanisms by which the pupils' learning is paced and controlled – testing, grading and measuring attainment – are not given prominence here.

Kentish Times, October 1983. Photographs: Ken Watt and Don Reed.

'Children are not born good,' declared Conservative MP and ex-headmaster Sir Rhodes Boyson, 'they have to be disciplined, otherwise they're a threat to the rest of society.' As a contributor to the 'Black Papers' on education, published as a response to Plowden, Rhodes Boyson was part of a long campaign which brought about a radical change in educational policy and culminated in the Conservative Education Reform Act of 1988 (described as the 'biggest shock to the school system in 50 years'). It was a change in which the desired image of schooling once more became an image of rows of children, seated at desks, paying close attention to a teacher. The 1997 Labour government intensified the drive towards disciplined schooling, structured teaching, regular testing, inspections, and the measurement of schools against nationally established criteria of success. But although the ideological battle had been won at the level of policy, the imagery continued to reflect conflicting views in the definition of childhood. What changed was the social-class alignment of these images.

In the period immediately after the Second World War, the perspective of the upwardly mobile segment of the working and lower-middle classes had dominated popular discourse on education. After all, these were groups for whom social improvement was attainable only through schooling. State schools were offering children a precious value that had not been available to their parents. Education promised a better life. But by the end of the century, the class location of the dominant narratives had changed. Now they were dominated by a successful middle class who sensed that their values and privileges were under attack, and feared that a state education would pull their children down. The concept of possible futures has changed, no longer aspirational and democratic, but individualistic and competitive.

The invention of tradition

To come into contact with the formal academic curriculum, English working class children have to pass through another 'symbolic universe' of uniforms, honours boards, prize days...etc...Any democratic conception of education has always had to be advanced in the context of educational traditions and practices that were produced by – and themselves serve to reproduce – the undemocratic political and educational thinking of the nineteenth century.

In each of its contexts the imagery of childhood is torn between a rather frightening orientation towards the future and a more comfortable backwards glance. This tension displays itself most strongly in the imagery of school, which harks back to the past with a confidence quite unlike the sentimental nostalgia of other forms of childhood imagery. In a powerful social construct fraught with paradox, one version of the history of education draws on traditional forms and image-laden rituals to create a spectacular display of visualised antiquity. This set of images refers further back in history than any other image associated with childhood, to a medievalism revived in the mid-nineteenth century, yet it still gives value to many newly commodified educational establishments. A resonant image for the concept of excellence in British education is the expensive and prestigious public school and its state-funded imitator, the grammar school, which both seek to distinguish themselves, not least by ritual and visual display, from everyday run-of-the-mill secondary schools (notoriously referred to by a spokesman for the British government as 'bog standard comprehensives').

As state-funded secondary education was hesitantly established at the beginning of the twentieth century, Robert Morant – the civil servant in charge of implementing the 1902 Education Act – wrote that 'uniforms, badges and latin mottoes' were the essential characteristics of a true secondary school, and many aspiring establishments set about providing themselves with these markers of antiquity. At the beginning of the twenty-first century, the ancient universities and the elite public schools continue to cast their magic shade. The visible signs of the 'best' education still include the teacher's gown, the monastic cloister and the gothic arch, all frequently hinted at in visual presentations of schooling. Within this image children are subordinated to the symbols they carry on their bodies (school tie, heraldic badge, school motto) and the positioning of their bodies within a ritualised space (lined up for assembly, standing when the teacher comes into the room). This is a *performance* of tradition, a visual marker of privilege, a theatre of ritual. It is certainly intended to make an impression on its participants, but in the contemporary, post-modern world, tradition also plays an ornamental and decorative role for an audience constructed as tourists.

Despite the excess of the performance (its tourist aspect), the visual reminders of an elite education enable a continuous elision between privilege and ability. The signs of wealth have come to stand for cleverness, those of exclusivity for excellence. Whenever ordinary, hard-working schools use such devices as badges, gilded lettering, panelled halls, archaic uniform, to represent themselves to their pupils, they are, willy-nilly, recycling the meanings of hierarchy and exclusion. They are also referring to an ecclesiastical past where learning is associated with godliness, and scholarliness is cut off from the melee of the everyday world. Refined places of learning can be presented as being above grubby politics, since their imagery refers to the dignified ranking of pre-industrial times with its hierarchically stratified society, outside the unholy scramble of capitalist exchange and grab. This lofty image has provided a conceptual framework for the whole of the British debate on education, which, according to Carr and Hartnett, is

conducted in 'a language which embodies educational assumptions and voc-
abularies which speak to pre-democratic traditions and prevent fundamental
concerns about the democratic role of education being adequately expressed'.

A school uniform in particular can invest its present wearers, with no effort
on their part, with a prestige brought by past wearers. The older and more
confident the school, the odder its costume and its symbols may be. (My postcard
collection includes a crocodile of Kings College Cambridge choristers in gowns
and top hats filing past the famous chapel.) In its claim to be an unchanging
inheritance from the past, school uniform must be the antithesis of fashion, with
little attention to convenience or comfort. Parents are informed that to produce
their child as a uniform image is a sign of social achievement. ('Spot the kid from
Bash Street,' challenged an Abbey Life advertisement above four neatly blazered
youngsters, while an ad for Woolworths asked, 'Are you as smart as your kids?')

Uniform is a convenient marker of schooling in other ways. It is a visible
sign of the multiplicity characteristic of school imagery, and it adds the important
ingredient of conformity. It gathers children together in an orderly fashion, gets
them literally into line, encourages a uniformity of stance and bodily control as
well as dress. It speaks of a uniformity of quality which will transcend individual
quirks and oddities. (The photographic image can be corrected, even when the
pupil resists. A GCSE student had her pink dreadlocks electronically transformed to an acceptable brown by the school photographer.) This is a reassuring
image for adults, for it tells them where children belong and who is responsible
for them. It has become an easily available shorthand to indicate school itself.
This image of conformity and exclusion is an unavoidable part of the daily lumber
of pedagogical meanings, visually imported even when unwanted. Through
uniform, the 'traditional' version of schooling has become an exemplar of all
education. Childhood is confined and defined.

Although this mythic image calls up the distant past, the politics of the 1980s
pushed it firmly into the present. When changes to the law allowed schools to opt
out of local-authority control, the resonant strength of the grammar-school
image contributed to its presentation as a more reliable alternative. The *Observer*
'Review' used a photograph showing uniformed teenagers in a shady cloister
beside the headline, 'The best for one's child?'. The *Daily Mail* featured a Skegness
school that was opting out. Its begowned headmaster and suitably uniformed
sixth-formers declared themselves proud of their newly adopted latin motto:
'Murus Aeneus Conscientia Sana' ('A clean conscience is like a wall of bronze').
Antiquity can be easily appropriated by a market model of education, for, unlike
the less visible qualities of the social-democratic public-service model, 'traditions'
can be constructed whenever needed and can be put up for sale. 'Now we are a

business,' declared the Skegness headmaster. The spectacle of education itself entered the marketplace, the more exotic signifiers of learning gained economic value, and the backward-looking iconography of traditional schooling was appropriated for a future-orientated world of competition.

The powerful claim of public schools and grammar schools to offer the 'best' education, accompanied by easy access to the 'best' universities and elite professions, has continued to mean that comprehensive schools which aim to offer equal opportunities to all have not been represented as an alternative vision but as a poor second best. No image has emerged to characterise the democratic aspirations of these secondary schools equivalent to the image of the Plowden primary classroom. Instead, in the narratives of the popular press, children have been described as abandoned in a comprehensive jungle. The image of youngsters in undifferentiated groups (dangerous coagulation) has been mobilised as a potential danger – and has characterised structureless and disorganised schooling. The blame has been laid, once more, at the door of the teachers. When 'tradition' was opposed by teachers they were condemned as 'trendy', while efforts to create a more equal regime were jeered at as 'political correctness'. 'We can't take a chance on teachers like this…' declared the *Daily Mail* in 1984 above a drawing of teacher with an afro hairstyle, a 'coal not dole' badge, a bomber jacket and trainers. More than a decade later, the *Independent* was still (partly tongue-in-cheek) characterising teachers as 'trendy' (young, female, in sweatshirt, jeans and trainers) or 'traditionalist' (middle-aged, male, in mortarboard and gown). But the *Mail*'s mood was more bitter. By 2001 its theme remained the same, even if fashions had changed. Now it claimed to reveal how teachers' 'stupefying political correctness wreaked havoc with children's lives'.

Shock reports and schools of shame

The image of school appears in the national press in two strikingly different contexts. In the 'quality' press, such as the *Guardian* education pages and the *Times Education Supplement*, the address is largely to professionals. These publications expect an audience conversant with educational policy and often directly involved as teachers, governors, academics or active parents. The imagery is realist and observational, sometimes illustrating an argument, sometimes exploring a practice. By contrast, the popular press addresses its readers as laypeople, highly suspicious of the obfuscations of professionalism. These readers are seen as parents with a straightforward, commonsense approach, who may not be well educated themselves but are worldly-wise and want the best for their children. They are assumed to have no stake in perpetuating education as a protected area, for it is an area from which they themselves have frequently been excluded. They are thought to see schools as places of restricted access, protected by arrogant and unaccountable teachers. Such readers, then, will not be surprised when they open their daily papers and are taken behind the scenes into the forbidden territory of school to find dreadful behaviour and scandalous goings-on.

In the daily sequencing of the national press, narratives develop over the weeks and years which gain their own momentum. These long-running dramas create a framework into which the individual news items are fitted. They provide a set of expectations, including familiar plot-lines and a cast of characters who move between the news, features and gossip pages. There are heroes and villains, victims and aggressors – archetypal roles waiting to be filled by whatever real individual is the subject of the next topical scandal. Readers follow developments as if following a soap opera, eager for the next instalment.

In the last decades of the twentieth century, a popular drama of this sort built up around education. The heroes were 'parents', cast as the losers in the struggle for education, who were campaigning for their 'freedom' – in other words for the right to choose their children's schools. The villains were the 'teachers', determined to thwart the parents and blinded to the children's interests by their devotion to ideology. Teachers, in this scenario, disguise political opinions as professional expertise and use fancy language to deceive and confuse. Against this background readers have been entertained with discipline scandals, sexual scandals, and scandals centring on improper teacher behaviour and uncontrollable pupils. They have been given shock reports (*Daily Mirror*) and schools of shame (*Evening News*). Stories have explored those margins of a school's activity which are largely unspeakable in the professional discourse. When inner-city 'sink' schools, with their almost insuperable problems of underfunding and disadvantaged pupils, hit the headlines, the popular press, led by the *Sun* and the *Daily Mail*, demanded more discipline and an assertion of 'standards' that they claimed could only be imposed by 'traditional' teaching methods.

Education made the front pages when conflict erupted into action, as with the extended dispute over progressive teaching methods at William Tyndale School in Islington in the mid-1970s – which led to teachers mounting a highly publicised picket of the school, and to a public inquiry – or the teachers' strikes of the mid-1980s. The relatively few pictures of children which accompanied these unfolding narratives reflect the secondary place that children have taken in the drama, even though the polemic has been centrally concerned with the nature of childhood. Children could legitimately play a part only as pawns in the game or as passive by-products of the system. When they do appear, the 'happiness' seen as characteristic of the primary school has changed to a sullen resistance, and rebelliousness has become a narrative theme. Sometimes children appear alongside angry parents; sometimes they are shown as pathetic figures, deprived of their schooling by militant or incompetent teachers. When allowed to speak up for themselves, they demonstrate their own need to be controlled. 'Please sir, don't be trendy,' ran a headline in the *Daily Mirror*. The humourless call was for a return to the delightfully ironic three Rs. 'The need to get back to the basics in education – that means the three Rs – is recognised by everyone. Everyone, that is, except the teachers in their ivory classrooms,' wrote the *Sun*, missing (apparently like everyone else) the joke embedded in the very idea of three Rs. (Since they are derived from spelling mistakes they tell us that educational incompetence is inevitable.)

When the Education Reform Act of 1988 introduced a national curriculum and regular assessments for all children at seven, eleven, fourteen and sixteen, the Conservative government could claim that the move was in response to public opinion, and particularly the opinions of 'parents', as expressed in the popular press. The debate continued to rage over the form of the national curriculum, as traditionalists feared that the progressives would hijack it for their own ends. A row over the teaching of reading led Education Secretary Kenneth Baker to describe 'modern' methods as 'cranky'. Traditionalists argued that children should gain access to the subversive power of the word through graded reading schemes and formal systems rather than through undisciplined access to 'real books'. Knowledge itself must be carefully controlled and designed in such a way that children may be graded, tested and marked for life. In what came to be the accepted wisdom, a new, visible disciplinary space was reasserted, with the teacher firmly back at the front of the class.

By the beginning of the 1990s, 'the dream of a more egalitarian education had turned into a nightmare', and the traditional image had been triumphantly reasserted. Deprived of political support as well as money and equipment, state education was accepted as second-class, abandoned by all who could afford to do so. By the end of the decade, a 'new' Labour government had adopted the rhetoric of competition, inspections, league tables and structured schooling backed up by private-enterprise initiatives. Labour Chancellor of the Exchequer Gordon Brown announced his desire to 'bring business into the classroom'. 'Failing schools' were to be 'turned around', in the manner of businesses, by 'superheads'. One 1998 paper showed 'superhead' William Atkinson pictured as a massive figure against a playground empty of children. Schools could even be taken away from 'teachers' and given to 'nominees'. The debate had moved from educational methods to the efficiency of schools measured by outcomes and competitive results. Many pages in the broadsheet press are now given over to publishing complete league tables of GCSE and A-level results – often ranked under photographs of suitably uniformed pupils. 'How well is *your* child's school doing?' they ask.

This is not the desired image of schooling. When children appear in contemporary newspaper reports we all too often see surly faces in the playground or, in an important new strand of imagery, children who have been excluded from school – at home watching television or hanging around on the streets. (In one striking case a mother was jailed for allowing her daughters to truant.) For those who remain in class, testing and assessment remain all-important. Michelle Cole wrote to the *Guardian* 'Education', 'I, along with many other children, get nervous and scared. Why us children? We should relax and be children for as long as we can – we'll have enough problems when we're grown up!'

NOTES ON CHAPTER 3

p.75   'In the mind of the child': Maria Montessori (1936) *The Secret of Childhood: a Book for all Parents and Teachers*, trans. Barbara Barclay Carter, London: Longman, p.3.
'Children are not born good': Rhodes Boyson, quoted by Bel Mooney, *Nova*, 1972.
Janine Weidel: Rob Walker and Janine Weidel (1985) 'Using photographs in a discipline of words', in R. Burgess (ed.) *Field Methods in the Study of Education*, London: Falmer Press.

p.76   struggle for democracy: John Dewey (1916/1966) *Democracy and Education*, London: Macmillan; David Rubinstein and Colin Stoneman (eds) (1970) *Education for Democracy*, Harmondsworth: Penguin; Wilfred Carr and Anthony Hartnett (1996) *Education and the Struggle for Democracy: the Politics of Educational Ideas*, Buckingham: Open University Press.

p.77   The end of childhood?: *Guardian* 'Education', 29 February 2000.

p.78   'my first day at school': *Parents*, 1975: Photograph: Graham Henderson.

p.79   Dangerous coagulation: reference to Michel Foucault (1977) *Discipline and Punish*, London: Allen Lane, p.143.
'Is this what they mean by "crammer"?': Diana Hinds, *Independent*, 9 November 1995. Photograph: Geraint Lewis.
'Each individual has his own place': Foucault (1977) above, p.143.

p.80   In harmony with the nature of the child: 'No advances in policy, no acquisitions of new equipment have their desired effect unless they are in harmony with the nature of the child', The Plowden Committee (1966) *Children and their Primary Schools*, London: HMSO, para. 9.
'Early Learning Goals': 'Branded school failures at four', *Daily Express*, 4 September 1998; 'Lessons too early "scare off infants"', *Independent*, 12 May 1999.
progressive educationists: Willem van der Eyken and Barry Turner (1975) *Adventures in Education*, Harmondsworth: Pelican; R.J.W. Selleck (1972) *English*

Primary Education and the Progressives 1914–1939, London: Routledge & Kegan Paul.

H. Cauldwell Cook: Selleck (1972) above, p.67.

Maria Montessori: Maria Montessori (1936) *The Secret of Childhood*, London: Longman, p.189.

Susan Isaacs: photographs of children at her school from a film directed by Mary Field for British Instructional Films in 1927 included pictures of children making pottery, working lathes and dissecting Isaacs's cat, which had just died. Van der Eyken and Turner (1975) above, p.55. See also p.101.

p.81 **'This distinction between work and play is false':** Plowden (1966) above, para. 523.

the teacher remains the controlling centre: Valerie Walkerdine has described this progressive pedagogy as an 'impossible fantasy'. She argues (1990) that, 'bourgeois culture is taken as "nature"'. 'Progressive pedagogy and political struggle', in *Schoolgirl Fictions*, London: Verso. See also Valerie Walkerdine (1984) 'Developmental psychology and the child centred pedagogy: the insertion of Piaget into early education', in J. Henriques, W. Holloway, C. Urwin, C. Venn and V. Walkerdine, *Changing the Subject: Psychology, Social Regulation, Subjectivity*, London: Methuen.

p.82 **a mask of seemliness:** Montessori (1936) above, p.189.

Many books of 1960s and 1970s: those I have picked up for 10p or 20p in second hand bookshops include: John Blackie (1967) *Inside the Primary School*, London: HMSO, in which the newly retired Chief Inspector of Primary Education gives an account of Plowden principles; Nora Goddard (1964) *Reading in the Modern Infants' School*, London: University of London Press, in which a retired headmistress lays out the principles of child-centred learning on which she had run her school; Cynthia Mitchell (1973) *Time for School: a Practical Guide for Parents of Young Children*, Harmondsworth: Penguin, one of an innovative series on progressive and alternative education under the imprint of Penguin Education.

'the degree of involvement': ILEA *Contact*, Primary Supplement, Issue 21, 1974.

p.83 **major achievement of discipline:** see Walkerdine (1984) above.

The 'social' eye of the documentarist: see Stuart Hall (1972) 'The social eye of *Picture Post*', Working Papers in Cultural Studies 2, Birmingham: University of Birmingham, an extract reprinted in Jo Spence and Terry Dennett (eds) (1979) *Photography/Politics: One*, London: Photography Workshop.

Gone are the two-by-two rows of desks: Joanna Patyna, 'What are they learning now?', *London Evening News*, 9 May 1978. Photographs: Jimmy James.

p.86 **'Black Papers':** C.B. Cox and A.E. Dyson (eds) (1968) *Fight for Education: a Black Paper*, and (1969) *Black Paper Two*, London: Critical Quarterly Society.

'biggest shock to the school system in 50 years': Judith Judd, 'The lost art of learning', *Independent*, 6 March 1999, a contribution by the paper's education editor to a series called 'Dumb Britannia' on the allegation of the 'dumbing down' of British culture.

Education promised a better life: for an expansion of this perspective, see Richard Johnson et al. (1982) *Unpopular Education*, London: Hutchinson.

The invention of tradition: Eric Hobsbawm and Terence Ranger (eds) (1983/1992) *The Invention of Tradition*, Cambridge: Canto.

'To come into contact with the formal academic curriculum': Wilfred Carr and Anthony Hartnett (1996) *Education and the Struggle for Democracy: the Politics of Educational Ideas*, Buckingham: Open University Press, pp.111, 120.

p.87   'bog standard comprehensives': *Daily Express*, 14 February 2001.
       Robert Morant: quoted in Carr and Hartnett (1996) above, p.94.
       the gothic arch: Robert Bell and Nigel Grant (1974) *A Mythology of British Education*, St Albans: Panther. These authors point to the links between Gothic imagery and the rise of Victorian anglicanism and Newman's *Idea of a University*.

p.88   **which embodies educational assumptions:** Carr and Hartnett (1996) above, p.12.
       Abbey Life: insurance advertisement, 1980; Woolworths' school clothes, 1986.
       A GCSE student: *Metro*, 22 February 2002.
       'The best for one's child?': *Observer* 'Review', 22 February 1981.
       Murus Aeneus: Ross Kinaird, *Daily Mail*, 23 February 1989.

p.89   **'We can't take a chance':** *Daily Mail*, 18 December 1984.
       characterising teachers as 'trendy': *Independent*, 16 January 1996.
       stupefying political correctness: 'Chilling indictment of British education', *Daily Mail*, 31 March 2001.
       Shock reports: a reference to the *Daily Mirror*'s occasional 'shock' issues including a 'Shock report on education', 22 May 1972, when the school leaving age was raised to 16, and 'Shock issue', a 'Mirror campaign for the future of your children', on the lack of facilities and funds, 25 February 1990.
       schools of shame: a reference to an *Evening News* headline on the dispute over 'progressive' teaching methods at William Tyndale School, Islington, 15 October 1975.

p.90   **These long-running dramas:** see Patricia Holland (ed.) (1977) *Lunatic Ideas: on Education and the Press*, London: Corner House Bookshop.
       William Tyndale School: Terry Ellis et al. (1976) *William Tyndale, the Teachers' Story*, London: Writers and Readers.

p.91   **'Please sir, don't be trendy':** *Daily Mirror*, 26 April 1976.
       'The need to get back to the basics': *Sun*, 29 July 1975.
       Education Reform Act of 1988: see Carr and Hartnett (1996) above, p.166.
       the dream of a more egalitarian education: Colin McCabe, *Independent*, 9 December 1990.
       bring business into the classroom: see Richard Ingrams, *Observer*, 24 June 2001.
       'superhead' William Atkinson: Vivek Chaudhary, 'Super Sir', *Guardian*, 23 February 1998. Photograph: Graham Turner. A character apparently based on Mr Atkinson was played by Lenny Henry in the television series about a charismatic headmaster. *Hope and Glory*, BBC1, June 1999, Script Lucy Gannon, Dir. Peter Lydon.

p.92   **a mother was jailed:** 'Jail for truants' mother', *Daily Mirror*, 14 May 2002.
       Michelle Cole: letter in *Guardian* 'Education' on SATs (standardised assessment tests), 13 April 1999.

4

The fantasy of liberation and the demand for rights

PART 1: THE IMAGE OF PLAY

The little ones leaped, and shouted and laugh'd

The little ones leaped, and shouted and laugh'd
And all the hills echoed...

The quotation from William Blake accompanied the section on children's play in the massive photographic exhibition *The Family of Man*, staged in New York in 1954. Pictures showed many types of play – some co-operative, some aggressive – but the key image which has echoed down the decades was that of children leaping, shouting and laughing, casting off constraints – and often clothing – expressing nothing but pure exuberance and *joie de vivre*. Near-naked children run over sand dunes in Bechuanaland – one is caught in mid-air, both knees up, an arm raised in a gesture of pure exultation; children throw long shadows as they race across the cobbles in a Swedish street; a naked child is about to splash into an expanse of water. In images heavily laden with adult fantasy, these children from many cultures seem to be leaping free from the containing institutions of home, school and nation. Only a short decade after so much public imagery had documented the devastations of war, the exhibition aspired to a form of global reconciliation. Children exemplified a reassuring vision, since children could be shown as outside the wars, rivalries and cultural hatreds of adult society. As the image resonates across the decades, children continue to leap free from problems of all sorts. 'Let the children play' was the headline in the Save the Children magazine *World's Children* (1997) above a photo-story by Julio Etchart seeking children at play around the world despite the most difficult of circumstances. The message is that play is children's birthright across cultural divisions, and evidence of the universal nature of childhood itself. *The Family of Man* had set a pattern for a celebration of the common rhythms of life. It aimed to be 'a camera testament, a drama of the grand canyon of humanity, an epic woven of fun, mystery and holiness'. 'There is only one child in the world,' it claimed, 'and the child's name is All Children'. This powerful assertion of universality was cynically rejected by Roland Barthes who, in a celebrated essay, attacked the exhibition's sentimental denial of historical contexts, 'placing Nature above History'.

As we trace the image, we find that the concept of childish play has been repeatedly re-negotiated over the twentieth century, pulled between 'nature' and 'history', between adult fantasy and children's activity, between instrumentality and a refusal to be appropriated for any end but its own. Its independence is celebrated, but at the self-same moment it is appropriated for learning or for therapy. We have already observed how the image of play is contested as it moves between the consumer paradise of the home and the learning environment of the school. For two psychotherapists writing in the late 1940s, it 'is an activity for its own sake, without a utilitarian significance, it is non-purposive and free,

Advertisement, late 1990s.

hence, perhaps, the peculiar delight which pertains to it', and yet their book is a discussion of play as 'child treatment'.

The liberatory aspects of play have come to characterise childhood as opposed to adulthood, but at the same time they throw all boundaries into question, including that between adult and child. With its promise of joyful and even ecstatic experience, play is increasingly seen as a value which adults seek to reclaim. Images of childhood play are shadowed by adult envy and adult fear: envy since play stands for non-utilitarian pleasures that adults must leave behind, and fear because moving beyond social constraints may provoke nameless dangers. Thus it is hardly surprising that when pictures of leaping, laughing children stand as a key image they tend to be separated from surroundings which would root them too closely into a specific social milieu. Their pure pleasure is not interrupted by too much grounded information and they have no qualms in representing nature rather than history.

Closely observed children and the irresponsible eye

Children at play seem absorbed in activities that are not pre-defined by adult society. They have an air of mystery and inaccessibility, like some exotic cult. Iona and Peter Opie, ethnographers of childhood, spent many years recording children's culture, talking to children in the playground and noting games and rhymes. These sometimes turned out to be of great antiquity, passed from one generation to the next, and sometimes very new, spreading across the country with remarkable rapidity and no apparent mediation by adults. Such secrets have long tempted the adult eye. Observation of children at play may well further the teaching or therapeutic process, but on other occasions it has no other purpose than to delight the adult viewer. Either way, observation reasserts adult control over childish spaces. I shall consider here three approaches to the image of children at play: first an argument for respectful observation; second a valuation of childhood which sees it as a resource for the rescue of a corrupt society; finally an irresponsible way of looking, in which adults appropriate childish values.

Observational photography has been strongly criticised for its voyeurism and denial of the photographer's presence. It has been seen as a form of repressive surveillance, capturing an image without the consent or collaboration of the participant. The observation of childhood is an extreme case of this inequality between observer and observed, since the relations of power between adults and children are so great. (Candid photographers are advised to keep a low profile and wait for 'that magic moment when the movement reveals the child'.) But, as

I have argued throughout this book, the meaning of an image may be modulated according to its context and use. In 1972, Leila Berg put a gloss on the documentary project in an eloquent argument for adults to respect children's privacy. A vocal advocate for child-centred education, she invited her readers to Look at Kids. The photographs which make up the book set out to reflect a respectful practice in which she urged adults to observe but to hold back from interfering or attempting to impose acceptable behaviour or formal constraints. Rather than studying children in order to teach them, Berg argues, they should study them in order to learn from them.

Moving a step beyond such humility is the view in which playful children are seen as the keepers of true values, including those values of community and rationality that adult society seems to have lost. 'How can human beings emerge in a society that has such rampant nihilism as does ours?' asked Paul Adams, writing in the same year as Look at Kids, '...where people grow up immersed in anomie, aloofness, relativity, absurdity, indefiniteness and non-participation?' In his view, if childlike values are allowed to develop freely, the world would stand a better chance of achieving a future of peace, co-operation and harmony. In this adult fantasy, children are owed a better society, but they themselves are expected to create it. These high expectations have led to a search for images in which children's play appears constructive rather than destructive, companionable rather than antagonistic.

At the same time, the popular imagery of childhood has produced a resonant image of play that is not particularly constructive or co-operative, but freefloating and anarchic. In this resonant image, playfulness is expressed in the movement of the body of the child through the open spaces of the countryside or the city. The geographical location is important here, for a background of home or school would imply constraint or pedagogic purpose which would negate the drive of the image. Rather than fitting a child to a pre-prepared childshaped space, this image offers the exciting prospect that children will be able to create their own space. Viewers are not addressed specifically as parents, teachers or caring professionals, but are invited to look with an irresponsible eye, feeding off the childlike values expressed. Unanchored in a daily negotiation with real children, this image serves to release the viewing adult from practical responsibility. It becomes susceptible to a different kind of projection of adult fantasy – an invitation to viewers to share the playful experience and take on the irresponsible qualities of childishness.

Increasingly adults have bought into the values of play. Rebecca Abrams describes it as 'a fundamental social good'. Contemporary imagery is more likely to find the child in the adult than the adult in the child. A double-page spread in *The Big Issue* which at first glance seems to be a collection of snapshots of children, turns out to be a group of adults, laughing, tumbling and chasing each other in outdoor games. An image of bicycles screeching out of control down a hill is actually a fashion spread by 'hot' young photographer Elaine Constantine, and the bikes are ridden not by children but by adult models. The current appropriation of childish values now finds adults on cornflake packets and euphoric values in car advertisements. Surprisingly often, children have been pushed out of the picture to be replaced by childlike adults.

Urban ruralism

As we have seen, many of our resonant images of childhood are linked to particular periods of history, and linger in the cultural image-bank long after their original significance has lost its contemporary charge. Their meanings may decay, so that they remain decorative or ornamental, or they may be recuperated and reconstructed through a new dynamic usage. The image of children at play has moved through both of these processes. We have already considered the decorative and seductive image which lingers from the turn of the twentieth century, and shows a world of quiet villages and peaceful village greens where children sing and play gentle games far from the corruptions of the town. Historically, the last decades of the nineteenth century were a time of rural depopulation and an unprecedented expansion of urban living. But despite the actuality of poverty and hardship in the lives of real children, it was a period when the cult of childhood took on a new significance. The fantasy of a simpler, more innocent period in history fitted well with the concept of childhood as a simpler, more innocent period in human life. Cecil Sharp sought out a type of rural folk song that he saw as 'the product of the spontaneous and intuitive exercise of untrained faculties', as opposed to 'the conscious and intentional use of faculties which have been especially cultivated and developed'. Similarly children's spontaneity and untrained faculties came to symbolise an aestheticised ruralism which celebrated the rhythms of a country lifestyle that was fast disappearing – if it had ever existed. The turn of the twentieth century saw revivals of children's games, maypoles, 'folk' songs and 'folk' festivals in the recreation of a largely mythological pre-industrial past. Popular imagery of all kinds has followed and exaggerated the trend.

(In the outer London suburb where I was brought up, carved out of the fields and parks of the landed gentry in the mid-1930s, children, mostly little girls, still dress up for an annual May Day festival, known locally as the 'May Queens'. The only time I took part, it poured with rain, and instead of dancing round the maypole on the local common we ended up in the Village Hall in wellington boots with navy gabardine macs over our flimsy dresses. Perhaps because it reminds me of those childhood extravaganzas, one of my favourite postcards is a photograph from some time in the 1920s entitled 'Free dancing for children on Tooting Bec common under an LCC scheme'. It shows a row of little girls in fairy dresses led, not very freely, by a rather stout lady in a long satin dress and bouffant veil. They point their toes and elegantly stretch their arms for the camera.)

An image of pre-industrial rural life lay behind the thinking of the free-schoolers of the early part of the twentieth century. By the 1970s the aim was to recreate a sense of organic community and find a creative space for children *within* the inner city. For example, Colin Ward's *The Child and the City* captured the last moments before major road and office redevelopments transformed the British urban landscape. Photographs show children playing on bomb-damaged wastelands, hiding in disused buildings and scribbling with chalk on the paving stones. The indulgent adult's desire not to interfere is strongly tested as children take risks with fire, piles of rubble and abandoned machinery, moving at the edge of danger. The self-conscious realism of this urban imagery sought to reject the moralism and romanticism which linked children with the rural and with nature, but in treating the town as a space for discovery it created its own form of urban ruralism. Children were not seen invading the centres of modernity and power. Instead they were shown seeking out quaint customs and craftspeople at work. The hiding-places, nooks and crannies of the inner city were for all the world like the lanes and copses of the countryside, peopled by elderly characters with a tale to tell. This imagery set its face against the hardness and reflective surfaces of the new city in a nostalgia for the manipulability of the old.

By the end of the twentieth century the idea that the back streets of the city offered spaces which children could explore seemed outrageous. The open spaces of city and countryside had become the subject of new fears – of ill-intentioned strangers, increasing traffic and the dangerous pressures of modernity. The consensus was that children should be supervised beyond as well as within the home. Readers of the concerned press now find articles on how to protect their children in that difficult period of the school holidays. 'Girls and boys come out to play … but where?' headlined the *Observer*, adding anxiously 'six weeks to go before they're back to school'. The photographs which accompany such articles tend to be carefully framed to contain playful children within a safe environment. 'Children to have safe "play-zones"', headlined the *Independent* above a photograph of two girls soaring high on chain-link swings. The swing is a useful photographic device. A form of equipment specially constructed for children's play, its delicate chain can hold them fast, suggesting both safety and energetic movement. Supervised local play areas, readers were told, will allay parents' fears.

Savagery and horror

Psychoanalyst Melanie Klein has described play as the central activity of child-hood, and one with a clear purpose. 'In their play children represent symbolically phantasies, wishes and experiences,' she wrote. Above another picture of a young girl on a swing, a Council of Europe publication expanded on her view: 'A child of any age who resorts to play is in a sense entering a private domain – usually secret, magic or sacred – a maintenance area in which every item is taken apart and put together in a genuine process of creation'.

For Klein the observation of children at play was an essential part of her pioneering child therapy. Susan Isaacs, an analyst herself and a friend of Klein, established the Malting House School in 1924, which she saw as a laboratory for the study of child development. She argued that if education should follow the nature of the child, it was important to explore that nature in all its aspects. Photographs of the children at the Malting House show them coping with functioning equipment – often much bigger than they are – and absorbed in their tasks. But pictures like these leave little space for the projection of adult fantasy. Rather than feeding a nostalgia for a lost past, these children give the impression of calmness and competence in the present world of adults.

But the psychoanalytically trained educationists of the early part of the twentieth century were also aware of the dangerous aspects of play. ('Here the children's crudities, the disorder of their emotions, their savagery even, are allowed to show,' wrote a contemporary of Susan Isaacs.) For the radical headmaster A.S. Neill, playfulness was definitely *not* to be harnessed to the educational process. In 1926 he founded Summerhill, 'that dreadful school' where children were left to make their own choices, including the decision on whether to attend lessons or simply to play. 'Most of the school work that adolescents do is simply a waste of time, of energy, of patience. It robs youth of its right to play and play and play,' wrote Neill. The attacks on the 'wildness' of Summerhill children continued throughout the life of the school. Despite the increasing formalisation of the education system, by the early 2000s Summerhill, now run by Neill's daughter, Zoe, continued to hang on by the skin of its teeth (on 20 March 2000 it appealed in the High Court against OFSTED the schools inspectorate).

In recent years the imagery of play that is not contained within home or school has been concerned both with dangers *to* children and dangers *from* them. Euphoric play that takes no account of the consequences can easily topple into equally careless forms of uncontrolled violence. The contemporary image which matches Colin Ward's celebration of playful children in the back streets is one of mayhem and destruction (see Chapter 5). When in 1992 the toddler James Bulger was abducted from a Liverpool shopping mall by two ten-year-olds, then murdered in horrific circumstances, one of the images that dominated the press was the terrifying face of a demonic doll. The boys were said to have been influenced by a film called *Child's Play*, whose plot heightened the irresponsible destructiveness of play by featuring toys that run out of control. Although it became clear that the boys had not, in fact, seen the video, an image that horrifies rather than attracts has become indispensable to the imagery of play.

PART 2: LIBERATION AND RIGHTS

Childhood is not a good idea

The mundane facts of children's everyday experience have meant that playful liberatory aspirations sit uneasily with the practical demands for children's rights. The one promotes a vision of childhood outside all cultural constraints; the other insists on a negotiation with culture, politics and everyday life. Yet, as with *The Family of Man* exhibition, the aspiration remains for a universal childhood which will be available for all children whatever their parents' culture, and will draw on their global similarities and potential freedom from entrenched hatreds. 'For better or worse, the world can be revolutionised in one generation according to how we deal with the children,' wrote Eglantyne Jebb in the aftermath of the First World War. Jebb had founded the Save the Children Fund in 1919, with the specific aim of transcending national enmities and aiding the innocent victims of war, in particular the children of enemy countries – Germany and Austria.

She went on to draft the first Declaration of the Rights of the Child in 1924 – but a formal international commitment to children's rights took the best part of a century to achieve. In 1959 the United Nations issued a Declaration, in the form of 10 succinct principles, whose worthy preamble affirmed, 'Mankind owes the child the best it has to give'. Twenty years later the International Year of the Child created a global opportunity to heighten awareness and to publicise the condition of children worldwide. But a further 10 years passed before the

General Assembly of the UN adopted the Convention on the Rights of the Child. It entered into British law in 1991.

Other campaigners for children's rights have been contemptuous of slow negotiations and modest claims. 'The first duty of a revolutionary is to build a society geared to children,' declared *Children's Rights* magazine, launched in 1971 by a group of adults and children who saw children's liberation as an obvious companion to the women's liberation and the radical student movements of the time. For them, children should not be satisfied with taking their place as junior partners in an adult society, they should set out to transform that society. In its short and controversial existence, *Children's Rights* attempted to hold together a heady call for social and sexual revolution with a re-evaluation of the nature of childhood itself. The project nearly ended in disaster when the magazine produced a 'Bust Book' which advised children to fight the police and resist arrest. It was rescued by its eminent board of advisers, including A.S. Neill and Leila Berg, who sacked the editor and relaunched it under a new title, *Kids*. They made it clear that the fatal mistake had been for adult editors to attempt to speak from the position of children. 'If the Bust Book article had been written by a group of kids,' wrote Leila Berg, '...it would not have been taken as a "practical guide" but as a demand to have attention paid'.

The dangers inherent in an inappropriate confusion between adult and child shadowed the movement. But many writers of the time continued to argue that boundaries must be readjusted despite the risks. Only then could society be both more free and more rational. Whereas nineteenth-century reformers such as Mary Carpenter had struggled to have children recognised as children, the progressives of the twentieth century pointed to those qualities children shared with adults. Writers such as John Holt insisted that children are not different from adults – or at least not in the ways that are commonly assumed. They are not less conscious of their rights, nor less sensitive to disrespectful treatment. Nor are they less able to assess a situation and make coherent decisions on their actions. The balance between childhood defined as different from adulthood and the ways in which children are similar to adults was up for negotiation. If adults desired the playfulness of childhood, children should be granted the privileges of adulthood. This was not a plea to protect an endangered childhood but to escape from childhood altogether. 'I decided that childhood was not a good idea,' wrote John Holt in the preface to his book of that name.

In this spirit, a new 'free-school' movement emerged in the 1970s, insisting that an appropriate space for learning should refuse traditional demarcations. 'All over the world school has an anti-educational effect on children,' wrote Keith

Paton in a densely typed pamphlet which featured an angry Dennis the Menace on its cover. He argued that schools shut off avenues of exploration rather than opening them up. They should not be the peaceful oases envisaged by Plowden but should be open to the surrounding world. The streets should be seen not as a place of danger and corruption but as one offering potential learning opportunities. Children should be free to wander where they will, invading adult territory, entering places of work, exploring and asking questions. 'There are plenty of learning situations outside, and there could be more if workers inside assisted in a mass jail break and turned their energies into making society more educative for everyone, not just kids.' Learning should take precedence over economic activity, and the values of childhood should permeate society.

For some the answer was 'alternative' schools, in which children would be participants as well as pupils. The White Lion Street Free School in London, one of the more long-lasting and articulate of these, aimed to break down many different kinds of boundaries – between holiday and term, between pupils and teachers, between teachers and other adults who worked in the school, between teachers and parents, and between school and the world beyond. A commitment to children's rights in education meant that childhood was to be a positive value even in the school context. Children should be allowed to evolve their own forms of expression and not be channelled into those already laid down by the adult world. Other education experiments included free schools on the Summerhill model, innovations such as learning exchanges, adventure playgrounds, often built by children themselves, 'schoolkids'' unions, radical teachers' groups, informal truancy centres providing facilities for school refusers who would otherwise be hanging around on the streets, and campaigns which aimed, in the words of a contemporary guru, Ivan Illich, to 'deschool society' and reject the strictures of institutions altogether. Children's centres were set up in crumbling urban spaces, often in squatted warehouses or other empty buildings, in which children could express the playful values that had gained such a symbolic weight, and where the heavy hand of adult guidance was restrained.

There was a prolific output of informal posters, pamphlets and magazines produced by children themselves, with names like *Braindamage, Fang, Miscarriage* (produced in Hackney) and *Blazer*. They were shortlived, but they shared a sense of urgency and drama, and evolved a dynamic imagery of their own. (A ragged pile of these magazines forms a special part of my collection, acquired through a bookshop where I worked at the end of the 1970s. Sometimes photocopied, sometimes stencilled, full of vigour and venom, I value this pile of magazines as a remarkable antidote to the all-too-smooth professionalism of mainstream imagery.)

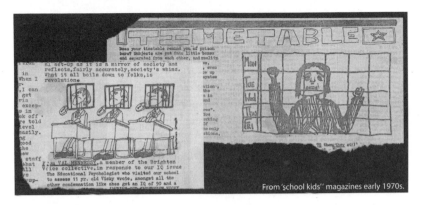

From 'school kids" magazines early 1970s.

The calm and orderly photographs which represented the progressive class-room (Chapter 3) were not pictures in which radical teachers and school students could recognise themselves. There was a yawning gap between the social-democratic documentary image and the helpless, chaotic experience of school expressed by the rebellious pupils of the mid-1970s. Their imagery showed the school system as mechanical and inflexible, directed towards a future that was equally limited. 'Schools imprison your mind and control your body...they don't encourage us to develop our potential but rather tame our natural inclinations, causing total apathy in most and rebellion in very few,' wrote the editors of *Braindamage*. For them it was a system in which individuals were reduced to mere items, crumbs from a mincing machine (the cover of *Libertarian Education*), or trapped within the bars of a timetable (in *Y-Front*). The imagery of prison was balanced by an energetic imagery of escape, both mental and physical. *Vanguard* used a photograph of children symbolically leaping from a classroom window.

The magazines did not totally reject school, but their demand was for 'schools not prisons'. They return again and again to a sense of deep injustice and impotent outrage when adult action fails to match adult rhetoric. Despite their anarchic streak, they are convinced that their approach is grounded in reason and justice. Although they see themselves as reasonable, they know that in the eyes of the school authorities this is an empty claim. Children's demands need not be taken seriously by those whose power does not derive from consent. In that sense teachers' power is bound to be arbitrary and irrational. Demands which were on the surface trivial, such as regulated hair length and the wearing of uniform, gained enormous significance as the centre of symbolic battles. The magazines contain letters and anecdotes which describe routine humiliations when 'reason-able' requests come to nothing. 'Have you ever been ticked off for bringing a paper carrier bag to school for your books because it is inappropriate or not strong enough?' wrote Skinners' School third-year pupils. 'Sometimes when you're at a table you're not allowed to speak, but why can grown-ups speak?' asked Karen, aged 10, both in *Children's Rights 2*.

The magazines are full of sexual innuendo and risqué jokes. Whatever their quality, their existence was a challenge, an assertion of pupils' right to address each other publicly and to speak aloud those things which are normally giggled over or muttered. Informal school culture was made public.

Irrationality and attitude

As children, the 1970s campaigners found that irrationality was expected of them. They were trapped by the ways in which they were defined. One tactic was to embrace irrationality as an appropriate expression of their situation. In the 'kidslib' magazines, irrational fury and rational solutions were presented together in a chaotic visual style. There was a need for an imagery that would represent children to each other and, at the same time, deny to adults the fullness of that representation. These children did not intend to gratify adults either with their visible innocence or with Montessori's 'mask of seemliness'. Instead they set out to antagonise and shock. 'The impossible generation bites deeper,' declared *Miscarriage*. With bad spelling, scribbled drawings and disorderly pages, adults' view of children was thrown back at them. The magazines drew on the language of the student movement, the proletarian image of the clenched fist, the dream imagery of hippiedom, and above all the anarchic imagery of children's comics.

Comics are traditionally complicit with children's interests. Their prices are low so that they can be bought with pocket money, and on the whole they are free from educational overtones. They tend to be frowned upon by adults and forbidden in class. Their inventiveness and irreverence remain icons of children's refusal to be shaped into an image acceptable to adults. Over the generations Dennis the Menace and the Bash Street Kids have come closer to expressing children's experience of childhood and school than many a more respectable medium. Dennis started his disruptive career in Scotland in 1951 and has kept his appeal into the twenty-first century, successfully competing with newer inventions. 'A menace never changes,' he declared in 1991, in a strip in which he refused to abandon his striped jersey to become updated with tracksuit and personal stereo. The characters in *Beano* and *Dandy* remain close to the spirit of the tramps and messenger boys in the very first comics of the

1890s, inhabiting a world that is unequivocally working-class and urban. Their one aim remains to outsmart adults and teachers. (For many years, publishers D.C. Thomson jealously protected their characters and refused all requests to reproduce them. But commerce conquers all. The Dennis the Menace Fan Club was launched in 1976 and brand merchandising began. An invitation to 'go menacing and win a Dennis the Menace make-over for your bedroom' turns out to be a 2001 Safeway's promotion for a new flavour called 'Baked Beano'. Clearly a menace *can* be tamed when promotional culture calls the shots.)

Comic-book kids traditionally take perverse pleasure in an image of childhood which rejects any form of attractiveness. The Bash Street Gang are weedy, ugly or oddball. They are reverse exhibitionists, mostly boys, but Beryl the Peril and Minnie the Minx are in a similar mould. By drawing attention to an unacceptable surface, they reject adult sympathy and attempts at understanding. Their appearance is designed to repel. Their chosen image erects an

Book cover, 1979. Magazine, 1990s.

antagonising shield of ugliness which may keep selfhood secret within it. It is an image which has been taken up by some children – particularly the shaven-headed hard ones who become visible elsewhere in the imagery of poverty and exclusion. It has also been appropriated by such pre-school favourites as the Tweenies, with their punky hairstyles and clumpy shoes, and by contemporary birthday cards, which often favour young toughies in the comic-book mode.

In the books and magazines of the children's liberation movement, the gaze of the adult is met head on with a challenging glare. A simmering aggression covers an underlying expectation of betrayal: the contempt in the eyes of the Rasta child on the cover of *Changing Childhood*; the calculating gaze of the boy on the cover of *Children's Rights* magazine. These are looks that refuse deference; which recognise but defy the demand for acquiescence. These children are shown as people who, in the words of Paul Adams, have the right to live in a meaningful world and to have a moral sense, but instead are offered 'opportunism, expediency, absurdity and non-participation'. The look from these pages is not an innocent one. It claims the right to express anger and refuses any sense of guilt. Leila Berg's injunction to look at kids in a generous and empathetic way becomes uneasy when children claim the right to glare back.

The assertive glare at the camera has become established as 'attitude' – a multicultural, post-colonial defiance. A semi-official Brixton magazine featured on its cover an oriental boy in a Mao cap and dark glasses. Readers were invited to purchase 'Attitude from Brixton to Hong Kong'. This vision of liberation poses a dilemma of power and control which is the more acute for adults who support its claims. For this image is anti-humanist. It does its best to reject the comforting assumption of a shared humanity, since that assumption can all too easily be sentimentalised or exploited. The image of Chucky, the murderous doll from the *Child's Play* films, is in the same tradition.

Participation and politics

Despite the theorising of the liberation movements, to the popular press children's politics simply means unruly demonstrations incited by subversive teachers. Only corporal punishment would be appropriate discipline for such riotous behaviour ('I will cane these lollipop rebels,' read one headline). But the mundane image of the democratic committee meeting had also played an important part in the challenge to unequal relations between adults and children. Decision-making at A.S. Neill's Summerhill was by school meeting, where, in theory at least, no one's voice would count for more than anyone else's, regardless of age or position. The practice was taken up by free schools such as the White Lion. Photographs show a heterogeneous group, adults and children of all ages, in intense discussion.

The 1979 UN Year of the Child brought the opportunity to expand definitions of children's rights beyond protection to include children's participation in the public sphere, claiming a legitimate presence in political space. It was formally recognised that children have the right to express opinions and have those opinions taken into account; to exercise freedom of thought, conscience and religion; to meet with others and form associations, and to have access to and share information. The Advisory Centre for Education (ACE) published a draft Charter of Children's Rights, which was grudgingly welcomed by the 'schoolkids" magazine *Miscarriage*, which described ACE as a 'mild, liberal group of people'. The Charter concluded, 'Children's rights are no different in nature, nor do they demand any different interpretation than is applied to the rights of adults'. Writers, such as Bob Franklin, supported children's right to vote. 'Arguments in favour of child suffrage have too frequently been ridiculed rather than met... [but] that position is a clear violation of the principle that no individual or group should be subject to laws which they have not participated in making.' Pictures which accompany such arguments are sober, without the spectacular qualities associated with childhood in other contexts. Photographs like that of a children's election meeting which accompanied Bob Franklin's *Guardian* article are far less gratifying to adult fantasies, depriving the viewer both of the heady opportunity to identify with a liberatory childishness or of an equally gratifying opportunity for violent denunciation.

By the 1980s, although arguments for children's liberation had come to seem hopelessly excessive and outmoded, the campaign for children's rights had made definite changes to public perceptions of childhood. The alternative-education projects and small-circulation magazines had closed down, no longer viable in the changing political climate. Nevertheless, children's voices had gained some legitimacy. Long-standing organisations in the field of child protection and child welfare sought to produce images of childhood that would reflect the shift from an adult-oriented welfare approach to a child-oriented participatory one. In 1989 Saatchi and Saatchi produced a series of role-reversal posters for the NSPCC. To persuade parents to pay greater attention to their children, they placed undersized adults on the laps of oversized children. The point was made without taking the risk of appealing outside the family structure.

Children's participation has become more widely accepted, and there are now more spaces where they are freed from the responsibility of being childish for the benefit of adults. Newspaper presentations and news broadcasts are more likely to seek out children's opinions. To encourage them, Save the Children issued a leaflet advising journalists on interviewing children respectfully ('tell [the photographer] to avoid clichéd camera angles...'). In 2000 Stirling Council published *Children as Partners: A Guide to Consulting with the Very Young*. Echoing Leila Berg, nursery staff are reminded that consultation is not enough. 'Once we have learned to listen to children, we must be prepared to change our own thinking as a result of what they have told us.'

In the 'Rosendale Odyssey', pupils between five and eight at Rosendale Infants School, South London, collaborated on a multimedia presentation of their lives, bringing together the 22 different languages spoken at the school. Visitors to the website were invited to click on a classroom and meet children whose pictures of themselves were inventively presented using photoshop technology; 'Me and my brother eating breakfast' has a snapshot crayoned over with specs drawn in, one eye mauve and the other yellow. Some children provided family histories with photographs of parents and grandparents, others showed pictures of the things they like: 'This is my bedroom. These are my toys. I have 100 Barbies.' Children who visited the site were invited to e-mail the participants and develop a dialogue.

The *Independent* newspaper featured portraits of schoolchildren from 12 to 18, whose opinions on morality were headed 'public sleaze is blamed for moral decay'. The comments echoed the schoolkids' magazines of the 1970s, but reflected the changing climate: '[My parents] have never said "no" to anything really and if they did I'd probably go and do it because they would be stopping me'. This shift in attitude means that adult fantasy may be defused by a different type of realism – not the traditional documentary realism in which an unseen observer peeps in on activities which would otherwise go unobserved, but a *participatory* realism, making space for a social group which has previously had no access to public modes of expression. Inevitably, children's meanings are expressed using linguistic tools honed over the centuries by adults, but it is becoming clear that children are able to articulate a perspective which is distinctive and particular to them as they gain greater access to the public arena.

Childhood is a good idea – perhaps

When the UN finally accepted the Convention of the Rights of the Child in 1989, posters showed not the glowering directness of the 1970s liberation movement, but a cheerful multiplicity. UNICEF imagery includes a poster in which cultural markers such as skin colour or a scrap of clothing identify groups of children gathered together within the shape of a globe, and a greetings card with multi-cultural children clambering on a globe as if a climbing frame. Drawings by children illustrate the children's version of the Convention as the dilemmas of conflicting cultures are smoothed over by the promise of childhood.

The multicultural image was taken up most strikingly by Oliviero Toscani in his advertising for the clothing company Benetton, which changed its name, under his influence, to 'United Colours of Benetton'. Prominent in crowded town centres, railway stations and on the sides of buses, posters showed children of many races, selected for the contrast, photographed in high-quality saturated colour. This engaging image added a level of excess to UNICEF multiculturalism, in the context of challenging Benetton images which turned racial stereotypes back on themselves: a black child as a devil, with a white child as an angel; a black woman breastfeeding a white baby.

In the spirit of *The Family of Man*, both these commercial and rights-based presentations of multicultural harmony look to a presentation of difference without conflict. But this is precisely where the image of childhood once more runs up against its limits. Childhood is sought as that space beyond conflict, before those rigid differences have taken hold, as a point where 'humanity' aspires to an impossible escape from 'society' and the bland but optimistic universal image smoothes over adult problems. (One advertisement claimed 'there's one place where there's no racism', with a picture of babies from many races.) But children's lives are embedded in the structures and imperatives of culture, gender and language. When the British press showed photographs of terrified young girls from the Catholic community in north Belfast forced to walk to school between crowds of screaming Protestants, both the parents who insisted on walking through opposition territory and those who fought to defend that territory were demonstrating in defence of what they saw as the historic rights of the children of their particular community. An effective demand for children's rights must deal with the prejudices and historical lumber of hatreds and exclusivity that accompany such divisions.

NOTES ON CHAPTER 4

p. 95   **The little ones leaped:** William Blake, 'The Nurse's Song' from *Songs of Innocence and Experience*, printed and illustrated by Blake in 1789 and 1794. 'The Nurse's song' is illustrated by a circle of dancing children under a lurid red sky. Oxford: Oxford University Press, 1970, p.24.

sand dunes in Bechuanaland: photograph: Nat Farbman.

race across the cobbles: photograph: Pal-Nils Nilsson.

splash into an expanse of water: photograph: Edward Steichen, curator of the exhibition.

p. 96   **'a camera testament':** Carl Sandberg (1954) *The Family of Man*, New York: Museum of Modern Art, introduction, p.4.

'placing Nature above History': Roland Barthes (1957/1993) 'The great family of man', in *Mythologies*, London: Vintage, p.100. Interestingly, when the exhibition was shown in Paris it had the word 'great' added to its title.

repeatedly re-negotiated over the twentieth century: a few examples can illustrate how the concept of (childish) play has been re-appropriated at different points in the century: alternative education projects of the 1920s, such as Caldwell Cook (*The Play Way*, 1920) and A.S. Neill (see below); the development of 'play therapy' by the psychoanalyst Melanie Klein and its expansion in the aftermath of World War II (see 'The psycho-analytic play technique: its history and significance', in Juliet Mitchell [ed.] [1986] *The Selected Melanie Klein*, Harmondsworth: Peregrine, and D.W. Winnicott [1980] *Playing and Reality*, Harmondsworth: Penguin); the idea of play as itself learning, expressed by the Plowden Report on Primary Education of 1967 (see Chapter 3); the aim of youth culture and the 'underground' to embrace 'childish' values' in, for example, Richard Neville (1970) *Playpower*, St Albans: Paladin; the 'children's liberation' movement of the 1970s, which made much of playfulness as a right of all children; and finally the contemporary appropriation of playful values for adults, both as part of a 'new work ethic' and as the basis of a consumer economy (Rebecca Abrams, 'Let's all go to and play', *New Statesman*, 13 November 2000).

two psychotherapists: Lydia Jackson and Kathleen M. Todd (1946) *Child Treatment and the Therapy of Play*, London: Methuen, p.8.

p. 97   **a value which adults seek to reclaim:** Richard Neville (above), p.224, quotes Norman O. Brown, *Life Against Death*: 'childhood is man's indestructible goal'. See also Frank Furedi (2001) *Paranoid Parenting*, Harmondsworth: Penguin, on 'the colonisation of the world of children by adults'.

Closely observed children: Michael Armstrong (1980) *Closely Observed Children, the Diary of a Primary Classroom*, London: Writers and Readers.

Iona and Peter Opie: (1959/2001) *The Lore and Language of Schoolchildren*, New York: New York Review of Books.

a form of repressive surveillance: John Tagg (1988) *The Burden of Representation*, London: Macmillan.

the movement reveals the child: Time-Life (1973) *Photographing Children*, New York: Time Inc., pp.92–93.

p. 98   **Leila Berg:** (1972) *Look at Kids*, Harmondsworth: Penguin.

'How can human beings emerge': Paul Adams (1971) 'The Infant, the Family and Society', in Paul Adams et al., *Children's Rights*, London: Elek, p.79.

Rebecca Abrams: (1997) *The Playful Self*, London: Fourth Estate, and in *New Statesman*, 13 November 2000.

p.99 *Big Issue*: Shelley Fannell, 'Playtime', *Big Issue*, 3–9 July 2000. Photographs: Amyand Tanveer.

Elaine Constantine: 'Girls on Bikes', *The Face*, 1997: 'It's one of my favourite images. I wanted to create an image that expressed the excitement that comes with adolescence and the independence it brings. Adolescence is all about seeing yourself as an individual... I loved Polly Banks' DIY styling – it's all about these girls experimenting. The bikes served to give an extra sense of things being out of control or reckless.' Quoted in 'Life', *Observer* 'Magazine', 30 June 2002.

a time of rural de-population: Alun Howkins (1986) 'The discovery of rural England', in Robert Colls and Philip Dodd (eds) *Englishness: Politics and Culture 1880–1920*, London: Croom Helm.

the actuality of poverty: Anna Davin (1996) *Growing Up Poor: Home, School and Street in London 1870–1914*, London: Rivers Oram Press; Hugh Cunningham (1991) *Children of the Poor*, Oxford: Blackwell.

cult of childhood: Peter Coveney (1967) *The Image of Childhood*, Harmondsworth: Peregrine, Chapter 10; Jaqueline Rose (1984) *The Case of Peter Pan, or the Impossibility of Children's Fiction*, London: Macmillan.

Cecil Sharp: writing in 1907, quoted by Dave Harker, 'May Cecil Sharp be praised?', *History Workshop Journal*, 14, Autumn 1982.

an annual May Day festival: Patricia Holland (1991) 'The old order of things changed', in J. Spence and P. Holland (eds) *Family Snaps: the Meanings of Domestic Photography*, London: Virago.

p.100 **Free dancing for children**: from the Hulton Deutsch collection. For a discussion of fresh-air schemes for children see Valerie Walkerdine (1984) 'Developmental psychology and the child centred pedagogy: the insertion of Piaget into early education', in J. Henriques, W. Holloway, C. Urwin, C. Venn and V. Walkerdine, *Changing the Subject: Psychology, Social Regulation, Subjectivity*, London: Methuen. On Margaret Macmillan, pioneer of nursery schools and advocate of 'Night Camps' and Open Air Nurseries, see Carolyn Steedman (1990) *Childhood, Culture and Class in Britain: Margaret Macmillan, 1860–1931*, London: Virago.

Colin Ward: (1977) *The Child and the City*, London: Architectural Press.

Girls and boys come out to play: *Observer*, 28 July 1996.

'Children to have safe "play-zones"': *Independent*, 3 August 1999, Photograph: John Voos.

p.101 **'In their play children represent'**: in Mitchell (1986) above, p.64.

A child of any age who resorts to play: Marie-Jose Leres-Richer (1979) 'The Child at Play', *Forum*, Council of Europe, February.

Susan Isaacs: Willem van der Eyken and Barry Turner (1969) *Adventures in Education*, Harmondsworth: Allen Lane.

'the children's crudities': van der Eyken and Turner (1975) above, p.43.

'Most of the school work': A.S. Neill (1968) *Summerhill*, Harmondsworth: Pelican, p.38. See also pp.67–70, on play. *That Dreadful School* was the title of one of Neill's earliest books, published in 1936. On 21 February 2000, *Le Monde* reported that its French translator had lived off the proceeds of *Summerhill* for the previous 10 years.

p.102 **a film called *Child's Play***: Patricia Holland (1997) 'Living for libido or Child's Play 4: the imagery of childhood and the call for censorship', in Martin Barker and Julian Petley (eds) *Ill Effects, the Media/Violence Debate*, London: Routledge; Bob Franklin and Julian Petley (1996) 'Killing the age of innocence: newspaper reporting of the death of James Bulger', in Jane Pilcher and Stephen Wagg (eds) *Thatcher's Children: Politics, Childhood and Society in the 1980s and 1990s*, London: Falmer.

Childhood is not a good idea: John Holt (1975) *Escape from Childhood: the Needs and Rights of Children*, Harmondsworth: Penguin. 'I have come to feel that the fact of being a "child", of being wholly subservient and dependent, of being seen by older people as a mixture of expensive nuisance, slave and super-pet, does most young people more harm than good', p.15.

negotiation with culture: P. Alston (ed.) (1994) *The Best Interests of the Child: Reconciling Culture and Human Rights*, UNICEF-ICDC, Oxford: Clarendon Press; Jo Boyden (1997) 'Childhood and the policy makers; a comparative perspective on the globalisation of childhood', in Allison James and Alan Prout (eds) *Constructing and Reconstructing Childhood: Contemporary Issues in the Sociological Study of Childhood*, London: Falmer, p.196.

Eglantyne Jebb: quoted by Yvonne Roberts in 'The Rights of the Child', *Observer*, 30 September 1990. See also Helen Jones (2000) *Women in British Public Life 1914–50: Gender, Power and Social Policy*, Harlow: Pearson Education, pp.79–82.

p.103   **Other campaigners for children's rights:** see Stephen Wagg (1996) 'Politics, childhood and the new education market', in Pilcher and Wagg (eds) above.

'If the Bust Book article had been written': Leila Berg (1972) *Kids*, no 1; see also Colin Wringe (1981) *Children's Rights*, London: Routledge & Kegan Paul.

Mary Carpenter: see Geoffrey Pearson (1983) *Hooligan: a History of Respectable Fears*, London: Macmillan, pp.179–82.

'All over the world': Keith Paton, *The Great Brain Robbery*, privately published and circulated by the author in the early 1970s.

p.104   **adventure playgrounds:** Jack Lambert, an inspired creator of adventure playgrounds, photographed children constructing weird and wonderful structures. His account is in Jack Lambert and Jenny Pearson (1974) *Adventure Playgrounds*, Harmondsworth: Penguin.

Ivan Illich: (1971) *Deschooling Society*, London: Calder & Boyars; Paulo Freire (1972) *The Pedagogy of the Oppressed*, Harmondsworth: Penguin; Everett Reimer (1971) *School is Dead*, Harmondsworth: Penguin.

p.105   *Libertarian Education:* no 11, April 1973.

Y-Front: no 3, 1972.

p.106   **'A menace never changes':** *Beano*, March 1991.

Beano **and** *Dandy:* were both launched by D.C. Thomson in Dundee in 1937.

first comics of the 1890s: George Perry and Alan Aldridge (1967) *The Penguin Book of Comics*, Harmondsworth: Penguin.

p.107   **'go menacing':** *Weekend*, Brighton, 20 May 2001.

p.108   *Changing Childhood:* Martin Hoyles (ed.) (1979) London: Writers and Readers. *Children's Rights:* no 1, 1972.

'Attitude from Brixton to Hong Kong': *Brixton Village*, vol. 2, no 2, April 1994.

'lollipop rebels': headline in *Evening Standard*, 17 May 1972, quoting Charles Kuper, Head of Emmanuel School, London, on the occasion of a schoolchildren's demonstration in Trafalgar Square.

p.109   **a heterogeneous group:** pictures of Summerhill taken by a 16-year-old pupil, Joshua Popenoe, illustrated his book (1970) *Inside Summerhill*, New York: Hart Publishing; *The White Lion Street Free School Bulletin* published minutes of its meetings, as well as photographs. On Wednesday 12 November 1980, decisions ranged from 'no more football in the basement' to 'the cook is responsible for calling lunch' and 'James agreed to show round a visitor from Melbourne, Australia'.

Miscarriage: no 2, Winter 1971.

'**Arguments in favour of child suffrage**': Robert Franklin in *Guardian*, 9 July 1986; Bob Franklin (ed.) (2002) *The New Handbook of Children's Rights: Comparative Policy and Practice*, London: Routledge.

p.110   '**tell [the photographer]**': Sarah McCrum and Lotte Hughes (1998) *Interviewing Children, a Guide for Journalists and Others*, London: Save the Children, p.26.

Children as Partners: *A Guide to Consulting with the Very Young* (2000) Stirling Council. Photographs: John McPake.

'**Rosendale Odyssey**': this interactive presentation made by pupils between five and eight at Rosendale School ran at the Photographers' Gallery in London in March and April 1997.

portraits of school children: *Independent*, 16 January 1996.

p.111   **Benetton**: but see Les Back and Vibeke Quaade, 'Dream utopias, nightmare realities: imaging race and culture within the world of Benetton advertising', *Third Text*, 22 1993.

girls from the Catholic community: Protestants demonstrated violently against Catholic parents taking their children to the Holy Cross Primary school, as the route was through streets from which they feared Protestants would be driven out. A typical headline was 'Riots as children run the gauntlet of hate', *Daily Express*, 5 September 2001. Photographs showed terrified schoolgirls protected by parents and surrounded by a barrier of police officers with protective helmets, visors and riot shields. *Observer*, 9 September 2001, extracted three faces of fearful youngsters from photographs by William Cherry, Kim Haughton and Justin Kernoghan.

An effective demand for children's rights: Jo Boyden writes, 'the human rights discourse tends to detract from careful ethnography, as often as not calling forth simplistic explanations and solutions, many of which are inappropriate or ineffectual'. Boyden (1997) above, p.220.

5

No future: the threat
of childhood and the
impossibility of youth

PART 1: BAD BOYS

Public space

In 1993 a low-key, blurry image was reproduced across the British media, captured from a frame of a security camera. It came to stand for a radical reorganisation of the relations of looking and being looked at which occurred in the final decade of the twentieth century; part of a drama of safety and danger, surveillance and protection, in which the concept of childhood played a central role – a drama enacted physically on the streets and reflectively in the media. The picture shows a busy precinct peopled with hazy figures. In the foreground, back to the camera, a tiny child is apparently holding the hand of another child, their relative sizes made clear in comparison with a shopper who is passing by. This is the abduction of two-year-old James Bulger, pictured as it happened. The picture records the beginning of a sequence of events which ended with the toddler's horrific murder by a pair of ten-year-old boys. It was one of a series of frames released by Liverpool police and enhanced by a local photographic agency at their request, so that the figures would stand out more clearly. As it was used and re-used across the national press, it was worked on further, sometimes cropped, sometimes coloured; sometimes the low resolution was further enhanced; sometimes the figures were highlighted by a frame within the frame. The original frame has the date and a code number superimposed across its base, and the illuminated name of a shop, Mothercare, is clearly visible across the top, acting like a heading to the picture. And yet this image represents everything that caring mothers dread

the most. The events and the deluge of publicity and debate which surrounded them became pivotal in the iconography of childhood, pushing contemporary attitudes to children in a darker, more pessimistic direction.

The original frame was automatically recorded by a camera set up to protect the interests of retail businesses in a public shopping mall. Millions of such frames are produced daily by security cameras across a nation which is increasingly apprehensive of crime and disorder – including disorderly children. In contemporary towns and cities there is a marked difference between types of public space and the ways in which children may be present in them. A suburban street refers to the powerful concept of 'home' (see Chapter 2), and children supposedly play there safely under the watchful eyes of their parents. (A website is devoted to 'Home Zones', streets which are traffic-free and child-friendly. The home page shows children between about four and eight years old filling an urban street with their scooters and tricycles under a brilliant sun with just a hint of mock-tudor in the gabled houses.) By contrast, the desolate spaces of inner-city estates – sometimes surrounded by ageing houses, sometimes by the repetitive balconies of 1960s tower blocks – are seen as unprotected and fraught with dangers. A third type of busy urban space, the shopping mall, is apparently open and welcoming to all, with its covered pedestrian arcades and brightly lit windows full of goods. However, although they masquerade as public space, shopping malls are usually gated areas, heavily protected by security staff and cameras. The retailers and businesses which control them seek to monitor the actions of all who come within their boundaries. This is definitely not a space where unattended children are welcome, for it is a space given over to a single activity, shopping, and children rarely have the economic status of independent shoppers. If they are simply hanging around they are probably up to no good – or they may themselves be at risk.

The image of James Bulger being led away by an older boy with murderous intent came to stand for both of these late-twentieth-century fears. It represented all those trusting young children who are in deadly danger when unattended in public places, and all those vicious and dangerous youngsters who pose a threat to society itself. The image was all the more powerful as it froze a moment before young James was attacked, a moment when the crime could have been prevented. The electronic eye of the security camera, cold and neutral, became a chilling indication of the world of the 1990s – an uncaring world, where surveillance is total, but disengaged. The automatic recording has none of the claims to artistry or journalistic judgement of a human photographer. Hence, although the abduction was *observed*, it was not *seen*. No one made sense of the image, and the recording did nothing to prevent the crime. Unlike Cartier-Bresson's 'decisive moment' – the moment when all the elements of a scene, driven by chance, come together to make the visually perfect picture which a skilled photographer can capture and transform – the moment captured by this frame has nothing to distinguish it from the moment before or the moment after. The quality which gives it its unbearable poignancy is precisely its own unknowingness. It is only with hindsight that the viewer knows what is to come. The almost unimaginable scenes of the murder itself, which were sometimes hinted at and sometimes partially described in the press reports, provide a dark undertow to the understanding of this low-key image. The ironic truth is that the apparatus of surveillance was as concerned to protect Mothercare as it was the child it unblinkingly recorded. The camera was scrutinising the scene with a commercial eye, for, in this semi-public space where children should not be without an attendant adult, a caring maternal eye was hardly appropriate.

Evil

'He was so evil they called him Damien,' headlined the *Daily Star* next to a school photograph of Robert Thompson, reporting the trial of the two accused ten-year-olds. The school photograph is the second type of low-key, empty image which came to characterise public outrage and deep perplexity around the event. Was there anything to be deduced from this simple image? After all, millions of children have school photographs posed exactly like this one. How could such a young, and – if the photograph is anything to go by – apparently ordinary child carry out such an atrocity? Like the electronic image, the school photograph is one which Marshall McLuhan described as a 'cool' image, giving up little to the viewer, waiting to be invested with meaning. But placed alongside the 'hot' image of the scowling Chucky from the horror video the boys were thought to have seen (see Chapter 4), the popular press had few doubts about the meaning of this picture. It was an indication of pure evil. And if such a bland expression could show that Thompson was evil, why not other children, whose expressions are equally disingenuous and inscrutable? 'We used to believe in the innate evil of childhood and we used to accept that it was the moral responsibility of all adults to keep it in check…By dismantling the concept of evil we've effectively disarmed ourselves…', argued columnist Janet Daley, and a mass of voices echoed her. Indulgence and child-centredness had gone too far, they claimed. The potential for evil springs from the very nature of childhood itself. Do not be taken in by youth and the appearance of innocence (the *Daily Mail* headed a 16-page special 'The Evil and the Innocent'). The concept of evil transcends and breaks free from social explanations. It can be called up as a final explanation, an end point, challenging rationality, a fact impossible to go beyond. The murder of James Bulger gave a new lease of life to this ancient view of childhood. 'The simple truth is that…we are staring pure evil in the face. Wickedness has existed since the dawn of man,' declared the *Star*'s leader. When Robert Thompson and Jon Venables were described as irremediably evil, the mere statement was enough to express the horror felt, justifying hysterical condemnation and excluding any attempt to explore the history or the context of the event. Evil behaviour was separated out. To seek social explanations or consider context was seen as excusing the deed or undervaluing the abhorrence to which it gave rise. Attempts to discuss a continuum of violent behaviour or a culture of violence were firmly rejected. The concept of evil was mobilised to legitimise hatred and vengeance.

When manifested in living children, 'evil' must be dealt with at the level of daily banality, and children's violent potential is largely repressed in a realist image of childhood. But 'evil' has a lively existence in fiction, fantasy and fairy stories. *Lord of the Flies*, a powerful book and a disturbingly convincing film, documented the systematic loss of 'civilised' values amongst a group of prep-school boys stranded on an island. Its naturalist mode suggested that civilisation is only a thin veneer over the natural savagery of childhood. But the sense of a supernatural force driving the demonic excesses of childish behaviour is let rip in the horror genre, particularly in films such as *The Exorcist* and the Damien series, in which the devil is born as a child. It was this fantastic imagery of horror that was harnessed to the case of the boys who killed James Bulger. It can be seen in the reference to Damien, but above all in the hysterical condemnation of *Child's Play 3*, a rather mild horror video in which a demonic doll is invested with supernatural powers of destruction. The popular press felt free to indulge to the full these mythical fears. In the broadsheets the horror tended to be deflected into the depressive drama of the surveillance camera and the simple school photograph.

Robert Thompson and Jon Venables (whose identities were only made public because the trial judge decided to lift the restrictions on naming juveniles) spent the next eight years in secure units for young offenders. When the parole board declared that they were rehabilitated and should be released rather than move on to adult prisons, a renewed outcry echoed through the popular press, accompanied by threats of vengeance. The boys were to be given new identities, and their appearance was not to be made public. The only new photographs of them to be released were also from 1993, and showed their frightened faces in police mug-shots. Their youth and childishness were emphasised by the measuring chart behind them, showing both to be hardly more than four feet tall. But within days of the announcement of their impending release, a picture which purported to show one of them was published on the Internet, apparently with the intent to provoke revenge. Once more the image was a frame snatched from a surveillance camera, captured during day-release from the unit. Once more the electronic medium provided an image invested with neither spectacular nor artistic qualities, which depended for its power on its seedy mundanity and its availability for illicit circulation and use. The insistent power of this low-resolution visual style had come to express a post-modern anomie which brings it close to the excesses of horror. In comparison, realist documentary seems over-studied and its humanist concerns inadequate.

Bad children and the savage streets

'The street is a playground for bored youngsters,' headlined the *Guardian*, dis-approvingly, next to a night-time colour photograph of a couple of adolescents, hands in pockets, outlined by the glare of a street light. Here, the values of play. have been turned upside down and a vision of a violent world of childhood opens up. This new resonant image is dominated by young boys – but increasingly it includes girls – who have escaped the constraining institutions of home and school, and burst unwanted into the lawless public spaces of contemporary towns and cities. Their presence is seen as illegitimate and threatening, and a series of public narratives have highlighted the violence and the dangers. In 1996, headmaster Philip Lawrence was stabbed to death by a gang of youths as he tried to protect a pupil outside his school gates; in 2000, ten-year-old Damilola Taylor was found bleeding to death on a South London estate; in 1994 six-year-old Rikki Neave was found dead near his home in Peterborough. Reports continue of children driven to suicide through bullying; of children who terrorise local estates, stealing cars, breaking windows, starting fires and terrifying elderly inhabitants; of gangs, whose rivalry is based on territory or race; of a growing drugs and gun culture and of suburban youth whose violence is casual and random. The mythological construction of childhood is interwoven with a cruel reality as newspaper narratives tell of children who are both damaged and damaging; of children who are aggressive, impertinent and out of control. As always, the childhood of these children is firmly constructed in opposition to adulthood, but now the spontaneity and irrationality of childhood, instead of being playful, has a savage and dangerous quality – giving adults the automatic right to call for punishment rather than understanding (Prime Minister John Major offered the opinion that society 'should condemn a little more and understand a little less'). An energy which in other contexts could be constructed as childish play is here displaced and re-directed. Such reports are struggling with a dilemma over the concept of childhood itself, trying to keep the qualities of innocence and violence firmly separated so that they do not contaminate each other.

Although it is often described as a new phenomenon, a sense of danger from children – particularly children from underprivileged social groups – has a long history in public discourse. In 1980 the *Sun* identified a 'vicious generation' which rejected any form of control. 'Terror is a modern fact of life. Increasingly Britain is a nation that walks in fear of its young,' it declared under the headline 'Aggro Britain'. In 1977 the *Daily Mirror* described a 'Savage Generation', and pictured young Geoff and Freddie, with a blank stare at the camera, posing in front of a brick wall indicating the inner-city wasteland. 'These young savages emerge as iron-hard, unfeeling boys and girls without any sense of moral values or sexual values, without any ambition or desire to be worthwhile citizens or to be part of a decent society,' wrote the *Mirror's* star columnist Marje Proops.

Geoffrey Pearson has traced back to the seventeenth century recurring outcries deploring the wildness of youth 'today', when they move beyond the control of their families. A 1910 report speaks of 'the gamins of our large towns [who] live a bandit life, away from their homes, free of all control'. Such complaints were invariably accompanied by regrets for a less turbulent adolescence 'twenty years ago'. It is thought that 'the manners of children are deteriorating, that the child of today is coarser, more vulgar, less refined than his parents were,' as the Stipendiary Magistrate for Brighton wrote in a 1898 report, the year the word 'hooligan' came into common usage. Pearson records how disturbances character-ised bank holidays in particular, when free time led to a celebration that could all too easily turn into a riot. And he notes the repeated dismay at the extreme youth of these uncontrollable youngsters. 'It is melancholy to find that some parents are not ashamed to confess that children of 7 or 8-years-old are entirely beyond their control,' declared the 1898 report. The sentiment was echoed a century later as the imagery continued to stress the youth of the wrongdoers: 'He is not yet 4ft tall and still only 7 years old. But for Anthony Scott it may be too late. His mother is convinced he will end up in prison.' Roy Hattersley noted children as young as 11 amongst those running wild on a Sheffield estate. In a feature headed 'The no hope kids: joy-riding on Britain's worst estate,' the *Mail on Sunday* review pictured a child, a woolly hat pulled well down over his face, a cigarette in his mouth, clutching the wheel of a car with its starting wires exposed. Other photographs in the feature show young boys pushing a stolen car or leaping in front of the flames, in a spectacular image of mayhem and destruction.

The image of such youngsters is most threatening when they are pointing a weapon – which may be a toy, or may be terrifyingly real – at the camera/viewer and apparently at the whole of adult society. A frame from an American home video showed Andrew Golden, aged six, pointing a handgun. 'Five years later he used his knowledge when he and his 13-year-old cousin, Mitchell Johnson, opened fire on schoolmates in Jonesboro Arkansas, killing four pupils and a teacher.' The cover of a thoughtful book on the effect of the conflict on the children of Northern Ireland shows a young boy wearing a gas mask, clutching a home-made petrol bomb. (The image became an iconic representation of Bloody Sunday, the traumatic occasion in 1972 when British paratroopers fired on a civil-rights march, killing 13 people. More than one photographer pictured the boy, and the image was used in a mural towering over the Bogside area of Derry 30 years after the event. 'The brawling children of Ulster...have passed prematurely from the innocent games of childhood to the deadly serious business of street warfare,' wrote the Belfast *Newsletter*.) Publications must be careful about the identities of children they show, especially if they are accusing them of misbehaviour or criminal activity, so the mask or scarf is a handy device which undoubtedly adds to the menace of the image. 'Balaclava Boy', the 11-year-old delinquent who terrorised a Hartlepool estate, cavorted in a ski-mask in front of the news cameras. His image, sticking up two fingers to the world, was taken up by the national press and used by a local rock band, the White Negroes.

The Guardian Monday May 15 2000 ● John Sutherland 5 ● Women 6 ● Marcel Berlins 9 ● Arts 10-13 ● Wheels 15 ● Crossword 23

A child in crime
The life and death
of Balaclava Boy.
By Emma Brockes

Frame from CCTV security camera, courtesy of North News and Pictures and *Guardian*.

(The combination of weapon and mask reminds us of the controversial photograph by the artist Tierney Gearon, in which two naked children point a banana at the camera. This was one of the pictures which almost brought about the closure of an exhibition at the Saatchi Gallery in 2001. Although the public debate focused on the nakedness of the children and the fetishistic implications of the mask, in my view what made them disturbing was their link to this key image of violent children – a directly threatening gesture at the viewer, but with identity concealed, so that understanding or empathy is denied.)

'We have never seen anything like them before,' wrote journalist Linda Grant, not of delinquents but of ordinary schoolchildren. The inscrutable faces that illustrated her article seemed almost as difficult to read as those hidden behind a balaclava or a mask. The blank look at the camera may equally imply a threat, a contest between viewer and viewed, challenging the adult desire to get behind the alienating surface. The confrontational glare which was one aspect of children's liberation – produced as a refusal of adult condescension – has, in this newer image, changed to something cooler and more intense.

When a 1996 survey recorded the social attitudes of 12- to 19-year-olds, the headline results judged 'the nation's young to be very, very boring'. However, the parade of characters and stories in the press continues to demand excitement rather than boredom, and condemnation remains more exciting than under-standing. 'Bad' children are news. Discussing the dubious ethics of picturing children who had been excluded from school, John Carvel wrote of 'media scrums outside schools' because 'school indiscipline had become a hot topic'. 'To be a "naughty" child today can mean national media exposure.' When in March 2002 a court lifted the ban on naming misbehaving youngsters, the *Mirror* pictured Ben, aged 17, and Robert, aged 15, on its front page above the caption 'VILE'. As well as losing their anonymity, these boys have exchanged the familiar blank expression for one of amused contempt (no doubt provoked by the *Mirror*'s photographer). In the *Mirror*'s words, 'The lawless teenagers are laughing at us all'.

One of the first acts of the 'new' Labour Government of 1997 was the attempt by Jack Straw, Home Secretary, to return youngsters who were out of place on the streets to their proper place in the home. The policy was to be 'zero tolerance', and the power of curfew over children under 10 was given to local authorities. On three council estates in South Lanarkshire 'from 8 o'clock every night teams of five police officers will tour the streets, stopping unsupervised young children and "escorting" them home if they are deemed to be a danger'. A typical photograph showed youngsters in the long shadows of the evening, oblivious of a billboard announcing '"Yes" to curfew on kids'. In practice, the order was never used. Even so, in 2001 the powers were extended to children under 15, and the condemnatory language employed by many journalists in the 2000s continued to echo that employed by Marje Proops in the 1970s. 'The sexual revolution, the permissive society and the abolition of marriage... have created this terrifying generation of murderous, morally blank wolf-children, fatherless, undisciplined, indulged one minute then brutalised the next,' wrote Peter Hitchens in the *Daily Mail*.

Punishment and parental control

But, as we have seen (Chapter 2), the restoration of imaginary family values is not the answer, since the image of the bad child has also invaded the home. Pictures of scowling children, screaming children, and children in mid-tantrum are no longer taboo. Difficult children and the problems of parental control are the subject of television programmes and features in parenting magazines and the concerned press. Tom Pilston's picture of a screaming boy in a supermarket trolley was captioned, 'Give in, cop out – a mother's confession'. 'What are we doing to our children?' asked the accompanying article. 'Bringing them up to express themselves freely in a way we never could, or failing them by refusing to teach them how to behave?' The question of physical punishment and whether smacking should be made illegal has occupied many a column inch. Family love may itself legitimate violence.

In today's commodified image of the middle-class family, to admit mayhem at home may give rise to sympathy rather than condemnation. The outpouring of commercial and advice-based literature for parents transforms the problems that go along with parenting into an acceptable lifestyle debate. Next to the picture of a charming three-year-old on the cover of *The Parents' Guide* are various indications of the contents of the magazine. Amongst them, 'Tantrums. How to keep your cool' figures prominently. This is not exactly a caption to the picture – but immediately the sweetness of the child is no longer sugary, and the enigma of her expression becomes a practical issue. Within this context, no stigma is attached to an inability to cope. The image is seen as a useful one, educational and functional, quite different from the frightening vision of radical violence.

But everyday naughtiness can imperceptibly merge into extreme behaviour, and fear of difficult children is a tangible undertow in the public discourse around families. Within the family context, 'understanding' is permitted. In contrast to the 'evil' or 'vile' wolf-children who roam the streets, truly bad behaviour at home may be recategorised as a medical syndrome or a response to intolerable experience. Magazines and newspapers tell of a variety of psycho-social problems, peaking in teenage years, including hyperactivity syndrome, unattachment syndrome, attention deficit syndrome. Children's suicide rates are increasing, as are depression, eating disorders and drug dependency. In their pioneering work on child abuse, Henry and Ruth Kempe pointed out that some abused children may become 'demon children': negative, aggressive, hyperactive, with the power to overturn the order of family life. Such devilish children can only be fully expressed by fictional characters – in films such as *The Exorcist*, *The Omen* or *Carrie*, in which children exercise demonic and destructive powers. In this safely fictionalised realm, the adult hatred of children and the adult fear of children's hatred can both be fully expressed. Marina Warner has demonstrated the ways in which fairy tales and illustrations deal in both of these dangerous emotions. Violence and uncontrollability are part of childhood too.

The available image of the bad child expresses an anxiety around the growing assertiveness which is now a recognised part of childhood. The obverse of the brazen, anti-authority attitude that commentators deplore is the uncomfortable fact that children themselves are now insisting that they must be taken seriously. Society has not adjusted to children's confident knowledge, to its strengths and its heterogeneity – many of the feared groups are from ethnic minorities. Real worries about an uncertain future may be displaced onto an exaggerated image of violent children. The sense of despair that such children are beyond both explanation and redemption echoes an adult powerlessness in a world where the vision of childhood leading to a better future is no longer convincing.

PART 2: THE IMPOSSIBILITY OF YOUTH

No future: the impossibility of youth

[The delinquent] is a little stunted man already – he knows much and a great deal too much of what is called life – he can take care of his own immediate interests. He is self reliant, he has so long directed or misdirected his own actions and has so little trust in those about him, that he submits to no control and asks for no protection.

So wrote the reformer Matthew Davenport Hill in 1855. In the second half of the nineteenth century, the aim was to get the children of the poor off the streets, where they had a precocious independence, begging, scavenging, working as crossing-sweepers or errand boys or at other odd jobs, as well as thieving and creating general mayhem. Proper legal protections and suitable institutions had to be created so that these children, too, could have a childhood. Hill concluded, 'He has consequently much to unlearn – he has to be turned again into a child'.

With the first glimmerings of twentieth-century prosperity after the Second World War, working-class young people returned to the streets in a different spirit, and once more the category of 'childhood' came under challenge. Theirs was a different sort of precocity, but it was equally deplored by respectable society. The 'teddy boys', with their sharp expensive suits, greased hairstyles and assertive ways were the first of the post-war spectacular youth cults, bent on leisure and consumerism. The neon and pinball machines of a seedy nightlife complemented the street corners and crumbling inner cities of this post-war phenomenon. An imagery of glitter and decay accompanied the attractions and moral ambiguity of a new youthful exploration of public places.

The public imagery of childhood has tended to take itself for granted. Only in recent years has it reflected on or commented on its own construction. Not so with the imagery of 'youth'. Since the emergence of the teddy boys, the pressure to redefine adolescents as 'youth' rather than 'child' has made this liminal state highly visible and problematic. In a system of meanings which creates rigid categorical differences, 'youth' is a non-category, nothing but the dividing line between two well-defined states – adulthood and childhood. It hovers on the margins of both, pulled first in one direction, then the other, so that, instead of being clearly distinguished from each other, the opposing categories appear uncertain and fluctuating. In 'youth', indications of childhood are no longer appropriate, whereas those of adulthood are withheld. But, paradoxically, these people who should logically be absent, since they hardly exist, have become strikingly visible. Again and again we have been invited to scrutinise them and consider the problem of their non-identity. Pictures of youth have been examined and dissected, catalogued and discussed, as if the image itself could give some clue to the nature of an elusive phenomenon. One way of understanding this prolific imagery is to see it as a set of strategies for coping with an impossible group and its all-too-possible freedoms. At the same time its very impossibility has made it a point of identification for adult fantasy in its promise of an escape from the strictures of adult rationality. It can stand for opposition, for transgression and for inexpressible freedoms.

There is a point in their lives when young people gain the right to be on the streets, and at that point they have emphatically drawn attention to themselves in a variety of ways – with rowdy behaviour, youth performance and carnivalesque values which all too easily topple into riot and disorder. Whether it is a group of raucous young girls in strappy dresses on their way to a nightclub, or anti-globalisation protesters holding up the traffic in fanciful costumes, 'youth', it appears, has not one manifestation but many. Newspapers have periodically provided their readers with visual inventories of young people on the streets. Strange exotic types have been identified, their characteristics analysed, their tastes in music and dance noted, their lifestyles distinguished each from the others. The tone has ranged from pleasurable amazement to something just short of moral outrage.

'Kids, just look at them. Rings through their noses, hair like porcupines. Men with earrings, girls in boots. Bloody kids! Who do they think they are?' exclaimed the *Daily Mirror*. The pictures which accompanied this outpouring responded to the spectacular values presented by their subjects and dwelt on the drama and wit of the costume, offering the rich and pleasurable surface of fashion photography. This was an exercise in decoding, a search for an understanding of youth through a reading of the signs – the tattooed cobweb, the spiked hair, the boots and braces – every item claiming significance. In similar presentations across the years, young people have been catalogued, sometimes with the aid of diagrams and charts, sometimes with photographs which attempt to record and pin down in a series of frozen moments the ever-changing language of self-presentation. The hunt was on for the weirdest of the weirdies, the craziest of the head-bangers, the challenges to social norms. In the 1980s there was the white make-up, blank expressions, tight leather, chains and hedonism of the 'goths'; in the 1990s the more earthy style of the eco-warriors caught the headlines, living in tree houses to protect ancient woodland and tunnelling underground to sabotage developments which would damage the environment. 'Swampy' became an icon for a generation, pictured emerging from a muddy tunnel, his hair in his eyes, a momentary hero. The jangling of different styles offers a pleasure Roland Barthes described as 'babel'. In Barthes's cataloguing of the pleasures of the text, 'babel' is a carnivalesque space where incoherence can momentarily be indulged. We can gasp with amazement, experience a frisson of horror, or laugh at the sheer cheek of it.

Growth out of childhood involves a challenge to adults' unlimited right to look and an unwillingness to accept the controlling gaze. And yet here is youth, forcing itself into view, demanding the attention of the lens. In Dick Hebdige's words, these young people are 'hiding in the light'. They engage in a visible negotiation with the powerful adult gaze, presenting themselves ready-made, as an image. The image may be designed to amuse, or it may deliberately set out to alienate the viewer, meeting adult indulgence with adolescent contempt, and searching for those signs that will shock the most. Punk took these tendencies to the extreme with its safety pins, swastikas, bondage gear, jackets embroidered with 'Belsen was a gas', facial distortion and two fingers at the camera. Bodily messages set out to challenge all that humanitarian society claims to value in

News of the World, 21 November 1982.

favour of the dark side of human history. The fashion for piercing – through the ears, the nose, the tongue, the navel, the nipples – focuses a lack of respect for social values onto the body itself, challenging the flesh to maintain its integrity. The drama of an impossible identity cannot be limited by mere bodily constraints. These people close to childhood fling into the face of the viewer everything children are supposed to be ignorant of and adults have learnt to express in carefully licensed ways. Knowledge suppressed in childhood is visible across the bodies of those who declare themselves not-child.

One genre of presentation has indulged a rhetorical attempt to recapture disaffected young people, and to reduce their challenge to mere bravado, returning them to the childhood they seem so anxious to shake off. This involves picturing them together with their parents. In a *News of the World* presentation, a father was captioned 'Proud of a punk', even though his spike-haired daughter wears a T-shirt that proclaims 'No future'. Since fathers' futures are conventionally expressed through their children, the daughter's visible denial of that future introduces a bizarre contradiction. The theme of 'No future' can both be cata-clysmic and point to an eternal present.

This type of imagery is not at the expense of its subjects. There is a visible collaboration, even if sometimes an uneasy one, between those who present themselves as performers and the photographers who enhance the performance in an entertaining way. But although the outrageous appearance seduces the camera, something slips away from behind the spectacular front. The young performers solicit adult attention, then refuse its implications. By making them-selves visible they make it clear that they cannot be known. Here there are no secret childhood moments for adults to peep in at. If young people cannot control the way their image is presented, they can at least make it both challenging and difficult to decipher. The role of the observer is itself called into question. An early youth chronicler, T.R. Fyvel, wrote of the insecurity of the teddy boys. But one of his informants warned him, while decked in his eye-catching gear, 'No one can look at the Boys and laugh and get away with it'.

From working-class resistance to spoilt brats

The claim to be defined as 'youth' rather than 'child' runs alongside the potent narratives of children who have rejected childhood in a variety of less acceptable ways. Headlines such as 'Affluent lifestyle leading children into temptation: "Drink, drugs and gaming are on the increase"' and 'So old yet so young, pity our lost children' introduce stories of premature sexual awareness, too much money to spend, precocious knowledge, dangers from new technologies and involvement in a sexualised pop culture which somehow summarises all these frightening attributes. The image of clubbing – ecstatic youngsters crowded together, waving their arms in a state of collective frenzy – rejects the dignity of the youth parade and puts aside the mask and the cool performance in exchange for an image of abandonment, not so different from the domestic image of children's parties.

For many left-wing sociologists and other writers in the 1960s and 1970s, a revalidation of working-class culture was the background for the identification of working-class youth as a special category. They saw a broader political and social purpose behind the apparent wildness of the youngsters. Unruly behaviour could be understood as resistance against the oppressive limits of both generation and class. Even when the young people themselves were unaware of it, solidarity and purpose could be recognised. The harsh disciplines of the working class, with its traditions of conformity and self-organisation, sustained a set of collective myths which gave dignity and a sense of identity. Misbehaving youths could unknowingly represent their class, even as they rebelled against their elders and the world of respectability. But this class configuration was dissipated as the heavy industries disappeared during the 1970s and 1980s. The trade unions weakened, male unemployment became endemic in certain areas, and the white working class was replaced by what was now described as an 'underclass', including second- and third-generation ethnic minorities. The nineteenth-century distinction between the 'deserving' poor – who earn their poverty – and the 'undeserving' poor – who are mere malingerers – was resurrected. A forward-looking image of struggle and class advance was replaced by the listless image of unemployment and despair. Ways of making sense of young people's, particularly young boys', unruliness changed too. There was a much greater readiness to condemn, and less inclination to explain or understand.

Youth cultures had arisen just at the point when increasing prosperity meant that young people were becoming a new target for marketing strategists. The creation of specific youth styles meant that visible class differentials could be reduced, and minority styles – particularly that of black Caribbean youth – could be absorbed into a media-conscious market. When Phil Cohen identified a 'youth spectacle' and Dick Hebdige defined punk as a post-modern style, a sort of glamour had been added to young people on the borders of delinquency. But as the 1980s became the 1990s, youth spectacle and youth resistance drifted apart. The spectacle settled into a commercialised pop culture and 'resistance' became more difficult to identify, while, as we have seen, the image of young delinquents became grimmer and more frightening.

Courtesy of Bournemouth University Student Union, 2002.

In 1988 an article in the advertisers' journal *Campaign* claimed that 'the teenage rebel is dead' and that 'Thatcher's youth' were caring and family-orientated. They looked forward to designer clothes, a successful career and a flashy car. By 1990 this reassuring picture had collapsed and a different sort of moral panic had ensued. 'Your son is 15. He lost his virginity two years ago, swills Carlsberg Special Brew and slouches in front of the television watching EastEnders.' The affluent conformists had become 'spoilt brats', reported the advertising agency Gold Greenlees Trott. By 2001, hedonism swept all before it. A 'junior rave outfit Teen Dreem' had a nationwide network of venues for under-18s only, from which adults were firmly excluded.

'Othering': degradation or nice kids

Adult society has employed many strategies to win back the right to look, to tear off the mask, to get into the club and to return young people to the disciplines of the childhood they have been rejecting with such impertinence. I shall consider three such strategies: a recourse to the imagery of the 'primitive' and the 'tribal'; a degradation of the child in the image; and the construction of an imagery of 'nice kids'.

Young people are frequently described as 'exotic', and youth culture has often been compared to that of a strange tribe with customs and rituals incomprehensible to 'civilised' understanding. In the *Sunday Times*, Ian Jack reported that his friends reacted to his interviews with young people 'as though one had returned from a long stay with the Marsh Arabs'. The approach is not new. In his survey of the reporting of delinquency and youth crime, Geoffrey

Pearson notes a centuries-old history of such 'othering' language, and Hugh Cunningham tells of nineteenth-century children described as 'hottentots' and 'street arabs'. There is an unavoidable continuum between children and adults which makes it difficult to describe young people as completely alien, but 'exotic' peoples can be presented as irreducibly different.

To look at the exotic is to look as a tourist, a travel photographer or an anthropologist. It is to look as a 'civilised' traveller at 'uncivilised' indigenous peoples, as a coloniser at the colonised. 'Primitive' tribes continue to be a regular ingredient of travel entertainment, and they continue to be presented as simpler, more emotional and less rational (even when they have cannily reconstructed themselves for the tourist trade). This vision remains woven into the language of racial subordination. A 'tribal' way of life may be spectacular and fascinating, but it may also be considered amoral, degraded and brutal. It is no coincidence that young people are regularly described as 'tribal' – with all the primitive licence that the word has come to imply. In 1956 the *Daily Mail* was outspoken in describing new forms of 'deplorable' popular music 'which surely originated in the jungle. We sometimes wonder whether this is the negro's revenge' (a 'revenge' which was amply recuperated in later music styles – including 'jungle'). In 1980 the *Daily Star* was more cautious about racist language, but the impression was similar. 'The "tribes" of youngsters who dance the night away across Britain all have their own distinctive style – in music, attitudes, dress… The beat goes on from midnight to breakfast time, inspiring complex and energetic feats of twisting, leaping and high kicks.' Even as they fight their way out of childhood with sophisticated irony, such language puts young people firmly back in their place, as their modern commentary on urban life is translated into primitive ritual. Studied self-presentation is rewritten as the least self-conscious of 'natural' behaviour.

Equating young people with the exotic ensures that they retain their childishness, and it also ensures that 'exotic' peoples continue to be attributed the qualities of childhood. Civilisation's 'other' remains necessary to civilisation's sense of its itself. Just like childhood itself, the image of those who are apparently beyond the constraints of the modern world can become an imaginary repository for qualities which 'civilisation' and adulthood must repress. It is an image with a long and ignoble history, and in twenty-first-century multicultural Britain such attitudes have dangerous consequences.

A second strategy for dealing with the impertinence of youth has been to produce an imagery which seeks to degrade its subjects. By the late 1970s, the use of drugs, which had given rise to the psychedelic dream of the 1960s, had become a sign of youth excess which could lead only to disaster. The impossible position young people are expected to occupy could result in early death – 'No

Is this the best future
we can offer our school leavers?

There are now more young people out of work than at any time since the war.

In some areas that's 1 in 3. And they're not work-shy hooligans, they're victims of the economic facts of life.

They've applied for jobs – in some cases they've applied for dozens – and they've been told that without a skill or work experience they haven't a chance.

Which makes them teenage rejects. Turned down without trial.

Youth Opportunities Programme.

The Youth Opportunities Programme is a new plan to help employers help young people, even if they can't offer any permanent jobs.

It's based on the best elements of existing schemes that have succeeded in helping as many as 8 out of 10 participants into jobs.

The idea is extremely simple: If you can take in young people for up to six months, introducing them to the benefits and disciplines of work, we will pay them £19.50 a week. And there are no National Insurance contributions or tax returns to worry about.

They get invaluable experience, training and the chance to earn a reference that proves their worth. You get a chance to give them a future without having to take anyone on permanently – unless you want to.

The alternative.

The only alternative is a growing number of young people who feel discarded by 'the system' and a smaller pool of trained and enthusiastic people for industry to draw upon.

And, if nothing's done, the inescapable truth is that by the end of this year the situation will be even worse.

Which is why the Programme is backed by the government, the CBI and the TUC.

How it works.

We have offices all over the country and our staff are eager to give employers every detail of the scheme. At the same time, these offices keep in close touch with all the bodies concerned with unemployed young people in your area.

Which makes them uniquely qualified to help you help young people.

If you're interested in participating in the Programme, our staff will help you plan an introduction to work for young people that will benefit them without disturbing the normal running of your business.

You are then free to choose the young men and women you feel have the most to offer – and whose future will be brighter as a result of training and experience under your guidance.

Then it's up to the Youth Opportunities Programme to make sure that your involvement is as trouble-free and rewarding as possible. Give a young person a chance, and we will do the rest.

What to do.

Get the full story from Roger Panton, Manpower Services Commission, Department G5, Selkirk House, 166 High Holborn, London WC1V 6PE Tel. 01-836 1213.

Our future workforce depends on it.

YOUTH OPPORTUNITIES PROGRAMME MSC

Advertisement, Manpower Services Commission, Youth Opportunities Programme, 1978.

future' at its most literal. A series of youthful performers acted out this scenario in public. 'I want to self-destruct myself,' Sid Vicious is quoted as saying. 'Look at my arms. That's a bottle scar from when I cut myself. Look at my chest... I'll probably die before I'm 25. But I'll have lived the way I wanted to.' His death was evoked by other young people. 'Charlie reckons he will be dead by his 21st birthday,' reported the Daily Mirror in a 1980 'youth issue', 'and he's happy to know he'll die a skinhead. "I want to die like Sid," he says.'

Self-destruction and the decaying body of the drug-taker apparently confirmed the despair which lay behind the claim to the ecstatic pleasure of being outside social categories, neither adult nor child. The huddled bodies and downcast eyes of the Daily Mirror's 'Shock report' of December 1985 were echoed in the Health Education Council's widely used advertisement showing a pale and wasted young man, 'Heroin screws you up'. By contrast with its jaunty 1983 feature 'Bloody kids', the Mirror's report on the 'Junk generation' presented a typology of despair. This time it introduced 'the dosser, the runaway, the racist, the hooligan, the thug, the rapist' in imagery which sternly refused any playful collaboration with its subjects. It sought to portray 'the depths of hell'. The language which accompanied the pictures used a bitter vocabulary of rejection: 'Joey Lamb is trash. A junk kid littering a junk world.' These young people 'are difficult to sympathise with and' – once more – 'impossible to understand'.

In previous years the Daily Mirror had produced issues which, in a mood of humanist realism, had presented a sympathetic view of youth unemployment, recognising that, in real life, many youngsters simply fell between the cracks of society rather than placing themselves outside in a deliberate act of refusal. But the image of degradation has a more powerful audience appeal than that of mere social disadvantage. In the late 1970s, government advertisements to promote its Youth Opportunities Programme (YOP) used pictures showing young people in dustbins, thrown aside like so much garbage. By the end of the 1980s, that metaphoric image had been overtaken by reality. Newspapers now carried reports of teenagers begging in railway stations, sleeping in cardboard boxes and sheltering in shop doorways as the problem of homelessness was added to that of unemployment. These young people were on the streets, not asserting their right to use those spaces but because there was nowhere else for them to go. It was an image recuperated by more fortunate youngsters, in what Angela McRobbie described as a 'dramatically "dirty" visual style', the fashion for ragged clothing and matted hair which evolved in the climate of Thatcherism, 'as young people staged "homelessness" or "the end of welfare"'.

Addiction and degradation does not only affect the poor. By the final years of the twentieth century many young people had abandoned a dramatisation of poverty for a visual style based on designer labels and a hedonistic commitment to leisure and pleasure. But however sleek their self-presentation, the narratives of youth have continued to reveal the underside of the image. The chilling possibility that youth excess leads to early death has created images that are even more shocking, as they indulge a new, intrusive realism. They include a photograph of 18-year-old Leah Betts, in a hospital bed with tubes in her nose, dying of an ecstacy overdose, and the pictured body of 21-year-old Rachel Whitear, the syringe with which she had injected herself with a fatal dose of heroin still in her hand. Both pictures were released by the girls' parents, in an attempt to draw public attention to the abuse of drugs.

Possibly the most effective strategy for bringing the image of youth under control has been a search for 'nice kids', even within the youth spectacle. Ripping away the mask may bring the 'real' teenager under public scrutiny. 'Are they really as horrible as they appear?' asked the News of the World, and, perhaps surprisingly, gave the answer 'No'. 'Underneath those mad mohican hairdos, startling make-up and way-out clothes are typical teenagers.' When a quieter, more 'realistic' photographic mode forces the image of young people back into the mundane world of trivial concerns, a much more reassuring view emerges. Particularly in the local press, where the subjects of the pictures and the purchasers of the paper are often the same, many photographs accept the ordinariness of young people. Unadorned by excessive make-up or fancy dress, they accept the gaze of the camera in a relaxed, if slightly tentative, way. Their challenge is defused, but the image has retreated from that mythological realm in which adulthood and childhood continue to confront each other in a never-ending drama.

Riots and stunted demons

'Everyone was having a pleasant morning here. Mums and Dads were sitting outside with their children enjoying the sunshine when these hooligans started running all over the place. It frightened everybody,' reported the Daily Express of a 'Day trip to terror'. On that bank holiday afternoon in 1980, 'children' who were sitting peacefully with their families were terrified by people at the limits of childhood, 'hooligans', 'young troublemakers' who had escaped parental control and started running all over the place. Adolescent anomie, youth entertainment and the delights of the youth parade – all these must be seen against a background of periodic and increasingly apocalyptic reports of youth disorder. Fears that are hinted at, dramatised or parodied by the youth parade, become brute facts when 'youth', which symbolises all that is chaotic and irrational, seems to throw off all constraint and act out its dreadful potential. From the 'mods and rockers' confrontations of the 1960s to the anti-capitalist demonstrations of the 2000s, from the inner-city riots that characterised recent decades to the periodic resurgence of football hooliganism, these most dramatic of public narratives have put the image of youthful riot at their centre.

Central to these dramas is the image of the crowd – young people gathered together in an undifferentiated, unstructured group, moving in unpredictable directions, no longer children but hooligans running all over the place, carried along by a euphoria similar to that of the clubbing image but now characterised as 'violence'. Feverish reporting casts these young people as objects of intemperate abuse and mortal fear. They are 'undisciplined, prejudiced and arrogant hooligans, dead set on overturning order, reason and free speech'. They are wreckers, young thugs and a threat to our sanity. They are 'stunted demons, emerging from the shadows with throwing arms raised'. (Pearson records the use of the word 'stunted' over and over across the years. As with the shocking smallness of the two boys who killed James Bulger, the smallness of these children adds to the awfulness of their actions.) They are animals, beasts. 'This dog is an extension of my right arm,' one police officer told the *Daily Express* in its account of the 1980 bank holiday riot, 'It's animal against animal'. The language pushes against the limits of humanity itself, provoking without examining questions about the division between humans and beasts and about forms of human behaviour which go beyond the margins of the tolerable.

The language of the tribal, the primitive and the savage gained a new significance when black youth played a prominent part in the urban riots of the 1980s. 'St Paul's, revolt of the lost tribe,' was how The *Observer* headlined the Bristol disturbances of 1980. The *Mirror* wrote of 'Tribal Warfare'. 'England' was regularly invoked as the epitome of civilisation, the antithesis of uncontrol. 'This is not England. It's just madness,' a policeman told the *Daily Express* after the Broadwater Farm riot in 1985. Blackness, primitiveness and a lust for violence were ideas which came together in an easy slide from metaphor to description. 'Many experts predict that life will only change for Britain's Blacks by bloodshed,' wrote Jean Richie in the *Sun*. 'Amazingly, some would even welcome it.'

Although later pulled back and knitted into the continuing flow of the narrative, in the imagery of riot certain hectic moments seem to arrest time itself and to stand for something beyond. Photographs search for this moment of action, the dynamism of movement, the 'throwing arm raised', waiting for the rioter to clutch the petrol bomb or the looter to smash the window. Devices to enhance the newspaper presentation include outlining a figure engaged in dramatic action, and pushing back the edges of the frame to include as many events as possible. In one notable example, a high-angle picture of a Brixton street – police behind their riot shields at one end and youths 'with throwing arms raised' at the other – spread across the front and back pages of the *Daily Mirror*, effectively wrapping the newspaper. Fire, dust and melee play an important role, in a landscape of broken windows and burning buildings and vehicles. Colour printing has meant that the searing orange/red of the flames has dominated more recent reports.

The image of riot is the most extreme of the images of escape from the mundane world of adult rationality. Safe in their armchairs, readers may take vicarious pleasure in the drama, in the experience of shock, and even in condemnation. But the chaos is rapidly pulled back into the flow of the narrative as the theme becomes the familiar one of control. The tactic is twofold: to reassert authority within the frame, and to use the news photographs themselves as evidence of crimes committed. 'If you know 'em, SHOP 'EM,' headlined The *People* after the poll-tax demonstration of March 1990, above mug-shots of rioters enlarged from news pictures. Readers are invited to become players in the drama, as collaborators in reasserting public order and adult values.

Within the photographic frame itself, order is seen to be restored. The imagery fragments the mobile crowd as photographers follow the police moving in to make arrests. When escape attempts take extreme forms, the visible repression may be violent. One of the most familiar images that accompany narratives of trouble on the streets is that of a young person, often black, struggling in the arms of several police officers. It is an image which detaches an individual from the mass and demonstrates their subjection to punishment. Youth is finally put in its place. 'A few moments before he was confident and aggressive. Now they drag him away screaming for Mummy.'

'He has to be turned again into a child,' wrote Hill in 1855, and respectable society in the ensuing hundred and fifty years has echoed his sentiments. The problem has been that disorderly, irrational behaviour, unacceptable to adults, always on the verge of becoming dangerous and violent, lingers as a defining quality of childhood itself. The idea of the innate evil of childhood may have taken a new form, but it has not been abandoned.

NOTES ON CHAPTER 5

p.116 **Public space:** Allison James, Chris Jenks and Alan Prout (1998) *Theorising Childhood*, Cambridge: Polity, Chapter 3, on childhood in social space. See also Virginia Morrow (2002) 'Children's rights to public space: environment and curfews', in Bob Franklin (ed.) *The New Handbook of Children's Rights: Comparative Policy and Practice*, London: Routledge.

a low-key, blurry image: Sarah Kember (1998) *Virtual Anxiety: Photography, New Technologies and Subjectivity*, Manchester: Manchester University Press, Chapter 3. The image was used by Nicholas Mirzoeff (1999) to typify the visuality of the contemporary world at the very beginning of *An Introduction to Visual Culture*, London: Routledge.

p.117 **a public shopping mall:** Rachel Bowlby (2000) *Carried Away: the Invention of Modern Shopping*, London: Faber.

'Home Zones': www.homezones.org.

p.118 **'decisive moment':** Henri Cartier-Bresson (1952) *The Decisive Moment*, New York: Simon and Schuster. Apparently, the reason *this* frame was selected was that this was the frame in which the toddler appeared to be holding the hand of the older boy.

'He was so evil': *Daily Star*, 25 November 1993.

p.119 **Marshall McLuhan:** (1964) *Understanding Media*, London: Routledge & Kegan Paul, Chapter 2, 'Media hot and cold'.

Chucky from the horror video: Patricia Holland (1997) 'Living for libido or Child's Play 4: the imagery of childhood and the call for censorship', in Martin Barker and Julian Petley (eds) *Ill Effects, the Media/Violence Debate*, London: Routledge.

'We used to believe in the innate evil': Janet Daley, quoted by Yvonne Roberts, *New Statesman*, 3 December 1993.

'The Evil and the Innocent': *Daily Mail*, 25 November 1993. See Bob Franklin and Julian Petley (1996) 'Killing the age of innocence: newspaper reporting of the death of James Bulger', in Jane Pilcher and Stephen Wagg, *Thatcher's Children: Politics, Childhood and Society in the 1980s and 1990s*, London: Falmer.

'The simple truth is': leader from *Daily Star* 25 November 1993.

daily banality: Hannah Arendt's influential characterisation of evil as banal was expounded in (1964/1994) *Eichmann in Jerusalem: a Report on the Banality of Evil*, Harmondsworth: Penguin.

fantasy and fairy stories: Marina Warner (1998) *No Go the Bogeyman: Scaring, Lulling and Making Mock*, London: Chatto and Windus.

***Lord of the Flies*:** (UK, 1963) Dir. Peter Brook. Based on William Golding's 1959 novel (New York: Capricorn). Phil Scraton comments, 'What an incredible irony this represents given the apparently insatiable appetite that much of the adult, patriarchal world has for violence, brutality, war and destruction'. Phil Scraton (ed.) (1997) *'Childhood' in 'Crisis'?* London: UCL Press, p.164.

p.120 **the horror genre:** Julian Petley (1999) 'The Monstrous Child', in Michelle Aaron (ed.) *The Body of Perilous Pleasures*, Edinburgh: Edinburgh University Press.

***The Exorcist*:** (US, 1973) Dir. William Friedkin.

Damien series: *The Omen* (US, 1976) Dir. Richard Donner; *Damien: Omen II* (US, 1978) Dir. Don Taylor. 'The antichrist who got rid of the whole cast of *The Omen*, now, as a teenager, starts on his foster parents. Once was enough,' was the disrespectful comment in *Halliwell's Film Guide*, 7th edition 1989, London: Paladin.

renewed outcry: 'The faceless killers freed into a world intent on seeking revenge...No matter where they go, someone will be waiting, says James's mum', *Daily Express*, 23 June 2001; 'These high-handed, out-of-touch judges are wrong, wrong, wrong', *Sunday People*, 14 January 2001.

close to the excesses of horror: which itself took over the casual, low-key visual style with *The Blair Witch Project*, purporting to be an amateur movie made with video cameras.

'The street is a playground': *Guardian*, 9 December 2000. Photograph: Christopher Thormond.

p. 121 **suburban youth**: 'Bromley: Teenage yobs hold a reign of terror over suburban streets; Residents are too scared of youths to leave their homes'; 'Help us name and shame them' included a series of frames from a CCTV camera on a no 261 Metrobus, as it was vandalised by a pair of young boys. *News Shopper*, 30 January and 27 February 2002. Thanks to Victoria Ruffle for showing me these references.

John Major: February 1993, quoted in Barry Goldson (1997) 'Children in trouble: state responses to juvenile crime', in Scraton (ed.) (1997) above, p.130.

'vicious generation': *Sun*, 'Aggro Britain', 26 August 1980.

blank stare at the camera: see Chapter 4.

'These young savages': Marje Proops, 'The savage generation', *Daily Mirror*, 19 September 1977.

Geoffrey Pearson: (1983) *Hooligan: a History of Respectable Fears*, London: Macmillan. 'the gamins of our large towns' is quoted from a 1910 government report on p.58; 'the manners of children are deteriorating' and 'It is melancholy to find...' are quoted from an 1898 Howard Association report, *Juvenile Offenders*, on pp.54–55; for the origins of 'hooligan', see p.74.

p. 122 **'He is not yet 4ft tall'**: *Sunday Times*, 22 September 1991.

Roy Hattersley: *Guardian*, 9 December 2000.

The no hope kids: *Mail on Sunday*, 'Night and Day', 19 November 1995. Photographs: Jez Coulson.

Andrew Golden, aged six: *Independent*, 27 March 1998.

the children of Northern Ireland: Morris Fraser (1973) *Children in Conflict*, Harmondsworth: Penguin. Cover photograph: Clive Limpkin. On p.22 Fraser quotes newspaper comments from these early years of the Northern Irish conflict: 'The parents who see them going berserk must surely discern that this is the Irish tragedy. It is profoundly tragic that the children of Ulster can no longer be called innocents.' *Daily Mirror*, 9 August 1972.

towering over the Bogside: photographed by Kelvin Boyes, *Observer*, 27 January 2002, on the thirtieth anniversary of Bloody Sunday, 30 January 1972. In that context, the boy is presented as a defender of his community, against the incursions of the police and the British troops, who are seen in the background of the mural.

'The brawling children of Ulster': *Newsletter*, 19 April 1971. Quoted by Fraser (1973) above, p.22.

'Balaclava Boy': *Guardian*, 15 May 2000; other examples include 'Asian teenage gangs', *Evening Standard*, 13 November 1996.

p. 123 **Tierney Gearon**: Jason Bennetto, 'Saatchi photographs are not obscene, says CPS' and 'Nudists join the show as Saatchi's carnival reopens', *Independent*, 16 March 2001.

'We have never seen anything like them': Linda Grant, *Guardian* 'Weekend', 6 January 1996. Highgate Wood schoolchildren photographs: Mike Smith.

a **1996 survey**: young people's social attitudes survey, sponsored by Barnardo's reported in *Guardian*, 19 March 1996. Eighty-two per cent of those surveyed said they had been the victims of crime.

p. 124 **John Carvel**: *Guardian*, 'Defiant face of class yob', 8 November 1996 quotes the Press Complaints Commission Code of Practice: 'Journalists should not normally interview or photograph children under the age of 16 on subjects involving the personal welfare of the child in the absence, or without the consent of a parent or other adult who is responsible for the children ... Children should not be approached or photographed while at school without the permission of the school authorities.' If the boy had appeared before a juvenile court, 'his anonymity would have been protected by law'.

'The lawless teenagers': *Mirror*, 20 March 2002.

the power of curfew: an intriguing insight into the pragmatics behind such decisions came from *Observer* columnist Nick Cohen, who suggested that Jack Straw had declared himself in favour of curfews in an off-the-cuff response during an interview with Cohen about crime prevention policies. Introducing them was then a face-saving strategy. 'Guilty as charged', *Observer*, 6 January 2002. For children's own views on curfews and public space, see Virginia Morrow (2002) above.

'from eight o'clock every night': *Guardian*, 24 October 1997. Photograph: Murdo Mcleod.

Peter Hitchens: quoted by Johann Hari, 'Yah boo to a *Daily Mail* myth', *New Statesman*, 23 September 2002.

'Give in, cop out': *Independent*, 24 September 1997.

p. 125 **The question of physical punishment**: Christina M. Lyon (2000) *Loving Smack or Lawful Assault? A Contradiction in Human Rights and Law*, London: Institute for Public Policy Research. See Chapter 6.

The Parents' Guide: May/June 2001.

psycho-social problems: Michael Rutter and David Smith (1995) *Psychosocial Disorders in Young People*, London: John Wiley and Sons; Peter Shrag and Diane Divoky (1981) *The Myth of the Hyperactive Child and Other Means of Control*, Harmondsworth: Penguin, on what they describe as the 'invention' of child behaviour disorders in the 1970s.

Henry and Ruth Kempe: (1978) *Child Abuse*, London: Fontana, p.50.

The Exorcist, The Omen: see above.

Carrie: (US, 1976) Dir. Brian de Palma.

Marina Warner: (1998) above; (1994) *Managing Monsters*, London: Vintage.

p. 126 **'[The delinquent] is a little stunted man already'**: quoted by Harry Hendrick (1990) 'Constructions and reconstructions of British Childhood; an interpretive survey 1800 to the present', in A. James, and A. Prout (eds) *Constructing and Reconstructing Childhood: Contemporary Issues in the Sociological Study of Childhood*, London: Falmer, p.43.

they had a precocious independence: Anna Davin (1996) *Growing Up Poor: Home, School and Street in London 1870–1914*, London: Rivers Oram Press; Hugh Cunningham (1991) *Children of the Poor*, Oxford: Blackwell.

p. 127 **promise of an escape**: Stanley Cohen and Laurie Taylor (1978) *Escape Attempts: the Theory and Practice of Resistance to Everyday Life*, Harmondsworth: Pelican, a work which they describe as 'profoundly self-indulgent', and which came out of the authors' studies of crime, deviance and youth cultures.

'Kids, just look at them': *Daily Mirror*, 25 April 1983.

This was an exercise in decoding: Dick Hebdige was the first to propose a semiotics of youth styles in *Subculture: the Meaning of Style*, London: Methuen,

1979. Since then, analysing sub-cultures has become a staple of the popular press and academic literature.

'goths': for example *Daily Star*, 'Weirdies!', 29 May 1980. Photograph: Simon Pythian.

p. 128 'Swampy': eco-campaigner Daniel 'Swampy' Hooper became famous in 1997 for his part in campaigns against the construction of a major by-pass in Devon and the extension to Manchester Airport by spending days in a tunnel under the sites. 'Anti-election special: Swampy for Prime Minister!', *Time Out*, 30 April–7 May 1997.

Roland Barthes described as 'babel': Roland Barthes (1976) *The Pleasure of the Text*, London: Jonathan Cape, pp.3–4.

Dick Hebdige's words: (1988) *Hiding in the Light*, London: Routledge.

swastikas: Hebdige quotes a punk asked why she wears a swastika. 'Punks just like to be hated,' she replied. Hebdige (1979) above, pp.116–17.

'Belsen was a gas': song by the Sex Pistols; see Hebdige (1979) above, p.110.

p. 129 'Proud of a punk': *News of the World*, 21 November 1982.

the insecurity of the teddy boys: T.R. Fyvel (1963) *The Insecure Offenders*, Harmondsworth: Pelican, p.36.

'Affluent lifestyle leading children into temptation': Louise Jury, *Independent*, 23 September 1996.

'So old yet so young': *Express on Sunday*, 24 August 1997.

p. 130 many left-wing sociologists: Stuart Hall and Tony Jefferson (eds) (1976) *Resistance Through Rituals: Youth Cultures in Post-war Britain*, London: Hutchinson; Geoff Mungham and Geoff Pearson (eds) (1976) *Working Class Youth Culture*, London: Routledge & Kegan Paul. For a historical account from the point of view of working-class young people, see Stephen Humphries (1981) *Hooligans or Rebels? An Oral History of Working Class Childhood and Youth 1889–1939*, Oxford: Blackwell.

what was now described as an 'underclass': see Zygmunt Bauman (1998) *Work, Consumerism and the New Poor*, Buckingham: Open University Press.

Phil Cohen: 'Aspects of the Youth Question', privately published pamphlets, 1970s.

punk as a post-modern style: Dick Hebdige (1988) and (1979) above.

p. 131 'the teenage rebel is dead': India Knight, *Campaign*, 13 May 1988.

'Your son is 15': Rufus Olins, 'Enter the superbrats, children of the 90s', *Observer*, 7 October 1990 discusses *Spoilt Brats*, the report by Gold Greenlees Trott.

Teen Dreem: Kirsty Robinson, 'Reach for the stars', *Guardian* 'Guide', 9–15 June 2001.

'a long stay with the Marsh Arabs': Ian Jack, *Sunday Times* 'Magazine', November 1981.

p. 132 'hottentots': Cunningham (1991) above.

they have cannily reconstructed themselves: many examples include the organisation of Maasai villages, with dancing displays put on for tourists, in Kenya; the development of Aboriginal paintings, music and artefacts across Australia.

'deplorable' popular music: quoted by Pearson (1983) above, p.24.

'The "tribes" of youngsters': *Daily Star*, 26 May 1980; see also 'Two tribes go to war', *Guardian*, 30 April 2001, on young May Day protesters.

'exotic' peoples continue to be attributed: Richard Appignesi (1979) 'Some thoughts on Freud's discovery of childhood', in Martin Hoyles (ed.) *Changing Childhood*, London: Writers and Readers. Also see Chapter 6.

p. 134 'I want to self-destruct myself': Sid Vicious interviews, *Daily Mirror*, 11 June 1977 and 19 December 1977.

'**Charlie reckons**': *Daily Mirror*, 8 April 1980.

Daily Mirror's '**Shock report**': 'The junk generation', *Daily Mirror*, 4 December 1985.

Angela McRobbie: (1995) 'Shut up and dance: youth culture and changing modes of femininity', in *Postmodernism and Popular Culture*, p.160.

p.135   **Leah Betts:** *Independent*, 16 November 1995; *Observer*, 3 March 2002.

'**Are they really as horrible**': *News of the World*, 21 November 1982.

'**Everyone was having a pleasant morning**': John Downing and Tom Smith, 'Day trip to terror', *Daily Express*, 8 April 1980.

p.136   '**mods and rockers**': see the classic study by Stanley Cohen (1973) *Folk Devils and Moral Panics*, St Albans: Paladin. The imagery of the set-piece battles on Brighton beach was recreated in *Quadrophenia* (UK, 1979), Dir. Franc Roddam, and the paraphernalia of both mods and rockers has been regularly recuperated, both as retro chic and as a form of homage.

the image of the crowd: Elias Canetti (1973) *Crowds and Power*, Harmondsworth: Penguin.

'**arrogant hooligans**': used to describe the student demonstration at Essex University: *Evening Standard*, 8 April 1974.

'**stunted demons**': used to describe street riots in Liverpool 8: Brian James, *Daily Mail*, 8 July 1981.

Pearson records: see Pearson (1983) above.

'**This dog is an extension**': *Daily Express*, 8 April 1980.

'**St Paul's, revolt of the lost tribe**': *Observer*, 6 April 1980.

'**Tribal Warfare**': *Mirror*, 8 April 1980.

'**This is not England**': *Daily Express*, 7 October 1985. Pearson (1983) above demonstrates a long history of describing such riots as 'un-English'.

'**Many experts predict**': Jean Richie, *Sun*, 11 November 1980.

p.137   **effectively wrapping the newspaper:** 'The shape of things to come', *Daily Mirror*, 13 April 1981.

'**If you know 'em, SHOP 'EM**': Jeff Edwards, *People*, 13 May 1990.

escape attempts: a reference to Cohen and Taylor (1978) above.

screaming for Mummy: 'Rough justice', *Daily Mail*, 13 August 1976.

6

Crybabies and
damaged children

PART 1: FASCINATING MISERY

Pathos, fear and the unhappy child

Without an image of an unhappy child the concept of childhood would be
incomplete. Real children suffer in many different ways and for many different
reasons, but pictures of sorrowing children reinforce the defining characteristics
of childhood – dependence and powerlessness. Pathetic pictures of children
create a desired image in which childhood is no longer a threat and adults are
firmly back in control.

Suffering children appear as archetypal victims, since childhood itself is
defined by weakness and incapacity. Children living in poverty, children who
are the victims of wars or natural disasters, children suffering from neglect or
disadvantage: all of these figure in the imagery as the most vulnerable, the most
pathetic, the most deserving of our sympathy and aid. This resonant image shows
children who appear to be on the receiving end of an oppression in which they
can only acquiesce. As they reveal their vulnerability, viewers long to protect them.
The boundaries between childhood and adulthood are reinforced as the image
gives rise to pleasurable emotions of tenderness and compassion, which satis-
factorily confirm adult power.

Pathos is an essential part of the romantic tradition that has been so
vigorously rejected by the cynicism of contemporary imagery. However, in an era
when many children did not reach adulthood, pathos – even when exaggerated
and exploitative – made a different sort of sense. Pathetic, dying children were

part of nineteenth-century reality as well as popular culture. Joshua Reynolds's portrait of Penelope Boothby, who died at the age of six, came to represent all children's tenuous hold on life. Her distraught father commissioned a memorial sculpture which moved viewers to tears and was described as 'drenched in sentimentality'. Children who died young preserved their childhood for ever. Fictional stories, such as those of Paul Dombey, Little Nell and William Carlyle of *East Lynne*, had a powerful appeal. Indeed, *East Lynne* became the best selling book of its century. Its author, Mrs Henry Wood, wrote that children should look 'with pleasure rather than fear on that unknown journey'. A soulful expression, with eyes uplifted to heaven, became an image that was a stock-in-trade of postcards and popular imagery of the second half of the nineteenth century. At issue here is the emotion which such pictures aim to arouse in the viewer, particularly when detached from the reality of the loss of a child. The pathos of childhood belonged to an age that valued sentiment as an aesthetic experience; at the same time, sentiment was a valuable way of dealing with the drab reality of child mortality.

The image of a short but holy childhood could represent a wealthy Penelope Boothby or a child from any class. However, poor children were the object of humanitarian reform accompanied by a frequently sexualised aesthetic thrill. 'Beggar maids' and street children were popular photographic subjects, with ragged clothes and appealing expressions. Oscar Rejlander's celebrated photograph of 'Poor Jo' was reconstructed in his studio, since those were the days before technology permitted candid photography, and resembles a tableau from a melodrama as much as a piece of reportage. The posture of the young boy, with body crouched and face hidden, has established itself as an archetype of neglected childhood. This sensibility should be seen against the teeming presence of poverty (there seemed to be no shortage of ragged children ready to act as photographers' models) but from it a resonant image has evolved in which a child who is deeply unhappy evokes an unfocused emotionality which is in danger of linking social concern with something close to prurience. Pity can be bound together with satisfaction at the confirmation of childish vulnerability.

Since its high point in the nineteenth century, the pathetic imagery of childhood has undergone various mutations, its significance shifting with the changing contexts. As health and welfare improved and the child mortality rate reduced, pathos began to take new forms. In one of its aspects the pathetic image of a weeping child has lingered as an integral part of childhood; in another the image has moved overseas and become more extreme – we find it in those pictures of degradation and disaster which have come to characterise the undeveloped world. Within the safe confines of the West, a familiar genre of press photography features pathetic children who have survived a serious accident or suffer from an incurable illness. But these brave little creatures are shown as battling against the odds rather than acquiescing in the manner of the other-worldly waifs of the nineteenth century. As, for example, in the specialist magazine *Disability Now*, cheerfulness in the face of adversity has taken the place of pathos. As more media spaces become available for the voices of those who might otherwise be seen as the objects of pity, pathos is vigorously rejected as condescending or demeaning.

Nevertheless, reducing children to something near pathos by inducing fear – even if playfully – remains part of the adult–child relationship. Marina Warner discusses a long tradition of gruesome stories, using illustrations which show fathers dressing up to frighten their children (usually daughters), and a sixteenth-century woodcut of 'the child guzzler', a popular carnival figure in the shape of a terrifying monster who devours young babies. Cruella de Vil, the scourge of Dalmatian puppies, is a recent incarnation of female terror. The picture of young Macaulay Culkin on the poster for *Home Alone* – a frightened, screaming child, desperate to be consoled – became a resonant image, used, for example, in an article on childhood depression (the image itself has much in common with the ironically popularised print of the expressionist work *The Scream*). 'Fear,' writes Marina Warner, 'is the defining flavour of the modern sensibility'.

Poverty answering back?

In the 1990s, home-grown poverty became the focus for a powerful set of images, as a new realism was mobilised to represent a growing concern over the 'new poor'. Channel 4 chose to introduce its series *Poverty Answering Back* with a cheeky wave from a small girl, but there was an echo of the key image of the pathetic child in the logo selected by the *Independent* for its series 'Breadline Britain'. This was an outline drawing of the head and shoulders of a girl around eight years old, holding out a plate with a very serious expression. In the manner of a resonant image, the logo was taken from a photograph in a hostel for homeless families. The isolation of the child from the figures who surround her in the original picture, together with her gesture of appeal, repeated daily at the head of a series of articles, transformed documentary realism into twentieth-century pathos.

In the 2000s the lives of the poor are well known, well publicised, carefully scrutinised and frequently pictured – sometimes with sympathy, sometimes with critical interest. A number of surveys and reports, many of them sponsored by organisations whose names proclaim their origins in nineteenth-century philanthropy – Joseph Rowntree Trust, Barnardo's – have confirmed a widening gap between the poor and the rest, and have documented the multiple disadvantages which poverty brings to children – more health problems, less nutritious food, greater chance of accidents in the home or in the street, worse educational opportunities and achievements, fewer recreational facilities, greater chance of unemployment. An Institute for Public Policy Research report in March 2000 argued that the UK was 'emerging as a serious contender for the worst place in Europe to be a child'. Such findings are reported in detail by the specialist press and the concerned press – particularly the *Independent* and the *Guardian*, whose expected readership includes members of the caring professions, social workers, teachers, health workers and educated parents. They tend to be accompanied by photographs in the new documentary mode.

New documentary makes a determined effort to avoid sentimentalism in its representation of poverty. It also rejects the voyeurism of which the documentary project has been accused – in which the privileged look at the underprivileged, the rich look at the poor, and the haves look at the have-nots. Usually black-and-white, often moody and rain-soaked, this contemporary genre focuses on children almost as incidental figures in a landscape. Unlike the pathetic image, these pictures do not place the burden of expressing disadvantage on the figure of a child. Instead, they accuse a gloomy environment of boarded-up shops, decaying tenement blocks, rows of unkempt houses and badly swept streets, while groups of young children preserve their childish sprightliness despite the odds. They may be on rollerskates, or striding along the pavement, or on a bicycle. In these loosely composed pictures, the children frequently acknowledge or play up for the lens. This contemporary, low-key image focuses on girls and young children, rather than the bad boys of the previous chapter.

A rather different twenty-first-century trend has also eschewed pathos, but this time in favour of extreme and shocking imagery. In 2000, Barnardo's launched an advertising campaign designed to draw attention to the effects of an impoverished and ill-cared-for childhood: a baby becomes a heroin addict, holding a string in its teeth in preparation for injection; a small girl beds down in the street; another is shown as a prostitute, soliciting by a car door; a small boy is about to jump from a tower block. In each case the caption projects a future for a damaged child. The use of digital techniques to create convincing pictures has opened up new possibilities of high intensity, closely worked images whose density of detail and the ability to create maximum shock effect pulls against the low-key aims of new realism. When the Barnardo's advertisements were first published, the Committee for Advertising Practice advised the media not to carry them. The creative director at the advertising agency responded, 'When I

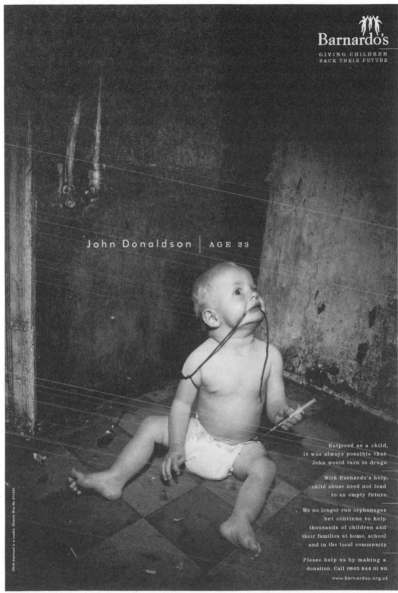

Advertisement, 2000, courtesy of Barnardo's.

used to work on the NSPCC account I'd actually see the police surgeons' log books, and let me assure you that the truth is so much worse than anything you or I could imagine'.

PART 2: VICTIMISATION AND
THE UNDEVELOPED WORLD

Save the children?

As the parameters of childhood are marked out and held firm – children are dependent, vulnerable, in need of instruction and protection – many other groups have been rhetorically bestowed with childish characteristics: women, people from ethnic minorities, and the whole of the previously colonised world have come to stand in a childish relation to the exercise of power. The globalised economy has brought a different international configuration, yet the non-white nations continue to be presented as if they lack potency in their very essence. It is amongst the children of the impoverished countries that we find the insistent imagery of childhood suffering. It stands in stark contrast to the well-fed, well-equipped mini-consumers of the domestic image.

The one area in which the British image industry has regularly and predictably produced pictures of black and other non-white children is in press reports of wars, famines and natural disasters and in the appeals for aid which accompany them. Over the last quarter of the twentieth century the wide eyes of the needy dark-skinned child have looked reproachfully out from news pages and from those advertisements that solicit rather than seduce. Particularly during the 1970s and 1980s, an image of a ragged child who is not ashamed to plead so dominated the available imagery of Africa, Latin America and the Indian sub-continent that the whole of that vast area beyond Western culture has been offered up as a place of distress and childish subservience ('All over the world children are dying for want of food'…'In the developing world, innocent children are dying…'). The expectation embedded in the image is that the viewer is from the industrial world, paternal, white and prosperous. Suffering in the undeveloped world continues to secure a sense of comfort amongst viewers in the 'developed' nations, by assuring them that they have the power to help – in the same 'natural' way that adults help children. That power is confirmed by the gaze of an appealing child. But the gaze must be carefully selected so that it in no way undermines the complacent certainty of a superior position. The children pictured in aid advertisements are not asylum-seekers challenging our borders; they are not armed guerrillas causing international disruption; they are without the stench of disease which might make their actual physical presence repellent; they are, apparently, without protectors from their own invisible culture. They are abandoned or orphaned. Their humble and submissive appeal protects the compassion of the viewer from the prosperous world and enables us to give.

The increased accessibility of visual and verbal information in the press and on television has made war, famine, drought and disasters of cataclysmic proportions familiar parts of everyday consciousness. The last quarter of a century has seen recurring famines across Northern Africa, the spiralling of the AIDS pandemic across the African continent, and increasingly serious floods and cyclones in the Indian subcontinent. At the same time, vicious wars have devastated the Middle East, East Timor, Colombia, Iraq, Chechnya, the Balkans, Afghanistan, Rwanda, Sudan and elsewhere in Africa and across the globe. In the image of the un-developed world, the pictures which document natural disasters have formed a continuum with those which show the results of human atrocity, and news reporting has come to share its imagery with ever-more-urgent appeals for aid. To walk into the annual exhibition of the World Press Photography Awards, held in the Royal Festival Hall in London, where the most striking news photographs of the year are enlarged to giant proportions, is to be overwhelmed by the fire, rubble and terrified faces of almost unthinkable human distress. The filtering and selection processes which led to decisions about which picture will make the front page and which photographer will be named photographer of the year all too frequently mean that photographers seek out the most vulnerable. Desperate children with wide eyes gazing helplessly at the viewer have been at the centre of a recurring image which has expressed the very depths of human degradation and suffering – but may well lead to a wrenching of emotion at the expense of understanding.

The question that runs through the imagery of distress, and which resonates between aid advertisements and the news pages, is who should take responsibility for these children? The pictures can be read as a series of reflections on that problem. When the presentation is part of an appeal for funds, viewers are invited to recognise themselves as both adult and Western, as individuals with the ability to 'change a child's life' for the better (in the words of an Action Aid advertisement) without changing their own for the worse. The only possible relationship posed for the pictured child in this resonant image is a relationship with the putative viewer. In a characteristic appeal, the black child is seeking a white benefactor, a surrogate parent who will be more effective than his own absent black parent. The appeal is to the competence of Western civilisation, seen not as a controlling father, imposing the harsh disciplines of international finance, but as a nurturing mother, the Mother Countries. The eyes of the child are at the centre of this image, as he looks to the prosperous world for help and succour: 'For God's sake help them – 80,000 children will die in Zaire in the next three weeks'; 'Sponsor a child and see the difference'; 'Be my postal parent! Help me!' The gaze balances hope and reproach as it constructs an impossible relationship.

In the resonance of the image, the child's adult relatives tend to be devalued, and men are the least visible. It is they who signify culture, whose presence locates a picture in its geographical context, who may themselves be fighters or oppressors. As the strongest group they are least likely to conform to the expected image of the victim and the most likely to be involved in attempts at reconstruction or resistance, confusing the clarity of the story, complicating a reaction of pity alone. One of the most powerful recurring images of disaster shows a mother and baby together, in which the weakness of the mother serves to intensify the plight of the child. In a 1970s advertisement, Oxfam captioned a desperate mother and child, 'Please sir, I beseech you, give me something for my baby'. The mother's breasts were drained dry so that she could not fulfil the only role that justified her presence. (A picture of the charity's sponsor, Winston S. Churchill, was inset as if to represent the generous white world.) The image recurs in many contexts. Pictures from war zones show innumerable sick and helpless mothers, or children caring for other children – this formed the logo of the *Independent*'s 'Children of War' appeal. But in the key image, a child appealing for help is separated from family and social context. If the children are not carrying any cultural baggage, then the children may be saved. The implications of the relationship between image and expected viewer go beyond a well-intentioned donation.

Child rescue plays an important part in the iconography of childhood. Gratifying pictures show children being brought from the rubble of earthquakes, being rescued from floods, fires and the aftermath of war, or simply being found when lost. The theme of child rescue runs through the history of childhood, particularly in accounts of nineteenth-century philanthropy, when Thomas Barnardo first raised money for his children's homes by selling 'before' and 'after' pictures of children brought in from the streets. But the theme of rescue has taken a particularly spectacular form in the development of narratives which describe relations between the industrial and undeveloped worlds. In such imagery, the role of the rescuer is routinely played by supportive white representatives of a technologised civilisation – doctors, nurses, aid workers. Succouring white hands support or feed the emaciated child.

Western civilisation may be seen to be effective through spectacular acts of charity – which also sell newspapers. '*Mirror* to the rescue,' headlined a picture story in October 1984, 'The *Daily Mirror* acted last night to boost the relief effort to Ethiopia's starving millions'; In May 1991, 'The *Mail* brings comfort to the cyclone children' (in Bangladesh). Since their community has apparently failed them and help appears only to come from outside, it seems logical to assume than these children may be most effectively saved by being completely removed from their communities. They may be adopted by Western families or given a Western education. In extreme cases, they may be airlifted out, like Ali Ismaeel Abbas, who lost his arms in the American bombing of Baghdad. The popular press has on several occasions cast itself in this god-like role. And the papers implicate their readers: 'How you rescued the orphans of Bogota,' asserted the cover of the *Sunday Express* magazine, showing a 'rescued' boy cuddling a dog – symbol of the 'civilisation' he has reached – and in 2003 several papers launched an 'Ali fund'. The prototype had been the *Daily Mail*'s 1975 airlift of 'orphans' (they were not all orphans) from Vietnam as Saigon fell to the North Vietnamese. It was organised in four days in order to scoop the official American airlift. The *Mail*'s photograph of editor David English carrying a sick baby from 'his' plane was on page 3, while the photograph of US President Ford carrying a rescued baby from the American plane was relegated to page 4.

A frequent visual device in the iconography of rescue is the intervention of the charismatic individual from the West – from showbusiness, royalty or politics.

Pop star Bob Geldof initiated the massive Live Aid concert, globally transmitted in July 1985. A series of what Zygmunt Bauman has described as 'carnivals of charity' have followed on television and across the media – Band Aid, Sport Aid, Comic Relief interleave images of suffering and rescue with entertainment and celebrity. Figures as diverse as Mother Teresa and Geri Halliwell have provided photo-opportunities in refugee camps and relief centres. Princess Diana's campaign drew fresh attention to landmines, which continue to mutilate children in many of the poorer parts of the world years after the wars which devastated them had finished. Pictures of children who have lost limbs are deeply shocking, and it is the more disturbing that it takes a special attraction, such as the presence of a Western media icon, to help them break through the news barrier and on to the front pages.

Shock tactics and the disgusting image

As familiarity has blunted their effectiveness, pictures of suffering have become less restrained. 'It is an unfortunate truism of famines, that by the time the pictures are horrific enough to move people, it's almost too late,' wrote journalist and film-maker Paul Harrison. But the use of distressing imagery for publicity and money-raising has been the cause of much soul-searching and debate within the aid agencies and amongst the press and other critics. During the genocide and civil war in Rwanda, journalist Richard Dowden wrote of 'the mad scramble for publicity as aid agencies begged journalists to visit their projects, gave them free plane tickets, put up attractive young females to represent them on television, and plastered huge areas of refugee camps with their logos in the hope of a flickering split-second of publicity'. Although, he added, 'Aid workers actually involved in the horrors of the camps were appalled'. Dilemmas over fundraising methods are not new. As far back as 1877, Thomas Barnardo was taken to court by the Charity Organisation because the photographic cards he sold to publicise his homes for destitute children were said to be faked. He did not photograph the children when he found them on the streets, but dressed them in rags especially for the camera after they had been rehabilitated, so that the cards could be sold as a 'before and after' pair. The International Save the Children Fund was itself launched in the midst of a controversy over an image. Just after the First World War, its founder, Eglantyne Jebb, was prosecuted for distributing a photograph of a starving Austrian baby. Under the draconian censorship laws introduced during that war, raising money for children of the enemy was ruled impermissible.

Today, aid agencies have expanded from their origins as small, voluntary groups to become major international, highly professional organisations, whose influence in the field of overseas aid and children's rights has rivalled that of states. They have been closest to events in disaster-prone areas, and have led the news media. In 1973 it was Oxfam which brought back the first pictures of the Ethiopian famine, and in 1991 a group of agencies toured journalists in parts of Africa that would otherwise have dropped out of media consciousness. But their main function of providing aid and assistance means that they must engage in a constant balancing act between passing on information which bears the full complexity of a situation on the ground and the need to penetrate the everyday parade of Western consumer images with presentations that will encourage the public to give.

By the early 1980s, pleading had given way to extreme tactics. Both Oxfam and Save the Children were using pictures of the emaciated bodies of very young children, surely only hours from death, against a stark white background. These advertisements appeared in shocking juxtaposition with the minutiae of everyday urban living – in the pages of newspapers and on hoardings above city streets. Unlike the children in the wide-eyed appealing image, such children were far too sick to fix prospective donors with their reproachful gaze. The focus was on the emaciated *body* of the child, rather than the eyes, which give at least some common humanity. Here the relationship between the dying black child and the viewing white adult is one of guilt by comparison. 'While you're eating between meals, he's dying between meals', 'You're not the only one with weight problems'. The viewer is forced to use the *text* as the only context. In the absence of more visual information, the power of interpretation is left to the controlling white eye outside the frame. The image was operating in a dangerous area between sympathy, guilt and disgust. In abandoning the attractiveness of childhood, such pictured children may well sacrifice the indulgence childhood commands. Without the flattery offered by the appealing image, they may arouse adult sadism without deflecting it, and confirm contempt for those parts of the world that seem unable to help their own.

The perceived need to deliver an imagery which would be adequate to the scale of extreme situations arose at the same time as a taste developed for shocking imagery of many kinds. In disaster movies and war films, mutilation and suffering was presented with an increasingly convincing realism. The technologies of animatronics and digital imaging were pushing the fantasy blood and gore of horror movies to greater lengths, while bloodthirsty computer games were invading teenage bedrooms. The pleasures of entertainment horror are routinely justified by their existence as fantasy, and by their audience's ability to recognise artifice when they see it. A problem arises when a similar psychic defence is summoned up against the power of extreme images which draw attention to real suffering. 'I want *you* to see this,' photojournalist Chris Steele-Perkins harangued his television audience while photographing a mutilated corpse in southern Sudan, recognising how little of his total experience would be reflected in the pictures.

By the late 1980s the sort of image which showed suffering children with no background and no context was coming under attack from several different constituencies, including people from the undeveloped countries, aid workers and journalists who were close to the realities of the situation, and photographers who were not satisfied with the way their work was being used. Black and Asian British groups argued that an imagery that stressed helplessness and dependence fuelled racism, and affected the way not only people from the undeveloped world but all non-white people were perceived. At a conference in 1998, disaster imagery was described as 'aid pornography' and Overseas Development Minister Clare Short argued that appeals for aid could deflect attention from political realities – particularly in countries which were overcome by civil war, such as Sudan.

As the groundswell of critique against the inequalities of global trade, the crippling indebtedness of the poorer countries and the policies of the international monetary institutions gathered pace, in some campaigning publications the familiar image of the starving child was turned to a new use in a bid to produce a political explanation for poverty. Instead of a context of supportive Western aid, these presentations placed the child amongst the symbols of Western exploitation – a baby-milk bottle, canned food or a roll of film, this last critiquing the role of photography in creating an over-simplified view. In 1987, War on Want, the most politicised of the agencies, commented on the dreadful repetition of images of starving children in an advertisement which declared 'the EC is running out of places to put its surplus grain' above an apparently infinite number of children's faces with open mouths. Its campaign was very successful, but the charitable status of the agency meant that it risked censure by the Charity Commissioners if its message was seen as overtly political.

In response to criticisms, most of the agencies adopted a strategy of 'positive images' and 'accuracy' of representation. In 1991, Save the Children's guidelines for photographers were based on the principle that 'the dignity of the people with whom Save the Children works should be preserved... portraying poverty and dependence as the norm is not accurate... The people with whom Save the Children works risk "exploitation by camera" if their identity or opinions are excluded in the promotion of development issues.' The cultural context was to be restored to the children for whom aid was requested. Smiling faces and expressions of resilience were to take the place of appealing eyes or starving bodies.

Nevertheless, the dilemma remained. When the public is said to be suffering from 'compassion fatigue', raising funds and raising awareness can seem like contradictory aims. Too much information can confuse the power of the image, and an understanding of political complexities deflects emotional response. Save the Children's advertising agency, Ogilvy and Mather, told the *Guardian*, 'Images of starving children have lost their appeal' at the same time as J. Walter Thompson, for Oxfam, insisted that 'a child will bring in more than an adult, a girl child who cries will bring in more than a boy who does not'. Save the Children called it a 'healthy tension'.

However, as many critics of documentary photography have pointed out, a realist style can only record what is in front of the lens. It cannot make the sort of analysis that War on Want's campaign had attempted. It can observe poverty and can suggest how those involved are coping, but it cannot even speculate about the invisible causes of the situation it observes. By the end of the 1990s, new analyses of globalisation and free trade made more emphatic links between the prosperity of the West and the increasing poverty and disorder of much of the rest of the world. Teresa Hayter wrote of the 'grotesque hypocrisy' of the rich countries' claim to 'help the Third World escape the poverty which they and their predecessors partly created and continue to create'. A new set of images began to seek out a different context, a way of showing children not as the victims of poverty-stricken communities but as the victims of global economics. In a different kind of visibility, images of children from the poorer parts of the world have shown sickness, child labour and brutalisation not as residues from a 'primitive' past but as new phenomena. Reporting had taken on a renewed sense of anger. The *Guardian*'s series on the debt burden was headed 'The new slavery'.

The clear distinction between the industrialised and the undeveloped parts of the world is visibly crumbling as photographers and journalists document the accelerated movement of human beings across the globe. 'All the migrants I photographed once lived in a stable way,' wrote Sebastiao Salgado. As an economist turned photographer, he is clear that he is recording a global change for the worse. Migrants become immigrants, asylum-seekers and unwelcome polluters of the streets. The image of a mother and child has gained a new meaning in the outcry from the British press against 'bogus' asylum-seekers. Women are said to 'use' their own children, or other children, to assist in begging. One photograph of a woman with a child, stretching out her hand to the passers by, was accompanied by a text which deplored a 'cynical exploitation of Britain's asylum laws' by people from 'a gypsy township in Romania'.

Brutalised children

Despite the actual relationship between children in the poverty-stricken parts of the world and the economic policies of the wealthier nations, the use of a child in news reports and in advertisements continues to refer to a value that, like Eglantyne Jebb's Austrian baby, claims to be outside politics. Children are seen expressing emotions that are universal, untouched by those other qualities – social and cultural as well as political – that make humanity so diverse. Not yet fully participant in divisions of language, nationality, culture or even race, the child is presented as uncontaminated by these antagonistic formations. As a symbol of common humanity, a child can be the bearer of suffering with no responsibility for its causes.

This view of a childhood which refers outside its cultural group – and must be protected, sometimes at the expense of its group – is in stark contrast to the practice of the starving nations, where the child is the most expendable. 'If a parent dies the family is doomed. The father eats first and dies last; the children eat last and die first,' wrote Richard Dowden of the aid camps in Ethiopia. The irony of the aid imagery, then, is that however accurate the picture, an appeal on behalf of the children may well operate against the interests of the community of which they are part, rather than on that community's behalf. Although the resonant image of a child humbly requesting help appeals to the richer, more powerful viewer, children's actual response to conditions of deprivation may well refuse the very qualities of childhood which give them their pathos. It is less easy for the imagery to deal with children who have become fighters, workers or aggressive dwellers on the streets.

The image of a child with a gun has been the subject of one of the biggest transformations from myth to reality. Guns are the ultimate symbol of male potency, celebrated in movies from the deadly but modestly sized pistols of the classic Western through to the massive armoury carried by Schwarzenegger or Stallone in 1980s action movies. Interactive video games take a further step, making the viewer a participant who is directly involved in the action. The image of a gun, placed in the centre of the frame, reacts like a real gun held in the hand of the player. Instead of empathising with the screen hero, the game's viewer/participant becomes part of a virtual gun-fight. The reality of children's actual proximity to guns and other weapons has become frighteningly clear in the atrocities committed by schoolchildren in the US and in pictures of child soldiers from many warring parts of the globe – particularly Africa. Yet the image remains fraught with ambivalence. The acquisition of power symbolised by a weapon may be a welcome sign of competence – for example by American parents pictured teaching their children to shoot – or it may seem like heroic resistance. I have a postcard showing a young Eritrean girl, parading with a wooden rifle as part of the 'children's militia'. A child with a gun may be shown as a disciplined young

Campaigning postcard, 2000, courtesy of Save the Children Fund. Photograph: Mike Goldwater/Network.

person playing a purposeful part in an organised force, a child who is not so much rejecting childhood as redefining childhood as part of a proud nationalism or justified resistance against an oppressor.

But such optimistic images are belied by cruel historical reality. As the brutalising effects of the wars that have raged across Africa have been publicised, the tactic of recruiting children to carry out atrocities has become horribly familiar. In countries including Sierra Leone and Uganda, numerous children have been trained to kill. Several British newspapers followed the story of 14-year-olds in Sierra Leone pictured with standard British-made rifles. A campaigning postcard from Save the Children uses a photograph by Mike Goldwater showing Ugandan children corralled into the 'Lord's army'. A column of blank-faced children, in combat fatigues, rifles on shoulders, stare intently ahead. The card is scrawled with the words 'I object' in crude red letters. A picture on the same theme in the *Daily Mirror* won the 2000 Amnesty International awards for photographer Mike Moore. Here, the youngster wears a dirty vest, sewn over with packages of ammunition which look like brightly coloured toys, and a bandage around the head which may be just for effect. A huge Kalashnikov stretches above his head. His expression may be one of surly aggression, or he may be about to burst into tears. The headline was 'Child victims of war'. Life in a violent society is far grimmer than even the most shocking of images can convey.

Street urchins, vagrants and murdered children

The image of the street urchin has an uneasy presence in the imagery of childhood – combining pathos with a sense of resilience and engaging impudence. Nineteenth-century photographers were fascinated by 'beggar maids' and street children; cheeky urchins have continued to play an indispensable part in travel imagery – on postcards as well as advertisements and brochures. In poorer countries, children working on the streets are part of the tourist economy and a tourist sight. A Western approach to the poorer parts of the world is rarely without aspects of a tourist gaze, which samples and then withdraws, indulging enjoyment without engagement. The holiday snapshot is part of this sampling and distancing process.

(And I do not pretend that it is easy to step outside this structure. My holiday snaps include a boy of about nine outside the Sultanahmet Mosque in Istanbul displaying his expertise with one of the spinning tops that he and dozens of others were selling to the tourists. Of course, he earned some extra money by posing for me.)

It needs only a slight shift of perspective to see the child on the streets as an undesirable vagrant. For many years the Western media have carried spasmodic reports on the street children of Latin America. They have created mild international scandal, but, seen from the distance of a continent, are quickly forgotten. But to many 'respectable' inhabitants of Rio and Bogota such children are like garbage, spoiling the attractiveness of the city, pestering tourists and robbing respectable citizens. By 1990 there were reports that street children were being routinely murdered by semi-official death squads. *Amnesty International Journal* published a picture of street children in Bogota, Colombia under a poster put up by local businesses inviting them to their own funeral. In July 1993 around 50 street children sleeping in the porch of Rio's Candelaria Church were attacked by three armed men who shot randomly into the group, killing eight and wounding more. Amnesty International created an outcry, but in Rio such killings were said to be 'socially acceptable'. 'When you talk about Brazilian children you must understand that they are not the same as European children. They really are savages here. Most of the time they are killing each other,' a Brazilian businessman told Zoe Heller of the *Independent on Sunday*. A high-circulation Rio daily, *O Povo*, took to publishing photographs of mutilated corpses as the only way of drawing attention to what was happening. Sometimes these are the only record of the deaths of children who have no parents, no birth certificates, no official existence.

This most shocking of images is by no means confined to children from the undeveloped world. 'The victimisation of children is nowhere forbidden,' wrote Alice Miller. 'What is forbidden is to write about it.' Imagery, sometimes the most extreme imagery, can put together meanings that words hesitate to express. Childhood is about impotence and weakness. Acceptable victimisation is part of the visual repertoire with which the concept of childhood crosses and influences the concepts of race and class. Whether starving child from the undeveloped world or helpless child from the domestic imagery of poverty, there is an easy shift of perspective from attractive gamin to foul-mouthed vermin. The image of the child as victim prepares the way for an open expression of adult hatred and cruelty.

PART 3: CRYBABIES AND DAMAGED CHILDREN

Tears

Tears are remarkable in men (the tears of football hero Paul 'Gazza' Gascoigne made front-page news), expected in women, but part of the very condition of childhood. They are the only bodily fluid that may legitimately flow in public, and the less an individual aspires to power, the less they need be restrained. Normal childhood tears are under adult control. Easily provoked by a shout or a prohibition and usually dried by a cuddle, they seem like an inevitable part of the relationship of training and care within which adults and children are entwined. Children will behave badly and adults will lose their temper. It is only to be expected. But, like the vast majority of the images of childhood, the relationship is largely imagined – and imaged – from the adult perspective. Pictures of childhood distress are judged in the light of adult experience. Uneasy promptings from our childhood selves tend to be repressed. Pictures in which tearfulness is comfortingly confined to children – and, what is more, where the tears are considered to be in the child's own interest – can only be reassuring. They keep both the pictured child and the internal childhood of the adult viewer firmly in place. A familiar form of neo-kitsch, pictures of weeping children may be reproduced purely for adult gratification on postcards or wall pictures, as examples of art photography or as anonymous symbols of misery itself. They may well carry a sexualised attraction.

(My postcard collection includes a pair of pictures of weeping children, reproduced from painted originals, signed with all the panache of an old master. In one, a pigtailed, dark-skinned girl of around six years old pouts as tears well from her exaggeratedly large and luminous brown eyes. In the companion card, a boy of similar age wears a gypsy scarf and broad-brimmed hat. He faces the viewer head on, with moist eyes and tear-stained cheeks. A more sophisticated image is the black-and-white card entitled 'La Tristesse'. A young girl of around five gazes upwards, eyes wide, hair in stylish disorder, while a huge and obviously artificial tear trickles down her cheek. The back of the card carries detailed credits: the model is Laura Baron from the Truly Scrumptious Model Agency; hair and make-up are by Tracy Townsend. The decadence of the romantic tradition is encapsulated in the knowing cynicism of this image – which at the same time evokes all the expected emotional responses to an image of a crying child.

A wall picture simply known as the 'Crying boy' is a popular purchase from cheap arcades and market stalls. My copy is printed on thin plastic pressed into low relief. Once more the boy wears a red gypsy scarf. His clothes are ragged, his

Postcards, France, 1970s.

hair in disarray and his voluminous tears gain prominence from the embossing technique of the picture. In one of its publicity stunts, the *Sun* ran a campaign against this picture – which, it claimed, could bring bad luck to its owners. (One copy had remarkably survived a major house fire.) Readers were invited to get rid of their copy by sending it in to the *Sun*. Thousands of readers responded and the *Sun* office, it was reported, was knee-deep in 'Crying boys' until they were carted off and ritually burned.)

Tears may be evidence of irrational adults, of harshly punitive relations between adults and children, or of a discipline which has run out of control. They may be evidence of neglect, cruelty or adult hatred. The *Daily Mirror's* 'Shock issue' of 1972, headlined 'Thank God we live here?' featured a crying child, at first hardly different from the kitsch of the postcards – except that real tears mean distorted facial features quite alien to the Truly Scrumptious model. The *Daily Mirror* was dealing with the growth in violent crime, and the child stood for all victims. 'Her face crumpled by unhappiness and fear. Her tears symbolise the agony of our present age of growing violence.'

There are all too few occasions when the viewer of a picture is invited to make a less welcome identification and see the image from the perspective of the child who is suffering instead of that of the adult who may either cause or relieve that suffering. Pictures of suffering children rarely allow their subjects to express the autonomy or resistance of Channel 4's cheeky girl in their *Poverty Answering Back* season. The reluctance to take this step becomes clearer when we consider another range of imagery, which pushes children's humiliation yet further. The crumpled face on the *Daily Mirror's* 'Shock issue' is not enough to differentiate between a child whose tears are part of the condition of childhood and a child who has been unjustly harmed. A second resonant image is evoked – one that has been repeated with remarkable frequency for more than a century. Reminiscent of Oscar Rejlander's 'Poor Jo' of 1860, this image shows children's bodies bent over with heads bowed, crushed by the weight of misery bearing down on them. Sometimes drawn, sometimes in a staged photograph, these children cover their faces as if tainted by the shame of their situation. This is an image of a child who is victimised, completely helpless and certainly not capable of answering back. This second image is not intended to be read as the normal consequence of relations between adults and children, but as evidence of cruel and perverted adults.

Yet these children, crouched or slumped, are not only crushed by the events which created their situation but also by the very image which seeks to represent their plight. Once more, there is a certain satisfaction for adults in envisaging such rejection – like a spitting out of unpleasant and unwanted elements. Attitudes that cannot openly be admitted have a shadowy presence in the image. Childhood and the residues of its devastating emotions are amongst those things we would dearly love to expel but which obstinately remain part of our very selves. We are left with the possibility of crushing those unwelcome aspects, of beating them down, just like the child in the picture. There is a danger that the resonant image of the slumped child, itself a temptation to adult violence, may become disgusting to us.

Broken bodies, tempting abuse

From babyhood, children are physically handled by their parents and carers (handling by doctors and other professionals has a different sort of legitimacy). Parents retain the right to caress or chastise, and to exercise a discipline modulated by these two extremes. The adult touch restrains and controls the child in a way that limits the movements of the child's body and evokes the expression of emotion on the child's face – laughter on the one hand, tears on the other. (Smiles and laughter make appropriate family pictures. As emotions shade off to express greater degrees of distress, their representation in personal photographs becomes less acceptable.) There remains no consensus about the point at which gestures of control become excessive and the infliction of physical pain unacceptable. The image of physical discipline has become a source of embarrassment.

In the absence of an easily acceptable image, articles on the topic of corporal punishment frequently resort to a humorous distancing device, using Victorian engravings of furious women with screaming and kicking youngsters over their knees. (James Kincaid has spelt out at length the prurient attraction and underlying eroticism of such an image.) Yet campaigners have pointed out that children who are physically chastised suffer humiliation as well as pain, which may sometimes be extreme. In 1998 the European Court of Human Rights ruled against a stepfather who had repeatedly beaten his stepson with a garden cane. An English jury had found him not guilty under the Victorian defence of 'reasonable chastisement'. Despite the European Court's conclusion that the boy's human rights had been violated, and that 'UK law fails to provide adequate protection to children and should be amended', the British government decided not to ban corporal punishment outright. This decision was challenged by a coalition of 140 child-welfare groups, including Barnardo's, the National Children's Bureau and the Royal College of Paediatricians and Child Health. They declared, 'hitting children is a lesson in bad behaviour'. 'If someone smacked me I'd feel like smacking them,' added Andrew, aged seven. The National Society for the Prevention of Cruelty to Children launched a poster campaign with cartoons which illustrated precisely this reaction; the child who had been hit goes off to hit a smaller child. Yet the arguments of the welfare groups were received with outrage by much of the press. If smacking were made illegal, it was argued, parents would be deprived of rights over their children, and children would be deprived of a firm upbringing when they are too young to understand what is good for them.

In a much more shocking set of images, adult power over children's bodies has been pushed to the extreme. Until the 1970s, these had been the most secret of pictures, available only to the medical and judicial professions, showing children whose bodies do not merely express sorrow or despair but, like the street children of Rio, have been mutilated and tortured. This resonant image shows children who are the broken objects of extreme physical abuse.

'The history of childhood is a nightmare from which we have only recently begun to awaken,' wrote Lloyd de Mause, one of a group of authors who argued for a new kind of history of childhood based on libertarian and psychoanalytic principles. Such a history would reveal centuries of violence and oppression. These authors describe habitual infanticide, mutilation, swaddling and other forms of restraint, enforced child labour, canings and beatings, sexual abuse and mental cruelty. 'Child abuse is so common that it may be a characteristic that comes close to being "natural" to the human condition,' wrote Bakan. Yet, he argued, the experience is so unbearable that subterfuges must be found to make it expressible. 'Hard thoughts which would be too unpleasant to think' underlie fantasy and fairy stories. 'There they are held fast in a frame of unbelief. Some things are simply too terrible to think about if one believes them. Thus one does not believe them in order to make it possible to think about them.'

It was literally necessary to look beyond the surface, and an expansion of radiology in the 1940s drew attention to fractured bones which could not be accounted for. A medical and forensic image turned child abuse into a social issue, as doctors, radiologists and paediatricians identified a 'battered baby syndrome'. A new range of pictures came into circulation, recording bruised and swollen bodies, bruises and abrasions on the skin and face. This is a medicalised image which does not deal with the child as a person, but with the child's body as evidence of a crime and in need of repair.

The narratives of child abuse have escalated over the last few decades, and their difficult expression has reflected the fears embedded in a recognition of such unbearable experiences, including the fear the strong have of the weak, and the fear that excessive use of power leads not to control but to a lack of control, not to a mastery of childhood but to a return to a childish lack of restraint. The damaged body of a child stands as evidence not of the child's painful accession to adult reason but of the unreasoning violence that adulthood cannot leave behind. The cases which gained prominence from the early 1970s made it clear that those who threaten children most are those closest to them. Recurring scandals centred on girls who died from injuries inflicted by their parents or carers – particularly fathers or stepfathers: Maria Colwell in 1973, Tyra Henry in 1984, Jasmine Beckford in 1985, Kimberley Carlile in 1986, Victoria Climbié in 2001. In 1994 Fred and Rosemary West were arrested for torturing and murdering at least eight girls and young women, including one of their own children. The subjectivity of the child is irrelevant in this relentless catalogue of damage. The photographs of these children are destined for practical use by the medical and legal professions, and their clinical nature increases the sense of shock when they appear in the pages of the press. Tyra Henry was shown in hospital, shortly before her death, her body cocooned in tubes and wires; colour photographs of Victoria Climbié's damaged and abused face and body were published with disturbing frequency during the enquiry into her murder during 2001 and 2002.

Such visible extremity unlocks the heavily defended space of the family to a wide range of professionals, but for much of the press, the well-meaning agents of the welfare state whose job it is to protect children from abusing parents have joined the ranks of those outsiders who threaten the healing powers of the ideal family. Social workers in particular have been condemned in tones which put the rescuers on a par with the abusers. In these obsessive narratives, the impersonal

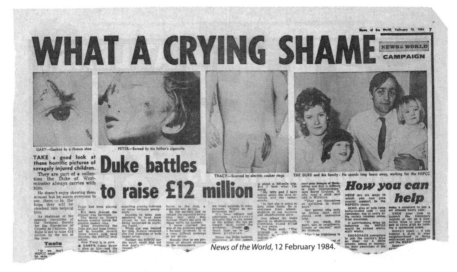

News of the World, 12 February 1984.

is opposed to the personal and the interfering state is contrasted with the privacy of the family. The press has continued to seek dangers from without rather than disintegration from within. In contrast to the accounts of Miller and de Mause, child battering has been seen as an extreme phenomenon, quite separate from the normal relations between parents and children. When the *News of the World* used pictures of children scarred and broken by their parents, it juxtaposed a classic family image of one of the richest men in Britain, the Duke of Westminster, with his arms around his wife and children. 'Duke battles to raise £12 million,' read the caption. The newspaper evoked a family that appeared to be better in every sense of the word, with the visual implication that the ideal family could charm away the horrors, both in the form of charitable donations and by the power of their contrasting image.

The dangerous world

Despite the evidence that children are far more at risk from relatives and carers, contemporary narratives have presented a world full of predators beyond the limits of the home. When children go missing, the whole nation follows every step of the police investigation. The parents of the children make appeals, newspapers offer rewards. A dreadful detective story unfolds in which no one seems to be above suspicion. A hazy snapshot or a school photograph on the front page of a newspaper, in all its bland ordinariness, comes to signal a terrible fear. With hindsight, these tentative or confidently smiling faces have acquired a compelling poignancy: James Bulger; Sarah Payne; Damilola Taylor; Stephen Lawrence; Rikki Neave; Holly Wells and Jessica Chapman. Their faces are instantly recognisable. Childhood always looks nervously towards an unknown future. For these children who have become household names, the future has proved too terrible to contemplate. Their foolish confidence appears to warn that what happened to them may happen to any unwary child.

The worst of fears was acted out in March 1996, when Thomas Hamilton burst into a primary school in the Scottish town of Dunblane and massacred 16 children and their teacher. This time it was a photograph of a whole class which filled the front pages. The incident gave rise to a media debate about the legitimacy of photographing shocked and grieving parents, and was quoted as an example of respectful journalism. Possibly the most disturbing picture to be used was a hazy frame from a home movie taken in a boys' club run by Hamilton. It shows him standing beside a vaulting horse, his hand supporting a boy as he leaps over. There is no indication of the identity of the boy – the face is blurred – nor of his fate. As so often with images that would once have seemed innocuous but are reinterpreted with hindsight, the effect, once more, is to suggest that not only this boy, but every boy, is in mortal danger.

Sexual abuse and paedophilia

By far the fattest of my bulging envelopes of press cuttings concerning child-hood is the one labelled 'sex abuse'. From the mid-1980s the scandals around child-battering were pushed off the front pages by even more dramatic revelations about the sexual abuse of children. At first these new narratives told of abuse within the family, but the emphasis moved, in what is by now a familiar pattern, to focus on the danger to children from the world beyond – usually in the shape of solitary and perverted men. The paedophile became the demon for the new century. The facts which have been exposed over the last twenty years have been the more shocking because of the scale and the extent of the abuse revealed. On the one hand the narratives have gained a mythological status, seeming to reveal an evil force beyond ordinary human comprehension. On the other, the brute reality is dreaded because its prevalence means that there has been a massive collusion in the secret. So much abuse by so many adults against so many children must be known to a large number of individuals – even though it had no public expression. Many people must have been involved in abusive relationships, as children and as adults. The exposure of sexual abuse, when it came, was built around fear, hysteria, denial and cries for revenge. This most secret of topics became the most public.

The image of the abused child, as we have seen, potentially holds within itself a complex of meanings and emotions. They include the construction of childhood as weak, dependent and completely within the control of adults, hence a child is always a potential victim. They also include an adult fear of children who may develop into demon children, so powerful that the child – or at least the image of the child – must be broken and crushed ('break their will,' in the Victorian saying). And they include an image of victimhood whose sexual nature is on the verge of becoming explicit. An image which will express such a complex of meanings is of necessity indirect and allusive. Readers of newspaper accounts, while dealing with the ambivalence of their own reactions, are once more invited to draw implications from the simplest of school photographs or snapshot portraits; or to read the possibility of abusive sexuality into any gendered image; or to return to fairy stories and mythology. The absent image becomes a collage of hints and implications. Newspapers use outline drawings, silhouettes or shadows. There may be a staged photograph of a cowed child; or a harsh rectangle blotting out a face; or pictures of the dolls that therapists use to diagnose and treat abused children – dolls which represent adults and children, with clothes that are easily removed, clear genitalia, rounded mouths and strange absent looks on their cloth faces. The one image which is forbidden is one that shows any form of sexual allure.

It is now accepted that abuse, both physical and sexual, is a long-standing aspect of relations between adults and children. There is no avoiding the pain recorded in oral and social histories. Harsh treatment in foster homes and children's homes has been all but taken for granted. But a new awareness of children's rights and a shift in the concept of childhood towards greater autonomy for children has led not only to an exposure of abusive practices, but also to a more rigorous definition of what counts as abuse. Adults who have been abused as children and children who are being abused have been given licence to speak, while feminist campaigns have replaced the concept of 'victim' with that of 'survivor'. In the mid-1980s, sexual abuse was featured in peak-time television viewing. Esther Rantzen's programme *Childwatch* was introduced in the *Radio Times* by a shocking quotation from an anonymous child: 'I was never frightened of walking home alone in the dark or of being raped or mugged. I knew what was waiting for me at home was infinitely worse than that.' The programme spoke directly to children and advised them how to protect themselves, if necessary against their own families. Under the slogan 'Speak to someone who cares', a presentation in the *Radio Times* showed a young girl calling for help by public telephone – a practical image which appealed beyond the family circle. The familiar prejudices against social workers and faceless state agencies were avoided, since a charismatic television star seemed to be providing an alternative to bureaucratic state interference. The programme launched ChildLine, a free and confidential telephone help line for children, whose logo is a smiling and unthreatening telephone. It was to become a major child-centred charity. In the first 12 hours after the programme went out, between 30,000 and 50,000 calls came in and up to 10,000 attempted calls a day followed. The National Society for the Prevention of Cruelty to Children reported a rise of more than 90 per cent in the numbers of new cases handled.

Sexual abuse within the family is private, secret and hardly spoken of between the participants. Those scandals which became headline news in the 1980s reached the public media because the abuse was alleged to be systematic and large-scale, and because concerned professionals – doctors, social workers and the police – took dramatic action by removing the children from their homes. First in Cleveland then the Orkney Islands, a large number of parents were accused of abusing their children. These new – yet old – and shocking narratives combined violence, illicit sexuality and sometimes occult practices. The question arose as to who was responsible for undermining that confident image so perfectly represented in the *News of the World* by the Duke of Westminster and his family. In feminist publications of the early 1980s the answer was, unequivocally, 'the Fathers'. This was the term used by Elizabeth Ward as the collective description for men in positions of authority – fathers, stepfathers, uncles, babysitters – who had abused girl children. She argued that incest is not separable from other forms of child abuse. It is simply an extension of 'a socially sanctioned sexuality that is coercive and unequal, committed by males against those weaker females who are available to them'. For Florence Rush, 'the family itself is an instrument of sexual and other forms of child abuse. The protector and the rapist are the same person.' Mary McLeod and Esther Saraga argue that 'Sex abuse happens in normal families, not deficient ones'. For these writers, the ever-present fantasy of incest is an extension of the power which welds the happy family together, throwing a shadow across its claim to perfection. While the image of a family is favourably contrasted with pictures of physically damaged children, the possibility of abuse forces a reassessment of the institution of 'family' itself. ChildLine's little girl with the telephone was a rare attempt to establish an image which would enable the voice of the child to be independently heard beyond the family group. But an image of a normally abusive family cannot be part of routine public imagery. In the Cleveland and Orkney cases the tabloid newspapers asserted their disbelief, voiced their condemnation of heavy-handed interference, and gave their support to parents' groups who claimed to be wrongly accused. Nothing was heard from the children themselves.

The only narrative of child abuse which legitimises a hint of pleasurable sexuality centres on a sexualised image of a young girl. This may be a narrative of seduction. 'Perhaps I stared at my father in a provocative way,' was a sub-heading in bold type in the *News of the World* magazine. A closer reading shows that the heading had rephrased a wry comment from the interviewee. Within the text she described the experience of her early childhood and added, 'Perhaps I wriggled my nappy at him in a provocative way'. The rewriting turns this ludicrous irony into a possible situation. An image of an adolescent girl, degraded and made available by premature sexual experience, is the only image which I have found accompanying features on child abuse in which the young person is regularly shown looking directly at the viewer. The impression is that, aware of her sexuality, she may well be provoking assault. Faced with this pressure from the image, the first incest survivors to speak out could hardly trust themselves. 'No one knows the inner torment I feel. I'm racked with guilt in case I provoked it. I'm a freak!' wrote 'Liz' in *Leveller* magazine.

The image of the girl child alone remains the most striking of contrasts with the image of the happy family group, for it is she who signals that the innocence of childhood is always deceptive. She is the one who holds immeasurable dangers for adult men. Her seductiveness may provoke them into betraying their dignity, and what is more, she knows their terrible secret. The position of the man at the apex of the family group is always under threat. He is exposed as capable of provoking total disruption at just that point where he claims to be the upholder of rationality and order.

Even at the high point of the sexual-abuse scandals, the popular press continued to preserve the image of a united family. The language was of 'parents' rights', and the aim was for children to be 'set free' and returned home so that the image could be restored. The *Star* showed a classic family – two parents, a boy and girl – at the time of the Cleveland scandal. The headline was 'Going home', as a judge had ruled that the children had been wrongly removed. It was a phrase that had gained a conscious ambivalence for those who dread what home may bring. But effectively what that picture showed was a *negative* of the classic family grouping, since, even reunited, this family were walking *away* from the camera, their identity concealed. They could only be photographed from behind.

By the mid-1990s the confusing ambivalence which attached to families and girl victims was less prominent an issue, since the narratives of sexual abuse were revealing the possibility of corruption in every institution which provides for children. The more closed the institution, the greater the danger. Scandals involved care homes, youth clubs, boarding schools, public schools, church groups, Scout troops and others. Most of these victims were boys, and the abusers were not relatives but professionals. In February 2000 Sir Ronald Waterhouse's report *Lost in Care* found that at least 650 people had been abused in children's homes in North Wales. A history of abuse was revealed in homes in Staffordshire, Leicestershire, East Belfast, Aberdeen and other locations around the country.

As the 1990s progressed, the blame was increasingly laid on a shadowy group of figures who, it seemed, plumbed the very depths of degradation. The 'danger from a stranger' meant that every child appeared to be at risk of abduction and abuse whenever they were alone on the streets. Hysteria peaked when the *News of the World* 'named and shamed' men previously convicted of paedophilia now living in the community. The publication of their mug-shots provoked riots in areas where they were thought to be housed – often deprived estates with very few amenities. Groups of residents – usually women together with their children – were photographed holding banners with violent slogans: 'Don't house them, hang them'. Excessive condemnation became an outlet for accumulated hatreds and resentments.

I have, amongst my press cuttings, several articles headlined 'Beyond belief'. The question of sexual abuse has consistently given rise to incredulity that such extremities should be so common yet so little known and so invisible. Questions arise around secrecy, denial, memory and false memory. Can children be believed when they tell of such outrageous events? Can adults who remember abuse accurately recall objective facts beyond the confusions of childish perception? What sort of image is being suggested? In this context, there was one image that was being hinted at which would have been central to the debate, but which had to remain a shadowy, mental image. It could not be formulated since it would make the unacceptable link between violence against children and sexual pleasure.

As the issue of sexual abuse throws doubt on a reliable moral framework within which childhood can be conceptualised, it forces a reinterpretation of all the other images we see of children. On the same page as an article by Nick Davies, beginning a *Guardian* series investigating paedophilia, was an advertisement for an airline, featuring a smiling, toothy, dark-haired boy. Here was an image of a young boy, possibly attractive to paedophiles, advertising flights to a part of the world where the law may possibly be easily avoided, where children are poor and where child prostitutes may be available. Such implications are no doubt entirely absent from the construction of the advertisement, but may be brought to an interpretation of the image by the publicity given to paedophile activities. The fact that sexual abuse can hardly be pictured means that smiles may become interpreted as seduction; childish sensuality interpreted in terms of adult sexuality; childish unknowingness as vulnerability; childish innocence as denial.

NOTES ON CHAPTER 6

p. 143 **'Fascinating misery'**: quoted from Jo Boyden (1990) 'Childhood and the policy makers: a comparative perspective on the globalisation of childhood', in Allison James and Alan Prout (eds) *Constructing and Reconstructing Childhood: Contemporary Issues in the Sociological Study of Childhood*, London: Falmer, p.196.

p. 144 **Penelope Boothby**: Anne Higonnet (1998) *Pictures of Innocence: the History and Crisis of Ideal Childhood*, London: Thames and Hudson, p.29.

Paul Dombey, Little Nell and William Carlyle: Paul Dombey in Charles Dickens, *Dombey and Son*, first published 1848; Little Nell in Charles Dickens, *The Old Curiosity Shop*, first published 1841. *East Lynne* was first published 1861. discussed by Peter Coveney (1967) *The Image of Childhood*, Harmondsworth: Peregrine, Chapters 5 and 7.

'Beggar maids' and street children: Graham Ovenden and Robert Melville, *Victorian Children*, London: Academy Editions. As an indication of how sensitive such material has become, in March 1993 the artist and antiquarian Graham Ovenden was arrested, and his negatives and collection of Victorian photographs were confiscated. Peter Rose of the *Daily Mail* reported that the Crown Prosecution Service believed he was the centre of a child-pornography ring. A petition signed by eminent artists and authors helped secure the return of his work. See David Newnham and Chris Townsend, 'Pictures of innocence', *Guardian* 'Weekend', 13 January 1996.

Oscar Rejlander's 'Poor Jo': Oscar Gustav Rejlander (1813–75), Swedish-born artist and photographer who worked in England from 1853, best known for his 'Two ways of life', a dramatic photomontage in the style of an allegorical painting, complete with artistic nudes and moral messages, made in 1857.

p. 145 *Disability Now*: published monthly by Scope London.

Marina Warner: (1998) *No Go the Bogeyman: Scaring, Lulling and Making Mock*, London: Chatto and Windus, pp.5, 10.

Cruella de Vil: in *One Hundred and One Dalmatians*, Walt Disney cartoon (US, 1961) with many live-action sequels.

Home Alone: (US, 1990) Dir. Chris Columbus.

childhood depression: Nicci Gerrard, 'What's worrying our kids? Psychiatrists suggest that one in five is suffering from depression and anxiety. Who stole our children's childhood?', *Observer* 'Review', 14 February 1999, a commentary on the Mental Health Foundation's summary of research on children's mental health, *Bright Futures*.

The Scream: the lithograph by Norwegian artist Edvard Munch (1895) has been ironically reproduced on pub signs, as a life-sized balloon and on Hallowe'en masks, as well as on numerous cards and illustrations.

'Fear ... is the defining flavour': Warner (1998) above, p.4.

the 'new poor': Zygmunt Bauman (1998) *Work, Consumerism and the New Poor*, Buckingham: Open University Press.

Poverty Answering Back: Channel 4, 'Broke' season, 1996. A contribution to the season were programmes by documentary photographer Nick Danziger, using still photographs, which made a point of explaining the background and the context for each picture.

'**Breadline Britain**': *Independent*, 15 October 1998. Photograph: Craig Easton.

p. 146 **Institute for Public Policy Research report**: *Independent*, 17 March 2000.

They may be on rollerskates: photograph: Steve Forrest, *Guardian*, 16 March 1998.

striding along the pavement: photograph: David Rose, *Independent*, 21 November 1994.

on a bicycle: photograph: Ted Ditchburn, *Independent*, 3 August 2001.

Barnardo's advertisements: John O'Keeffe, creative director at Bartle Bogle Hegarty, quoted in *Guardian*, 24 January 2000.

p. 148 **the undeveloped world**: the first version of this book, published in 1992, used the formulation 'Third World', which has lost its specificity after the collapse of the Soviet Bloc. Specialists in the field have discussed replacements – including developed/developing, majority/minority, industrialised/non-industrialised, North/South – all of which have their problems. As a non-expert I have settled for my own formulation, using '*un*developed', since lack of 'development' (whether industrial or otherwise) is a major issue in relation to poverty and 'otherness'. At the same time I do not want to imply that these countries are 'developing', since many of them, patently, are not. My thanks to Heather Montgomery of the Open University for useful information on this topic.

press reports of wars, famines: Jonathan Benthall (1993) *Disasters, Relief and the Media*, London: I.B.Tauris.

'**All over the world children are dying**': from a Save the Children advertisement, 'While you're eating between meals, he's dying between meals', 1980.

'**In the developing world**': Plan International UK, 2001.

p. 149 **World Press Photography**: Stephen Mayes (ed.) (1996) *World Press Photo, this Critical Mirror*, London: Thames and Hudson.

p. 150 '**change a child's life**': an Action Aid advertisement from the 1980s was headed 'Change this child's life', over the face of a dark-skinned girl with big, appealing eyes.

'**For God's sake help them**': *Daily Mirror*, 9 November 1996.

'**Sponsor a child**': Plan International UK, 2001.

Winston S. Churchill: at the time Churchill was roving correspondent for the *Times* and had reported on the war in Biafra. He provided a moving account which formed the text for the advertisement. The whole presentation thus communicates in more than one way, as the relationship between images, text and intended viewer shifts between different contexts.

p. 151 '**Children of War' appeal**: December 1995.

accounts of nineteenth-century philanthropy: see Hugh Cunningham (1991) *Children of the Poor*, Oxford: Blackwell, for a critique of this particular historical narrative.

'*Mirror* **to the rescue**': *Daily Mirror*, 27 October 1984. The report, by Alastair Campbell, describes the organisation of a flight carrying food as the personal effort by the *Mirror's* publisher and owner, Robert Maxwell.

'**The** *Mail* **brings comfort**': 13 May 1991.

given a Western education: for example an advertisement for Pestalozzi International Children's Village, 1979, showed young people with a distinctly tribal look next to the heading 'We'll give them the best survival training money can buy. An English education'.

Ali Ismaeel Abbas: see Patricia Holland (2003) 'Little Alice and Other Rescued Children' in David Miller (ed.) *Tell Me Lies: Media and Propaganda in the Attack on Iraq*, London: Pluto.

'How you rescued the orphans': *Sunday Express* 'Magazine', 19 May 1991.

***Daily Mail's* 1975 airlift**: 7 April 1975. Roy Greenslade, 'Mercy mission – Daily Mail style', *Guardian*, 6 August 2001.

p.152 **'carnivals of charity'**: Zygmunt Bauman (1998) *Work, Consumerism and the New Poor*, Buckingham: Open University Press, p.78.

Geri Halliwell: the Spice Girl pop singer was appointed 'good will ambassador' by UNICEF. On charity and celebrity see Andrew Smith, 'All in a good cause?', *Observer* 'Magazine', 27 January 2002.

'It is an unfortunate truism': Paul Harrison and Robin Palmer (1986) *News Out of Africa*, London: Hilary Shipman, p.97.

'the mad scramble for publicity': Richard Dowden, *Independent*, 21 December 1994.

Thomas Barnardo was taken to court: Valerie Lloyd and G. Wagner (1974) *The Camera and Dr Barnardo*, Hertford.

Eglantyne Jebb was prosecuted: Helen Jones (2000) *Women in British Public Life 1914–50: Gender, Power and Social Policy*, Harlow: Pearson Education, p.108.

p.153 **rivalled that of states**: Boyden (1990) above.

the emaciated *body* of the child: a rare example of a domestic appeal using a similar technique was part of the 'Wishing Well Appeal' from Great Ormond Street Hospital for Sick Children (Collett Dickenson Pearce, 1987). The advertisement showed a desperately sick premature baby in an incubator. The picture was a snapshot taken by the baby's mother two years previously, as the hospital was unwilling for the agency to photograph a child currently in an incubator. 'It had to be heart-wrenching,' said art director Neil Godfrey. The advertisement won the 1988 individual black-and-white *Campaign* Press Award (*Campaign*, 25 March 1988).

p.154 **'While you're eating' and 'You're not the only one'**: advertisements for Save the Children, 1980.

'I want *you* to see this': Chris Steele-Perkins, *Video Diary: 'Dying for Publicity'*, on his photojournalism in Somalia and Sudan, BBC2, 25 September 1993.

was coming under attack: including my own article '"Save the Children" or how the newspapers present pictures of children from the Third World', in *Multiracial Education*, Vol. 9, No 2, Spring 1981, which contains material I have drawn on for this chapter.

'aid pornography': Bridget Harrison, 'Is this aid pornography?', *Times*, 29 May 1998; Anthony Bevins, 'Does this picture make you flinch? Clare Short says graphic images like this stop people caring', *Independent*, 29 May 1998.

p.155 **baby-milk bottle**: War on Want (1979) *The Baby Killer Scandal*, 'A War on Want investigation into the promotion and sale of powdered baby milks in the Third World'.

or a roll of film: cover of *New Internationalist*, January 1987.

'the dignity of the people': Save the Children, *Focus on Images*, 1991.

'Images of starving children have lost their appeal': see Stanley Cohen (2001) *States of Denial: Knowing About Atrocities and Suffering*, Cambridge: Polity, Chapter 7.

'grotesque hypocrisy': Teresa Hayter, 'Aid: The West's False Handout', *New Socialist*, 24 February 1985.

p.156 **'The new slavery'**: *Guardian*, February 1999.

'All the migrants I photographed': Sebastiao Salgado (2001) *Children: Refugees and Migrants*, London: Aperture.

'cynical exploitation': Keith Dovkants, 'Town that lives off London's beggars: Standard exposes racket of spongers from Romania', *Evening Standard*, 14 March 2000.

'If a parent dies': Richard Dowden, 'Dying by Darwinian logic', *Independent*, 17 July 1991.

p.157 **fighters, workers or aggressive dwellers on the streets**: in her study of child prostitutes in Thailand, Heather Montgomery (2001) writes that these children 'exist in an ambiguous category which challenges notions of childhood and threatens Western constructions of children' (p.133). They 'do not need innocence. They need knowledge of their rights, appreciation of all their options, and ways of protecting themselves' (p.136). *Modern Babylon? Prostituting Children in Thailand*, Oxford: Berghahn Books.

American parents: *Independent*, 27 March 1998.

Eritrean girl: children's militia in Segeneti, Eritrea. Photograph: Mike Wells.

p.158 **pictured with standard British-made rifles**: the photograph, by David Crump, was used by British newspapers, including *Daily Mail*, 30 May 2000, and *Evening Standard*, 30 May 2000. Amnesty International's *In the Firing Line* (1998) estimated that at least 300,000 under-18s were actively engaged in over 30 armed conflicts, most of them in rebel armies. In a poignant comment on contemporary globalisation, a heavily armed boy in Liberia was pictured wearing a Benetton T-shirt. *Guardian*, 19 May 2001. Photograph: Guenay Hlutuncok.

Amnesty International awards: *Amnesty International Journal*, July–August 2000.

combining pathos: Hugh Cunningham has explored this theme in relation to images of children in the nineteenth century. Cunningham (1991) above.

tourist gaze: John Urry (1990) *The Tourist Gaze: Leisure and Travel in Contemporary Societies*, London: Sage.

p.159 **a poster put up by local businesses**: *Amnesty International Journal*, AIBS, January–February 1994.

'When you talk about Brazilian children': Zoe Heller, *Independent on Sunday*, 5 May 1991, accompanied by a photograph of sleeping children, literally piled on top of each other, by Ben Gibson/Impact Photos. Historian James Walvin (1982) wrote of the nineteenth century, 'it was hard for the middle class to regard the children of the poor as *children*': *A Child's World: a Social History of English Childhood 1800–1914*, Harmondswoth: Pelican, p.15.

'The victimisation of children': Alice Miller (1985) *Thou Shalt Not Be Aware*, London: Pluto, p.192.

p.160 **neo-kitsch**: see Michelle Henning (2000) 'The subject as object: photography and the human body', in Liz Wells (ed.) *Photography: a Critical Introduction*, London: Routledge, p.237. In the 1870s, Oscar Rejlander's photograph of a crying infant sold over a quarter of a million copies. Beaumont Newhall (1982) *The History of Photography*, New York: MOMA, p.74.

'La Tristesse': 1990, Athena International.

p.161 **the *Sun* ran a campaign**: Peter Chippindale and Chris Horrie (1992) *Stick it Up Your Punter: the Rise and Fall of The Sun*, London: Mandarin, p.157–61.

'Thank God we live here?': *Daily Mirror*, 19 September 1972. A 'Shock issue' headed 'Every ten minutes an act of criminal violence happens in this country'.

Poverty Answering Back: Channel 4 (1996) above.

p.162 **a spitting out of unpleasant and unwanted**: see Julia Kristeva (1982) *Powers of Horror: an Essay on Abjection*, New York: Columbia University Press, for a discussion of the notion of an 'abject' (neither subject nor object), a part of oneself that one wants to be rid off, but cannot.

p. 163 James Kincaid: (1992) *Childloving: the Erotic Child and Victorian Culture*, London: Routledge.

the European Court of Human Rights: Christina M. Lyon (2000) *Loving Smack or Lawful Assault?: a Contradiction in Human Rights and Law*, London: Institute for Public Policy Research, p.1.

'a lesson in bad behaviour': *Independent*, 23 September 1996.

a poster campaign: *Daily Mirror*, 29 April 2002.

Lloyd de Mause: (1976) *The History of Childhood*, London: Souvenir.

a group of authors: Beatrice and Ronald Gross's (1977) *The Children's Rights Movement*, New York: Doubleday Anchor, was a libertarian polemic; Lloyd de Mause's *The History of Childhood* (above) argued that historical changes are brought about by 'psychogenic factors'; Alice Miller's influential *Thou Shalt Not Be Aware* (above) came from a practising psychoanalyst who had come to doubt the validity of psychoanalysis.

'Child abuse is so common': D. Bakan (1971) *The Slaughter of the Innocents*, San Francisco: Jossey-Bass. On knowing and not knowing, see also Cohen (2001) above.

p. 164 A medical and forensic image: John Grady, 'The manufacture and consumption of child abuse as a social issue', *Telos*, 56 (Summer 1983), pp.111–18.

'battered baby syndrome': Henry and Ruth Kempe (1978) *Child Abuse*, London: Fontana.

those who threaten children most: NSPCC (1999) *Out of Sight*, London. Between one and two children are killed by care-givers each week: 40 per cent before the age of one, 33 per cent by the child's mother, 49 per cent by the father, step-father or mother's partner.

Tyra Henry: *Guardian*, 19 December 1987.

Social workers in particular have been condemned: Meryl Aldridge, 'Poor relations: state social work and the press in the UK', in Franklin (ed.) (1999) above.

p. 165 dangers from without rather than disintegration from within: Jenny Kitzinger (1999) 'The ultimate neighbour from hell? Stranger danger and the media framing of paedophiles', in Bob Franklin (ed.) *Social Policy, the Media and Misrepresentation*, London: Routledge.

The dangerous world: Ben Neasmith, brought up near Cromwell Street in Gloucester, the home of Fred and Rosemary West, writes, 'The discoveries at Cromwell Street made us realise, all those years later, that our parents were right. The bogeyman, the evil stranger really did exist and he was more terrifying and depraved than we could have ever possibly have imagined.' *Bournemouth University Student Press*, January 2002.

Despite the evidence: NSPCC (1999) above.

newspapers offer rewards: during the search for Holly Wells and Jessica Chapman, Express Newspapers offered £1 million reward, the *Sun* and the *News of the World* offered £150,000. However, the *Guardian* noted that 'little, if any, of the £2 million offered in rewards by five papers over the past six years has been paid, prompting claims that such offers are simply commercial ploys'. 10 August 2002.

A hazy snapshot or a school photograph: it is the job of a picture agency or a newspaper to approach the family for a photograph of a murdered or missing child. A moving account of the difficulty of this task is given in the television programme *The Troubleshooters*, about the Pacemaker photo agency based in

Belfast (Granada for ITV, 14 March 1995, Prod. Jeff Anderson). In an extra twist to post-modern communications, in a snapshot reproduced across the media during August 2002, Holly Wells and Jessica Chapman were both wearing T-shirts with an eye-catching logo advertising Vodaphone, which at the time was sponsoring Manchester United football club. The company saw it as 'brand contamination'. Johann Hari, 'How tragedy damages a brand', *New Statesman*, 9 September 2002.

p.166   **photographing shocked and grieving parents**: Jon Snow, 'What should the message be', *Guardian*, 18 March 1996.

a boys' club run by Hamilton: *Independent*, 15 March 1996.

the danger to children from the world beyond: in 1991, press coverage contained 47 items on the prevention of sexual abuse outside the home, and only two discussing 'incest-prevention'. Paula Skidmore, 'Gender and the agenda: news reporting of child sexual abuse', in Cynthia Carter et al. (eds) (1998) *News, Gender and Power*, London: Routledge, p.211. See also Kitzinger (1999) above.

p.167   **'break their will'**: 'Break their will betimes: begin this great work before they can run alone, before they can speak plain, or perhaps speak at all...make him do as he is bid, if you whip him ten times running to effect it,' wrote Susannah Wesley to her son John in 1828, quoted in M. Jobling (1978) 'Child abuse: the historical and social context', in V. Carver (ed.) *Child Abuse: a Study Text*, Milton Keynes: Open University Press.

oral and social histories: for example in many television programmes produced by Stephen Humphries at Testimony Films, Bristol.

what counts as abuse: see Allison James, Chris Jenks and Alan Prout (1998) *Theorising Childhood*, Cambridge: Polity, p.152, on the emergence of a concept which had previously been 'unseen or unintelligible'.

'I was never frightened of walking home alone': *Childwatch*, BBC1, 30 October 1986. *Radio Times*, photograph: Judy Goodhill.

p.168   **after the programme went out**: after its first year of operation, ChildLine estimated that 8000 calls were made daily, of which about 800 got through. *Guardian*, 14 September 1996.

First in Cleveland: Beatrix Campbell (1988/revised edition 1996) *Unofficial Secrets: Child Sexual Abuse, the Cleveland Case*, London: Virago.

the answer was, unequivocally: Elizabeth Ward (1984) *Father/Daughter Rape*, London: Women's Press.

Florence Rush: (1980) *The Best Kept Secret*, New Jersey: Prentice Hall.

Sex abuse happens in normal families: Mary McLeod and Esther Saraga, 'Abuse of Trust', *Marxism Today*, August 1987.

p.169   **'Perhaps I stared at my father'**: Ellen Petrie, 'Incest', *News of the World* 'Magazine', early 1980s. Photograph: Conrad Hafenrichter.

'No one knows the inner torment': 'Liz', 'Too afraid to speak', *Leveller*, No 78, 2–15 April 1982.

'Going home': *Star*, 1 July 1987, 'For this family the ordeal was over...for now. But for other parents the nightmare goes on. The youngsters must stay in care.'

p.170   **Lost in Care**: see Christian Wolmar (2000) *Forgotten Children: the Secret Abuse Scandal in Children's Homes*, London: Vision.

'named and shamed': *News of the World*, 23 and 30 July 2000.

'Don't house them, hang them': *Independent*, 26 September 2000. Photograph: Tom Pilston.

'Beyond belief': for example *Guardian*, 1 August 1998.

Questions arise around secrecy, denial: Jenny Kitzinger, 'The gender-politics of news production: silenced voices and false memories', in Carter et al. (eds) (1998) above.

an article by Nick Davies: 'A terraced street in suburbia that shrouded a guilty secret', *Guardian*, 25 November 2000.

where child prostitutes may be available: Judith Ennew (1987) *The Sexual Exploitation of Children*, Cambridge: Polity, Chapter 5; Montgomery (2001) above. Sex tourism has been exposed in many part of the world, such as Sri Lanka and Thailand. At the same time these are working children, making a contribution to the tourist economy of poverty-stricken states.

7

Gender, sexuality and a fantasy for girls

'Part little girl': girlhood and female sexuality

Lipstick smeared across a sulky pout, tousled hair, a crumpled gingham dress, an absent, heavy-lidded look: this is not a picture of a child, yet this 1990s fashion spread is dealing in the mythology of childhood. 'If Alice was a modern heroine she would wear these clothes,' says the caption. They are 'part folk, part gypsy, part Bohemian and part little girl'. The myth of Alice, the girl child of unstable size, puzzling her way through a mysterious Wonderland, returns constantly in the imagery of little girls – not least because of its undertow of barely suppressed sexuality. (A network of child pornographers, arrested in 2001, described themselves as the Wonderland Club.) Alice's image is fixed for ever by the inspired drawings by John Tenniel which accompanied the first edition. Her long, swept-back hair – even if not actually held in place by an Alice band – and her mid-Victorian pinafore dress, are instantly recognisable. The myth has another dimension, since portraits of the real Alice are amongst the best known photographs of the nineteenth century. Lewis Carroll, author of *Alice in Wonderland* and a respected Oxford don, was also a celebrated photographer who kept a cupboard full of dressing-up clothes and transformed his many 'child friends', including the original Alice, into beggar maids, popular characters and oriental princesses. An image which is 'part folk, part gypsy and part Bohemian' would certainly have appealed to him – especially as it remains 'part little girl'.

Unlike the even lighting and calm decorum of Lewis Carroll's girl children – even his nude studies achieve a cool distance – the young women playing at being children in this fashion spread have parted legs, open mouths and theatrical gestures. The chiaroscuro presentation throws half the face into deep shadow. The sophisticated styling and knowing references to cultural history play with the titillations of child prostitution and corrupted girlhood. This is the 'kinderwhore' look, part of a fashion repertoire which has included such styles as 'heroin chic', sexual ambiguity and a cult of the very thin – all of them constructions which bring into play the complex relations between childhood, sexuality and femininity. Post-modern cynicism, reflexivity and playfulness in the face of moral danger legitimise presentations that touch the edge of acceptability.

Such pictures are embedded in highly attractive, ornamental presentations, crammed with pleasures of the text. They are part of an all-pervasive re-alignment of sensibility and morality, an aestheticisation of everyday life which belongs to consumer culture. And being part of consumer culture is another way of distancing them from seriousness. As promotional images they are not for themselves alone, they are primarily for selling: 'frill hem asymmetric dress £300, voile dress £125…,' continues the caption for the 'modern Alice'. A fashion spread from the 1970s uses a 15-year-old model to sell nightwear to those who are 'too old for toys, and too young for boys'. The viewer of a fashion spread may purchase and wear the clothes and fantasise the roles on offer. The model in this genre of photograph, whether child masquerading as child or adult woman masquerading as child, is herself a commodity with a price on her head.

Fashion spread, *Observer 'Magazine'*, 1978. Photographs: James Wedge.

The 1990s image pushes excess and knowingness even beyond that of the 1970s. It is no accident that images of this sort have developed in parallel with a growing awareness of the reality of sexual abuse and a greater protectiveness towards real children. The obsession with sexuality which characterised the last decades of the twentieth century was partly a consequence of feminist and psychoanalytic explorations which brought to the fore issues that had previously been unspeakable. Women's greater confidence in the public sphere had allowed private sexuality and the borderline between childish and adult knowledge to be publicly discussed – and also to be playfully exploited. Unexpectedly, the fashion image discussed above has much in common with the picture on the cover of Jane Gallop's influential *Feminism and Psychoanalysis*, which was subtitled 'the daughter's seduction' (the theme of the book is that the daughter – feminism – can seduce the father – psychoanalysis – 'out of his impassive self mastery'). This is a picture of a child, and it too plays on the borders of the permissible. This little girl also has long hair – held in place by an Alice band – and looks directly at the viewer with an expression of profound ambiguity. She clutches a bitten apple. Once more the chiaroscuro suggests unnamed dangers held by the darkness, but in this picture the child's legs are together and they are curled away from the viewer.

The visible sexuality of young girls has had immense consequences for the imagery of childhood. Lindsay Smith points out that Lewis Carrol wanted his child 'friends' to stay young and small ('you'd better grow a little younger – go back to your last birthday but one,' he wrote to one of them) just at the time when there was agitation for the age of consent for girls to be raised from 13 to 16 in England and Wales (it was raised in 1885). Smith here points to a recurring theme. In order to keep childhood separate from adulthood there must be a continuous effort to repress or redefine children's sexuality. Girl children in particular must not be seen to explore sexual knowledge on their own terms. Instead they must *perform* childishness as if unaware of their sexual appeal. This disavowal has added another fold of interpretation to pictures of pre-pubescent girls (and, in an extra twist, to pictures of young adults playing the part of pre-pubescent girls). Like all taboos, it draws attention to itself and tempts playful – and sometimes dangerous – experiments with the image. Post-modern reflexivity works on the borders, taunting the taboos with kitsch and excess.

Doubling the image

Although the moment of transformation from child to adult is laden with significance, I want to go back to a point which is arguably even more radical: the point at which a gender-differentiated childish identity is constructed and the available imagery creates a set of distinctions which ensure that the image of childhood is not one but two – always crossed by the firm categorisations of male and female. So much hinges on this difference that distinctions built into the language make it a condition of humanity itself. It is only when we are told whether a newborn is a boy or a girl that we can allow the child to enter the social world and refer to 'it' with one, and only one, of those mutually exclusive, domineering, erotic and culturally explosive terms 'him' or 'her'. It is only in relation to these two apparently opposing categories that social behaviour becomes appropriate. Despite heated debates around the possibility of transgressing sexual boundaries and the important distinction between (biological) sex and (social) gender, we continue to live in a divided society in which the (still) unequal division of gender is underpinned by the difficult relations of sexual desire and power. 'Even at play, today's children are practising skills they'd have needed 10,000 years ago,' wrote a child psychologist in *Woman*. He was rehearsing an increasingly familiar theme that is sometimes stated triumphantly, sometimes regretfully. It asserts that Western society is to be congratulated on modernising gender relations and painlessly adjusting the grosser inequalities, and it concludes that we can now settle back into a post-feminist world where the brute facts of difference continue to impress us with their old, immutable forms. No amount of tinkering with cultural patterns can affect those inbuilt relations of power and desire. 'Men don't want their sons to be effeminate, so they go for masculine toys,' the National Association of Toy Retailers told *Woman*.

But things are never that clear-cut. As sexual difference is explored with relish across the range of public imagery, our attention is drawn again and again to the effort that goes into maintaining it as a fact and to emphasising its apparently natural social consequences. It has been subject to endless exploration, experimentation and reshaping within changing circumstances. The imagery seeks to produce two alternative types of individual, and in doing so it restates and overstates differences that at one moment seem oh so natural, so obvious and inevitable, and at the next so fragile that they must be strictly enforced.

To build my collection I tend to buy greetings cards in pairs, since they are produced that way. Even the image of babies tends to be doubled, with striking differences between congratulations cards for the birth of a baby boy and those for a baby girl. Two cards from the 1980s show the male baby self-reliant and

Greetings cards, Sharpe's Classics, 1980s. Simon Elvin, 2000s.

upright, while the female baby is lying on her back, passive and relaxed, legs apart. A birthday card for six-year-olds from the 1970s has a boy posing with a football. He is photographed from below, giving a sense of height and power – which, admittedly, has some irony to it. But it is contrasted with a girl who crouches beside a dolls' house and is photographed, without irony, from above. By the year 2000 the difference could not presented with such straightforward innocence. A much more dramatic pair of birthday greetings (described as 'boggle-eyed peepers') have cartoon-style drawings of both boy and girl with clumpy trainers, swivelling 3-dimensional eyes and huge toothy smiles. Nevertheless the girl is surrounded by flowers while the boy zooms along on a scooter. On another card, an energetic five-year-old on rollerblades, fairly androgynous at first glance, could only be a girl once we note her wispy hair and the flowers and hearts that float across the background. The difference continues to be created as it is lived through, in interaction with the image.

Although there has been a greater willingness to accept biological determinants in recent debates around gender difference – sometimes from feminists endeavouring to bring up boys in a non-sexist way – when I look at the changing imagery in my collection, it seems that the depiction of difference may now take it for granted that an enjoyment of femininity need not automatically lead to social disadvantage. There is a world of difference between the grinning girl and boy on the 'boggle-eyed peepers' and the upstanding boy and crouching girl of the 1970s cards. However, despite the glimmerings of a weakening link between masculinity and power, as strategies of visual differentiation shift and change, there are always new opportunities for that linkage to sneak back and claim its 'natural' status.

Strategies of differentiation

Conventions which indicate the sex of children range from the minimal, in which a line drawing eliminates all but the essentials, to the maximal, usually in advertising images which draw on huge resources to pack information into a dense presentation (a technique which Erving Goffman described as 'commercial syncretism'). Either way, the image seeks a recognition that will be instant, involuntary and unquestioned. A line drawing by the inimitable children's illustrator Dick Bruna on the front of the *Observer* 'Magazine' used only the starkest indicators. Two children are represented by heavy outlines: circles for heads, strokes of the pen for hairs, dots for eyes. As is frequently the case, the difference between them centres on the depiction of the girl. She is recognised by an *addition* of visual elements, in the form of six extra lines to stand for hairs. She is what is described in linguistics as the 'marked' term, in which an addition to a word indicates a deviation from its basic form (child, child*ren*; man, *wo*man etc). Those extra lines reinforce the impression, already embedded in the cultural environment, that femininity is a variation on a masculine norm. By indicating the girl's collar with curves, while the boy's has straight lines, this very simple diagram of difference also manages to suggest that femininity is softer and more decorative.

Any reading of an image of this sort inevitably calls up an active distinction between male and female which is part of everyday practice. Looking at this rigorously simplified presentation, a viewer is forced to make a series of judgements and understandings across the emotional and social spectrum. This live network of assumptions includes expectations about social roles, child-rearing practices, living arrangements within households, power relations between the sexes, sexual attraction, erotic relationships and our very sense of personal identity. A social and moral universe hinges on six little hairs. A single picture, by enforcing a positive act of differentiation on the part of the viewer, brings into play multiple biological, psychical and social structures, and secures the viewer's own place as part of those structures. The whole complex of overlapping and inter-related systems is emotionally underpinned by the forces of sexuality and desire. It is only when we pause to consider the process more closely that its instability becomes suddenly, startlingly visible. Despite the occasional exploration of sexual ambiguity, there seems to be a need to state, restate and overstate the strategies of differentiation, particularly when children are the subject of the presentation.

In the rich imagery of advertising, differentiation between the sexes is elaborated in great detail across the spectrum of consumer goods, ensuring that sexual difference is confirmed in the moments of purchase and consumption. In their consumer activity, children repeatedly reconstruct their gender roles. Advertisements celebrate present pleasures and open themselves to challenging and critical meanings at their peril. A promotional message must ensure that information is precisely directed, and must hold every element firmly in place to ward off any possible escape of meanings. However, in a critically aware society, overstatement may shake the security of the message, hence the increase in advertisements which are ironical or deconstructive. An example from the late 1970s gives an impression of the fullness of the genre.

A pair of advertisements for Heinz tinned foods appeared at the height of feminist campaigns concerning the representation of women and girls. They set out to persuade mothers to buy processed food, which was presented as

There will always be something kids enjoy more than Heinz Beans with Beefburgers.

But when they feel hungry, there's nothing they enjoy more.
Baked Beans with Beefburgers are more than just kids' favourites, they're nourishing, too.
And that's just what a lady needs to help her through a busy day.

There will always be something kids enjoy more than Heinz Beans with Frankfurters.

But when they feel hungry, there's nothing they enjoy more.
Baked Beans with delicious Mini-Frankfurters are more than just kids' favourites, they're nourishing, too.
And that's just what a chief mechanic needs after a busy morning.

Advertisements, late 1970s.

nourishing, convenient and enjoyable. They use photographs which employ a casual naturalism, making it seem as if viewers are catching the children unawares, as is the adult's right. Yet these are no documentary pictures, snapping the world as it passes before the lens. They have been expensively set up, carefully lit and framed, with every detail controlled to construct a heightened realism. Both presentations are organised around gender, the numerous props creating a space that in the one case could only be filled by a boy, and in the other only by a girl. Nothing confuses the viewer's expectations, nor hampers the task of discriminating between the two. The girls are in a bedroom, the younger one pulling clothes from an open drawer, the other trying them on in front of a mirror, playing at being an adult woman. The boys are in a garden shed full of tools, oil cans, paintbrushes and the paraphernalia of masculine activity. Unlike the girls, they are not pretending but are engaged in authentic work. They really *are* mending a bicycle. The activities and positioning of the bodies in the two presentations follow patterns recognised as characteristically male or characteristically female. One girl has her head bent back, admiring her reflection and, incidentally, displaying her body to the viewer in a double performance – for her own eyes and for others. The boys lean forward over a purposeful task, their heads bent away from the viewer of the image. The controlling opposition between male and female has brought into play associated oppositions between indoors and outdoors, clean and dirty, play and work, self-absorption and object-absorption.

Confident in its aggressive statement of difference, this presentation – and many others like it – assumes a reading by viewers who are themselves secure in their own sex/gender positioning. Viewers are expected to allocate each object securely to its place – bikes to the boys, dressing-up clothes to the girls – and to repress any slippage between the two. A sense of social maleness or femaleness is established, regardless of any insecurity in living out those categories in real life. Homosexuality, lesbianism, sexual non-conformity, seem inconceivable in this comfortably divided world. Pictures like these calm our anxieties, helping us to be aware, as Stephen Heath put it, 'of the absolute fact of difference', despite 'needing to deal with the simultaneous absence of difference in any one individual'.

'The absolute fact of difference' is visually stated again and again. Loveable, grubby young boys, each with a bold and impudent grin, are placed beside coy young girls, whose soulful expressions pose the enigma of sexual knowledge. Girls may bend their heads to one side; boys almost always face the camera/viewer directly; boys grin, girls simper; in a pair of advertisements for Nesquik, the girl puckers her lips to suck at her straw with a wide-eyed look at the camera, whereas the boy tucks his into the corner of his toothy smile; girls lean back, boys lean purposefully forwards. But the imagery of gender differentiation has proved infinitely flexible. It has its progressive moments (young girls in dungarees, boys in less aggressive postures) but the old distinctions continuously reassert themselves, ever seeking a form which will adapt to a changing social climate.

The promotion of toys is gender divided from the earliest years. Manufacturers may show both sexes playing with building bricks or Lego, but from the toddler stage boys have Action Man and dumper trucks, girls have Barbie dolls, fairy wings and toy prams. Boys do not have tea sets, dolls' houses, Care Bears or My Little Pony. Girls do not have weapons of war, micromachines or radio-controlled cars. Non-sexist parents faced with this chasm are caught up in acts of discrimination eagerly embraced by the children themselves. 'Lots of manufacturers advertise and package their toys for both girls and boys. But research tells them that sometimes it can be a waste of time and money. Girls simply don't buy the toy and manufacturers also risk alienating boys by linking them with girls at all,' wrote toy retailer Gerry Masters. The continuing problem is to disentangle gender differentiation from a masculine fantasy of dominance. Boys simply do not want to be linked with girls.

The image of the 'tomboy' (George/Georgina in Enid Blyton's 'Famous Five' books is an archetypal example), in which a young girl resists the markers of femininity and subordination (George 'wore her curly hair short' and was 'very fierce') has, in contemporary imagery, been pre-empted by unisex fashions and a veneer of equality. In promotional material for clothing, girls and boys are both shown wearing jeans, tracksuits, clumpy shoes and T-shirts. However, the principle remains: girls must also have skirts and frilly dresses – even though, in the 2001 H&M catalogue, the little girl in the lace collar and velvet skirt plays as energetic a part in the tug-of-war as those dressed in trousers and jerseys. Girls may learn welding along with the rest of the class, but their shoes must have a more decorative shape, as they had in a shoe advertisement headed 'Times are changing'. Times may well change, but the feminine remains the marked term in a difference that continues to subordinate. The indicators of difference, like those decorative hairs in the Dick Bruna drawing, remain on the feminine body. And that body must display itself in such a way that reveals its awareness (even if the child is 'unaware') of its sexuality, for, in this rigorously heterosexual visual regime, a drab differentiation based on housework, childcare, unequal pay and all those other mundanities is secured by the thrilling potential of sexual excitement.

Sex and gender: children and adults

Within many of the social contexts in which childhood is pictured and defined, the imagery is chiefly concerned to police the boundary between children and adults. At school or in the home, childhood is constructed as that which adulthood is not. However, in the broad scope of the imagery, the indicators of childhood are always crossed by the pervasive markers of gender and sexuality, which confuse distinctions based on age and generation. When the focus is on gender, the image of a child is confirmed not by the characteristics it has in common with all other children, but by its *contrast* with children of the opposite sex and a more complex set of relations with adults.

Advertisements and promotional imagery make use of the *childishness* of children as a justification for adult behaviour and patterns of consumption. But they also show children as trainees, displaying the characteristics they *share* with adults, learning to take their place in an appropriately gendered adult world. Imagery which confirms a girl's training for domestic labour and child-rearing has been modified by powerful critiques from feminist voices, but it continues to figure in advertisements for consumer goods from washing machines to toys, and from foods to toiletries. Modulated by a new sense of independence and dynamism in the children themselves, mothers are still helped by daughters around the house and initiate them into the use of clothes and cosmetics. The role of boys has expanded slightly. Just as men now figure much more frequently in a childcare role, boys are more likely to be encouraged to engage in domestic duties such as washing their own clothes – especially as those duties can now be shown to be simple and undemanding with the use of appropriate household technology. Even so, boys are far more often seen together with their fathers in training for physical activity, intellectual control and leisure choices. They appear in advertisements for cars, sports equipment, TVs, insurance and other 'masculine' fields. An imitative relation with the adult of the same sex – children as little men and little women, sharing the visual indications of masculinity and femininity – has remained remarkably consistent, despite the arrival of a free-flowing independent childhood and the 'new man' about the house.

Images of cross-gender relationships between children and adults bring a range of different problems. Within the context of the home, the image of a charming young boy may be used to give rise to motherly feelings in the viewer. Mothers are seen serving their sons with food, medicine and other forms of care, while sons accept and indeed demand their services. But there is more at stake than parenthood when the image of a young girl is viewed by an adult man. The image of a girl child inevitably reaches beyond the family, beyond men as fathers, to address men in general with an appeal which is potentially sexual. In the Heinz advertisements discussed above, the boys' world is shown as self-sufficient, while that of the girls is centred on a mirror. The older girl is looking at herself – and preparing to be looked at by another. Her angled position, just off-centre in the picture, causes her to display her framed and decorated body to the viewer, at the same time as she displays it to herself. The mirror is a central icon of femininity, and the little girl in the advertisement is rehearsing her adult role, styling her body to conform to the expectations of her gender. But the mirror suggests more than a future relationship with a viewing male. It creates a *present* link between the child in the picture and any of the grown men who may catch sight of it. 'I just look into the mirror and I'm an ordinary girl, but I am aware others see my looks,' 12-year-old model Elizabeth Preston told the *Daily Mail*. From the earliest years, the feminine body is constructed for display.

Questions about imagery which implies childhood sexuality have been forced to the forefront of public discussion in the context of scandals around paedophilia and incest. 'As soon as you are sensitised to the reactions of paedophiles you start to see unhealthy images of children where before you might only have seen cute ones,' wrote Geraldine Bedell. What begins as a fantasy for a little girl dressing up in front of a mirror may be transformed into a quite different fantasy for adult men. From flirting bimbos to pouting babies, we have been trained by the imagery itself to read pictures of girls in an erotic way. Little girls have a difficult route to negotiate as they actively engage in the process of becoming women.

Catalogue, 2000s.

Girl Heaven

At Christmas 2000, a mail-order catalogue called *Girl Heaven* offered little girls the opportunity to transform themselves into an angel, a fairy or a bride by choosing a veil, a posy, a halo or some sparkling wings. Any of these could be added to a ruched top and a net tutu – a bargain at £35. Other goodies on offer included a wand and tiara set, pink sequinned shoes and a heart-shaped bag. Really generous parents may spend another £35 on a pink satin ball gown with a hooped skirt. The girls who appear in the catalogue modelling these fantasy clothes are clearly delighted with themselves. They hold up their net skirts with their finger tips, stretch out their wands and display their tiaras – all in a leaflet of intense pinkness.

Girl Heaven is a recent manifestation of a fantasy for girls that has long resonated through the imagery of childhood. It appears in girls' books and comics and is filtered through advertisements and magazine features. It is the fantasy of the fairy princess who becomes a bride. In the storybooks she wears a white dress, often down to her ankles, which makes it difficult to do anything more than romp gently in the palace grounds. Long golden hair and a fair skin are axiomatic – this princess is almost never black. She wears a crown or a tiara, and servants and admirers pay homage to her status and beauty. Frequently she is a ballet dancer as well – she may be the Sleeping Beauty or may strap on her wings to transform herself into the Sugar Plum Fairy. Dressing up, being treated as someone special, being beautiful, putting on a show, being magic – these themes still pervade the fantasy world of healthy, assertive twenty-first-century girls.

The image of pre-adolescent girliness owes much to the romantic image of girl children in the nineteenth century in which beauty and vulnerability add poignancy. (I have a postcard from around 1910 in which a long-haired girl is surrounded by a cornucopia of flowers and fruit – an excess of sensuous abundance.) It also owes something to the image of the fairy, which in a popular genre of Victorian paintings and book illustrations transformed an earlier more adult supernatural being into a creature who was small, light, sexless and magic, borne up by little insect wings. The swirling graphics of girls' comic books of the 1970s and 1980s picked up on the iconography of stars, flowers and flowing hair for girls as they entered their teens. Angela McRobbie's 1978 analysis of the magazine *Jackie* revealed narratives in which girls' lives were dominated by their emotions, and where every girl was transformed into a romantic heroine. The imagery was taken up in the airbrushed style of Athena posters in the early 1980s, whose 'Unicorn Princess' decorated hundreds of bedroom walls. In more recent years the narratives of romance have largely disappeared, but the image remains – acted out by girls over many generations. This is not so much a 'masquerade', in the sense that true feelings are concealed and hidden behind an acceptable front, as a lived fantasy. It may be a performance, but it is one that is personal and self-absorbed.

Feminist critics have noted how the specialness of the princess prefigures the moment when her prince arrives and she colludes in her own subordination by becoming a bride, surrounded by more little princesses/bridesmaids. But I would argue that it is not necessary to pose this forward-looking, teleological interpretation of the image, since that harsh critique, while aiming to be liberatory by undermining the deceptive magic and revealing the covert workings of social expectations, nevertheless overlooks the ways in which the image is used –

particularly by pre-teens. Even when acting out the visual fantasy of the bride, the little princess may not be living in anticipation, but revelling in present performance and present enchantment. Her future is by no means determined. As with all imagery, the meanings of this image are observably re-constructed and re-appropriated within changing social circumstances.

Dancing on the boundary

The central questions asked by this book when considering an image are: *what* is it for? *Who* is invited to look at it? *What* has been made of it? What emerges is a contest over use. While we discuss images of girlhood as they are enjoyed by girls themselves, we know that girls are by no means the only envisaged audience for a group of pictures which have frequently evoked criticism and sometimes even demands for censorship. As boys reach manhood they tend to be represented in ways which are sometimes comic, and often, as we have seen, threatening. But the image of the girl child reaching puberty is all about sex. At this transitional point, the image of the young girl becomes a taboo image, surrounded by signals, fears and warnings, scrutinised for its dangerous potential and dissected for its move-ment into risky territories. In a real and active struggle over construction and meaning, parallel themes feed off each other. There are concerns about the processes of creating the pictures and the role of children as models; concerns about the part played by the image itself in a changing moral climate; and concerns about the possible use of the image by adult men with dubious motives. A central issue is the degree of knowledge expressed by the child in the picture. Is sexuality just in the eye of the viewer, or are we observing a precocity in knowledge and behaviour which leads to a premature loss of childhood?

Popular imagery shows many pictures of confident young girls who look the camera in the eye with an unembarrassed directness, but it needs only a slight adjustment, a slight tilt of the head to one side, to add a bashful self-awareness. One strand of the imagery routinely seeks to bend the head of the girl, to sexualise her image and to exploit the fascination of that transitional time when she is 'too old for toys, too young for boys'. The imagery of girl children balances childhood and femininity in contradiction and competition. At the same time, a fascinating exchange between knowledge and ignorance reaches beyond the boundary between girl and woman towards the forbidden attraction of innocence itself, the sexuality of the child. A little girl may be denied knowledge of sex, but as a feminine creature – for those who choose to look at it that way – her image cannot fail to indicate sex. I shall be discussing several strategies adopted by the

LITTLE GIRLS HAVE ALWAYS LOVED DRESSING UP

SO WHAT'S WRONG WITH PUTTING THEM ON THE STAGE? **NICCI GERRARD ON PAGE 5**

Observer 'Review', 31 August 1997. Photograph: Evan Corbis Sygma.

available imagery in which sexuality and femininity are contested, in a struggle in which children themselves are by no means passive.

First, the pleasures of a five-year-old may be adapted to charm adult eyes. The child's enjoyment in trying on adult roles, decked out with the earrings, high heels and other paraphernalia of a sophisticated woman, can be transformed into a major performance for an adult audience. Familiar images include over-dressed infants strutting through a mini-beauty contest; the five-year-old trophy winner having her diamante necklace fixed; the six-year-old American beauty queen Jon-Benet Ramsey facing her audience in mascara, lipstick and feathers. In a strange way, by enacting a femininity which is itself an excessive performance, such an image effectively keeps the concepts of adulthood and childhood sharply separate, even though the symbols of both of these states are brought together within the frame of the picture. These little girls would not convey their ironic message if they did not retain something of the unaware childishness that viewers have come to identify as signifying childhood itself.

A more ambivalent game of hide-and-seek is played with an image of girls close to adolescence whose youthful freshness is sought by adult model agencies. In 1988 Milla Jovovich, at the age of 12, was described as the 'hottest new American fashion model', remarkable for the contrast between 'her siren's head' and 'pre-nubile body'. Kate Moss was signed up by the Storm model agency at the age of 14, and was at the forefront of a 1990s trend for 'superwaifs'. In 1998, pictures of 12-year-old Elizabeth Preston leaning towards the camera in a light, strappy dress were reproduced in both the popular and the broadsheet press and provoked a spate of articles which lamented the loss of childhood. 'What sort of a message is it giving out to paedophiles? The fashion for very young girls looking sensual must be a terrible temptation to these sick individuals.' While the image of infants dramatising the sexual display of adult women is an ironic comment on the impossibility of keeping categories of femininity and childishness together, the presentation of young models like Milla and Elizabeth as if they were women, draws attention to the impossibility of holding them apart.

(There is a sense of judgement and retribution in the narratives which make the headlines. In a strange way the shortened lives of pure Victorian innocents are paralleled by the endangered lives of exploited twentieth-century child performers. In a moral lesson for our times, child stars have frequently been unable to cope with the pressures, and have either destroyed their health in an orgy of drugs and sex or have died young. Child singer Lena Zavaroni is a notable example; Sue Lyon – who played the original Lolita – is another. Jon-Benet Ramsey was murdered at the age of six in mysterious circumstances. The excess of the child spectacle becomes the more exciting for the sense of danger that accompanies it – both to the child and to the moral regime of which she is part.)

A third strategy in staging the tension between feminine sexuality and childhood is the drama of transition – observed with relish by the popular press, frequently with the willing collaboration of the adolescents concerned. A familiar theme is the escape from institutional constraints. Teachers voice their disapproval as a young girl abandons the constriction of school uniform and enters a public world where men may openly respond to her sexuality. 'My figure has always brought a lot of comments,' said 16-year-old Samantha Fox when her career as a Page Three girl was launched in 1983, 'so why not show it?' The *Star* followed a 15-year-old model in a series of pin-up pictures which, despite protests, culminated in a topless pose on her sixteenth birthday. The visual transformation was presented as a masculine triumph. School uniform itself may become a salacious joke. Young women in uniform can turn sensible shoes into sexy ones; they can advertise 'men's' magazines; they can poke fun at the 'prudes'. The joke is that the uniform attempts to control bodies that now refuse to be controlled. Breasts and buttocks burst out and insist that femininity will not be contained by the limits imposed by the institutions of childhood. Severe gymslips are lifted to reveal stocking tops, frilly knickers and suspenders. Forbidden parts of the body are indicated by old-fashioned underclothing that has itself become part of the stock-in-trade of pornography. (There is a porn magazine called *Schoolgirl.*) The uniform brings with it a sado-masochistic fantasy of school as a place of sexualised discipline.

Relations of power through sexuality underlie a game of provocation and denial, titillation and outrage, played around the unstable division between adult woman and girl child. The word 'girl' can refer to a woman of any age, implying a continuation of her defenceless availability. The pin-up girl, the chorus girl, the girlfriend – a word which stands for a child in whom sexuality must be repressed also stands for a woman at those very moments when she is defined by her sexuality. The word summons up childhood as a paradigm for dependency, vulnerability and subordination, and imputes those characteristics to the whole female group. The domination–subordination relationship between men and women is paralleled and reinforced by the domination–subordination relationship between adults and children.

The image of the child-woman balances that of the too-knowing child. In the first case, seductiveness seems an innocent condition of a woman's being which she does not choose and cannot reject; in the second, seductiveness may be consciously displayed but its consummation is tabooed. As adulthood and childishness merge and blur, what disturbs is the disappearance of the boundary. 'I lead an adult life, but I won't throw childhood away,' said a 15-year-old model who admitted that she first had sex at 13. 'I'll still be a child at eighty and have Coco Pops for breakfast.'

At the end of the 1970s a spate of American films worked a genre pioneered by *Lolita* in the previous decade and produced a more overt and disturbing image, that of girl children whose loss of innocence made them openly seductive. At the age of 12, Brooke Shields played a child prostitute in *Pretty Baby* (1977). At 13, Jodie Foster leaned provocatively against a lamppost in *Taxi Driver* (1976). By the time *Lolita* was re-made in 1997, with 14-year-old Dominique Swain, the reality and extent of child abuse had been publicly debated and the production of the film was accompanied by concerns for the well-being of the child actor. But the image of a child who has chosen to be sexually available continues to fascinate, and continues to be reinterpreted. Two teen magazines in summer

2001 featured articles on prostitution, both using the resonant image of a young girl in cropped shorts bending over a car, negotiating with a client.

It may be that a loss of innocence is the best protection against exploitation. In that spirit, a newer fantasy for girls, prominent in teen magazines and pop culture, sets out to shock the moral purists and to dramatise their worst forecasts. Using the strategies of camp, a familiar image of teenage girlhood challenges morality by pushing it to its limits and throwing it back at the accusers. Magazines such as *Mizz*, *Smash Hits*, *Shout*, *Bliss* and *Just Seventeen* are full of ordinary teenagers who are as sexy and knowing as the celebrities. An archetypal teenager, created in a montage in The *Observer*, is wearing a cropped top with bellybutton exposed and the words 'porn star' across her slight bosom (the word is slightly blurred, perhaps deliberately?). She wears a diamante choker in Edwardian brothel style, blue make-up on her heavy lids and has a partially open mouth. Despite – or rather because of – its excess, the distancing force of such an image is instantly recognisable, particularly to an audience familiar with female performers from Madonna to the Spice Girls.

Campaigns to preserve the purity of childhood risk turning their backs on precisely those areas most in need of a playful, if fearful, exploration. The little girl tottering on her high heels in front of the mirror is trying on adult identities but is also experimenting in turning them to her own advantage. An exploration of childhood sexuality and its rapid transformations will inevitably venture near the edge of what is acceptable. The consequent sense of transgression is undoubtedly pleasurable in itself – even when the pleasure is expressed as outrage.

Feminised boys

The image of the girl-woman is a threat to the masculine position in several ways. A familiar popular narrative tells of men who are seduced into transgression either by the irresistible innocence of the feminine or by rapacious Lolitas. Another tells of young males who are in danger of becoming feminised because they too stand in a subordinate relation to adult male power. This makes the sexuality of boys an even more impossible topic than that of girls. A masculine sexual assertiveness poses a dangerous challenge to adult males, while passivity and softness tends to be seen as feminising and homo-erotic. Unlike the 'tomboy', who is destined to abandon her resistance to female positioning, a feminised boy may risk losing his claims to masculinity.

However, the image of the feminised boy has an important place in the public repertoire. The image of a young boy in ruffled collar, velvet suit and curly hair

" BUBBLES.
By Sir JOHN MILLAIS, Bt., P.R.A.
After the Original in the possession of Messrs. PEARS

Postcard, 1910.

displays all the qualities of softness and sweetness usually associated with girls, and is still a recognised figure appreciated for its kitsch appeal. Little Lord Fauntleroy, first published in 1894, was made into a BBC television serial just over a century later. One of the earliest images of children to be commodified was *Bubbles*, the popular Victorian painting by John Everett Millais which became an advertisement for Pears soap and continues to be one of the most reproduced pictures of children (the postcard I have was posted in 1910). But in a climate where the power differential between boys and girls is under challenge, such visual ambivalence tends to be combated by masculine toughness. The contemporary image of the pre-adolescent boy needs to be strongly defended against feminisation, and also against fears of homosexuality and paedophilia. Thus the symbols of power are marshalled to secure the boy as the inheritor of the dominant position of the adult male. In contemporary advertisements, boys are much more likely to distress, threaten or judge their mothers. Their choice of toys involves tools, machines and weapons. They are rarely shown in repose. Instead they run, leap, throw, climb or engage in effective activity. The image of the young toughie has become the regular face of an engaging boyhood. His knowingness is not sexual, but a cheeky naughtiness. Amongst my collection of greetings cards I have a choirboy whose angelic face is belied by the catapult in his pocket, and a birthday card which shows a golden-haired youngster amongst some foliage – shooting with a toy bow and arrow.

It is not until boys reach their teenage years, when male potency is assured, that the image can afford to play with an effeminate look. Then the girls' magazines go for male pin-ups and boy bands who may well be floppy-haired and doe-eyed. A late 1990s fashion sought out 'male waifs' who exhibited a *Brideshead Revisited* foppishness.

Evidence of a crime

The cheeky face of a smiling boy may be read as an invitation to pornographers and paedophiles. A low-intensity image such as a school photograph or a snapshot may have meanings projected onto it that resonate beyond the bounds of social acceptability. However, there is another group of pictures which moves beyond the mere implication of paedophilic attraction and shows children actually involved in sexual acts or as sadistic or fetishistic objects. Such pictures are illegal and hidden from public view, and yet their very possibility provokes intense public fascination as well as horror. They appear to establish a link between a sexual attraction for children and abusive behaviour which divides paedophiles and 'perverts' from the rest of society. And yet the forbidden questions are implied: are images of physical punishment also linked to sexuality? Is the disgust aroused by degrading images part of a continuum of sexual response?

Secrecy and prohibition are central to the social structure which contains such images. When television personality Carol Vorderman followed a police investigation into child pornography on the Internet, she repeatedly reminded her audience that she could not broadcast the pictures she was calling up on a computer screen. Instead their disgusting nature was relayed through her expressions of revulsion. But the prohibitions have been gradually relaxed. When a group of men who called themselves the Wonderland Club was traced and arrested, the press could only indicate the nature of the pictures that had been circulated. They published hazy images with blanked-out faces, which nevertheless made it clear that the children shown were being appallingly maltreated – several of them appeared to be bound and chained. When the BBC transmitted *The Hunt for Britain's Paedophiles* in mid-2002, some of the pictures of children hoarded by the convicted men were transmitted in a far more explicit form.

These are pictures which hover at the very edge of available imagery, judged to be only for the eyes of criminals and those who would prosecute them. They are seen by the police as evidence of a crime, since it seems obvious that, at the moment the picture was taken, a child was actually being abused.

The situation is more problematic when the suspected abuse is in the mind of the beholder. Even if a photograph does not document abuse taking place, it may nevertheless be offensive to some viewers, who consider it abusive *in itself*. A picture of a naked boy sitting gazing at the camera with his hand covering his crotch was considered to be illegal in Western Australia, under a law which only requires a person who 'looks like' a child under 16 years of age to be photographed 'in a manner that is likely to cause offence to a reasonable adult'. The judgement was made even though the photograph had been taken by the boy's mother, as part of her course work as a photography student. Although they were outraged by the incident, the publishers of the academic journal *Continuum* hesitated before using it on their cover. The picture is a reversal of a notorious photograph of 'Rosie', taken by Robert Mapplethorpe in 1976, in which the child is fully dressed but reveals her private parts, not only to a particularly sensual photographer, but to those following generations who continue to gaze at his work. The Australian student remained on remand for more than two years, but the photograph of her son made it onto the cover of the journal. In London, the Hayward Gallery left 'Rosie' out of its 1996 Mapplethorpe show.

In the UK, the law states that 'It is an offence to take, or permit to be taken, any indecent photograph of a child', and, in a 1988 Court of Appeal judgement, 'indecency' was defined as whatever right-thinking people understood it to mean by 'applying the recognised standards of propriety'. In 1989 another Court of Appeal judgement stated that pictures suspected of being indecent must be judged *outside the context in which they were created*. No witnesses could be called to explain the motives of those who took them. The assumption is precisely the opposite to that argued in this book. My position, which is explained at length in the Introduction, argues that the meanings of imagery are always fluid. It is in the very nature of a visual presentation to shift and change its meanings according to context and usage.

In my view, these problems can only be untangled by distinguishing three different phenomena; first, the *process* of making a picture, which may well be an abusive act, whether or not the abuse is visible in the final image; second, the picture itself, usually a photograph, accepted as a record, as *evidence* of a crime; and third, an offensive picture, which may not have been abusive in the taking, and may not record a criminal act, but whose content is considered deserving of criminal prosecution because of present or future *effects*. These distinctions are thrown into greater relief by the use of electronic imaging, in which a present-ation may create, with apparent photographic exactitude, an event which never happened. (In 2002 two policemen were charged with possessing and making 'pseudo-photographs' of children under the age of 16.) The fact that an image is shocking does not remove the need to treat it as an *image*, rather than taking its evidential qualities at face value. It is of crucial importance to trace the history of its construction, its context and its past use. In the case of a picture which is censured because it may be 'offensive', questions are posed about a possible *future* use. But, as I have argued throughout, images may be put to many uses and their meanings modulated by different groups of users and in different contexts. There is no way of predicting that a picture which neither records abuse nor was abusive in the taking will, in the future, give rise to abuse. If it merely 'gives offence' it may well be amongst many challenging images which legitimately test the boundaries of contemporary meanings.

Wealthy, intelligent, passionate and have-it-all

The drama of childhood sexuality is taken a step further when shocking, familiar, but less spectacular public narratives tell of young girls' bubbling sexuality bursting forth in the disaster of unwanted babies or an otherwise ruined child-hood. This image tends to be heavy with moral judgement. The teenage mother is often shown head in hands, slouched and unkempt. Viewers are forcibly reminded that a girl is no longer alluring once she is degraded by prostitution or becomes a 'gymslip mother'. The transformation from child to adult is often presented in punitive terms. 'Thirty-six hours in labour, which is common, changed them dramatically', the principal of a school for teenage mothers commented grimly.

By the mid-1980s, the views of Mary Whitehouse, Victoria Gillick and other moral purity campaigners achieved a new credibility as the backlash against 'permissiveness' gained momentum and the advent of AIDS introduced new cautions. Yet AIDS made it possible to speak of sex to young people, with the discourse of danger sometimes coming perilously close to a debate on pleasure. Even so, in the view of the campaigners, too much knowledge deprived children of their innocence and, indeed, of childhood itself. 'How young is too young for love?' demanded the *Daily Express*. 'If kisses were not forbidden in school', said one headmaster, 'twelve- and thirteen-year-olds would be making love in the corridors'.

'Is there anybody in this country who really cares about our innocent children?' asked Barbara Jones in the *Mail on Sunday* of the relationship between

50-year-old Rolling Stone Bill Wyman and 13-year-old Mandy Smith. 'To hear the story as I did from Mandy's own lips as she curled up childlike on the sofa in her mini-dress would bring tears to the eyes of any decent mother or father.' But the other side of Mandy's spoilt innocence was her assertiveness. She was presented as the archetypal 'bimbo' – one of a new and shameless breed of exploitative girl-women, the gold-diggers of 1986, planning to trap wealthy middle-aged men. In subsequent years Mandy Smith regularly appeared in *Hello!* In June 2001, aged 30, she was showing off her new baby. There is always more than one way of understanding a picture, and the narrative of spoilt girlhood tells a quite different story when the perspective is switched around and the image is seen, not with the eyes of a sexually interested male, but with those of the inventive and assertive girl herself.

Yet, playing with their image is a risky business for young girls as they balance welcome pleasures with dubious pressures. 'We speak their language, they respond,' IPC told advertisers of its young women's magazines in the mid-1980s. 'Romance is here. Your message can reach her at her most receptive.' Adolescent femininity, they argue, is about living for the moment and for a future made up of similar moments, 'Today is what you make it. Tomorrow will be even better.' The point about romance is that sex is deferred or implied. But at the beginning of the twenty-first century, a joint report by the UK Houses of Commons and Lords into teen magazines had branded many of them 'immoral' in their focus on sex, and a Teenage Magazine Arbitration Panel was set up. Seven- to eight-year-olds leave *Girl Heaven* and *Princess World* and rapidly move on to publications which feature celebrity photographs and beauty tips, and have little time for romance in its traditional forms. They adopt a frank, if cheeky, attitude towards teenage health worries and body problems – and are open about sex. 'There is a new breed of girl out there – wealthy, intelligent, passionate, have-it-all. *Cosmo Girl!* will do for her what *Cosmo* did for older women 29 years ago,' declared editor Claire Baylis when *Cosmo Girl!* was launched in 2001, aimed at 11–16-year-old girls. 'Girls these days still crave privacy and are interested in boys but they are more media savvy, more cynical, take sexual equality for granted and are more aware of the competitive nature of the adult world.'

Young femininity has been commodified, but partly on its own terms. Girls' magazines now come under fire from those who would preserve romantic girl-hood and who deplore their explicit information and their refusal to accept the decorum of previous ages. This fantasy can be lived through with the aid of clothes and make up, and there's still a 'prince' in the shape of a young pop star plastered over the bedroom walls. Girl power – personified by the Spice Girls in their mid-1990s heyday – sees no contradiction between assertiveness and old-fashioned sexiness, and the 'ladette' of the 1990s set out to match the boozy, leery culture of boys becoming men.

A final fantasy for girls is expressed in the lusty energy of contemporary magazines; a challenging, provocative, come-and-get-me look; girls who are open about their sexual experiences, who look the camera in the eye and turn up to jeer the male stripper. The confidence of childhood, instead of being transformed into nervous coyness, has taken on board the sexual knowledge of the adult world and refused to be cowed by it. Paradoxically, such a new rumbustiousness may preserve rather than break the values of childhood.

NOTES ON CHAPTER 7

p.178 **'If Alice was'**: *Independent* 'Magazine', 12 December 1998. Photographs: Justin Smith.

A network of child pornographers: 'Warped world of Wonderland', *Daily Mail*, 14 February 2001.

John Tenniel: *Punch* cartoonist who collaborated closely (and argumentatively) with Carroll. Jackie Wullschlager (revised 2001) *Inventing Wonderland: the Lives of Lewis Carroll, Edward Lear, J.M. Barrie, Kenneth Grahame and A.A. Milne*, London: Methuen, Chapter 2.

p.179 **an aestheticisation of everyday life**: Mike Featherstone (1991) *Consumer Culture and Postmodernism*, London: Sage, Chapter 5.

p.180 **Jane Gallop**: (1982) *Feminism and Psychoanalysis, the Daughter's Seduction*, London: Macmillan, p.xv.

'you'd better grow': Lindsay Smith (1998) *The Politics of Focus: Women, Children and Nineteenth Century Photography*, Manchester: Manchester University Press, p.101.

p.181 **'Even at play'**: Dr John Richer, quoted by Karen Farrington, 'Would you buy your son a doll?' *Woman*, 20 December 1988.

'Men don't want their sons to be effeminate': Gerry Masters of the National Association of Toy Retailers, quoted by Farrington (1988) above.

p.183 **recent debates around gender difference**: for example Lynne Segal (1990) *Slow Motion: Changing Masculinities, Changing Men*, London: Virago; Angela Phillips (1993) *The Trouble with Boys: Parenting the Men of the Future*, London: Pandora.

'commercial syncretism': Erving Goffman (1976) *Gender Advertisements*, London: Macmillan.

A line drawing: *Observer* 'Magazine', 5 November 1978. Illustration: Dick Bruna.

p.186 **'the absolute fact of difference'**: Stephen Heath (1982) *The Sexual Fix*, London: Macmillan, p.139.

a pair of advertisements for Nesquik: Nesquik milkshake mix, mid-1980s.

'Lots of manufacturers advertise': quoted by Farrington (1988) above.

'wore her curly hair short': Enid Blyton (1947/1967) *Five on Kirrin Island Again*, London: Hodder and Stoughton.

p.187 **the 2001 H&M catalogue**: *The Last Days of Summer*, catalogue for children's clothes.

'Times are changing': advertisement for K shoes, mid-1980s.

p. 188   **styling her body:** Frigga Haug (ed.) (1987) *Female Sexualisation*, London: Verso, is an account of a group project by which a group of women explore the minute detail of the construction of femininity in their own bodies (specific projects focus on hair, legs and the slave-girl myth), relating visual imagery to lived experience.

'**I just look into the mirror**': *Daily Mail*, 23 February 1998.

'**As soon as you are sensitised**': Geraldine Bedell, 'This girl is for sale', *Independent on Sunday*, 22 July 1990.

p. 190   **the fairy princess who becomes a bride:** Marina Warner (1994) *From the Beast to the Blonde: on Fairy Tales and their Tellers*, London: Chatto and Windus.

romantic image of girl children: explored by Anne Higonnet (1998) in *Pictures of Innocence: the History and Crisis of Ideal Childhood*, London: Thames and Hudson.

the image of the fairy: Jeremy Maas et al. (1997) *Victorian Fairy Paintings*, London: Royal Academy of Arts. This was a catalogue to an exhibition in 1997–98; Susan P. Casteras (2002) 'Winged fantasies, constructions of childhood, innocence, adolescence and sexuality in Victorian fairy paintings', in Marilyn R. Brown (ed.) *Picturing Children: Constructions of Childhood Between Rousseau and Freud*, London: Ashgate.

Angela McRobbie's analysis: (1978) *Jackie: an Ideology of Adolescent Femininity*, Birmingham: Centre for Contemporary Cultural Studies Occasional Paper; and 'Just like a Jackie story', in Angela McRobbie and Trisha McCabe (eds) (1981) *Feminism for Girls: an Adventure Story*, London: Routledge & Kegan Paul.

'**Unicorn Princess**': designed by Robin Koni for Athena posters. Lindsay Baker, *Guardian* 'Weekend', 10 November 2001.

the narratives of romance have largely disappeared: Angela McRobbie (1991) *Feminism and Youth Culture: from Jackie to Just Seventeen*, London: Macmillan; and (1995) 'Shut up and dance: youth culture and changing modes of femininity', in *Postmodernism and Popular Culture*, London: Routledge.

colludes in her own subordination: Valerie Walkerdine (1990) 'Some day my prince will come: young girls and the preparation for adolescent sexuality', in *Schoolgirl Fictions*, London: Verso.

p. 191   **the only envisaged audience:** Valerie Walkerdine (1991) has discussed at length the complex family relations behind a snapshot of herself as a 'Bluebell Fairy'. See 'Behind the painted smile', in J. Spence and P. Holland (eds) *Family Snaps: the Meanings of Domestic Photography*, London: Virago.

p. 192   **five-year-old trophy winner:** *Radio Times*, 27 January–2 February 1996, stills from *Under the Sun: Painted Babies* (BBC2, 31 January 1996) showing young Brooke Breedwell, who has won more than 600 trophies.

Jon-Benet Ramsey: Tim Cornwell, 'Too much too young', *Independent*, 13 January 1997.

p. 193   '**hottest new American fashion model**': Glenn O'Brien, 'Milla Dollar Baby', *Sunday Times* 'Magazine', 1988.

What sort of a message: 'Outcry over sexy photos of girl aged 12', *Daily Express*, 23 February 1998; 'What kind of mother would allow a daughter of 12 to pose like this?', *Daily Mail*, 23 February 1998.

Lena Zavaroni: 'I was to marry Lena', *Daily Mirror*, 4 October 1999. The singer died at 35 following depression and anorexia.

Sue Lyon: was quoted as saying 'my destruction as a person dates from that movie. I defy any pretty girl who is rocketed to world stardom at the age of 15 in a sex-nymphet role to stay on a level path': *Radio Times*, 15–21 September

2001, p.61. By contrast, Shirley Temple, the most famous child star of all, went on to a successful career in diplomacy. Shirley Temple Black (1988) *Child Star, an Autobiography*, London: Headline.

'My figure has always brought': Shan Lancaster, 'Sam, 16, quits A-levels for Ooh-levels!', *Sun*, 22 February 1983.

p.194 sensible shoes into sexy ones: advertisement for Clarks shoes, late 1970s.

they can advertise 'men's' magazines: 'Our class of '78' was a double-page colour spread in *Campaign* showing eight dishevelled young women partying in high heels, stocking tops and crumpled school uniforms, inviting advertisers to *Men Only* and *Club*.

The image of the child-woman: see Goffman (1976) above for a discussion of women's 'childish' gestures in the advertisements he studied.

'I'll still be a child at eighty': quoted by Bedell (1990) above.

a spate of American films: *Lolita* (US, 1962) Dir. Stanley Kubrick; *Pretty Baby* (US, 1977) Dir. Louis Malle; *Taxi Driver* (US, 1976) Dir. Martin Scorsese; *Lolita* (US, 1997) Dir. Adrian Lyne.

Two teen magazines: 'Dirty Money', *More!*, August 2001; 'I was a teenage prostitute', *Bliss*, September, 2001.

p.195 An archetypal teenager: *Observer*, 19 August 2001.

Madonna: E. Ann Kaplan and John Fiske both have extended discussions of Madonna and her image in Robert C. Allen (ed.) (1992) *Channels of Discourse, Reassembled*, London: Routledge. Kaplan discusses two videos by Madonna, 'Express yourself' and 'Justify my love', pp.272–76. Fiske quotes Judith Williamson that Madonna 'retains all the bravado and exhibitionism that most girls start off with, or feel inside, until the onset of "womanhood" knocks it out of them', pp.306–18.

in danger of becoming feminised: in the context of a discussion of child abuse, Florence Rush (1980) argues that the social bisexuality of children is female. See *The Best Kept Secret*, New Jersey: Prentice Hall.

p.196 Little Lord Fauntleroy: by Mrs F.H. Burnett. (My copy has a dedication, 'To dear Daisy with love and best wishes from Nell', 1896.) The television serial was on BBC1 in January 1995.

p.197 'male waifs': Dominic Lutyens, 'Move over Schwarzenegger', *Independent on Sunday*, 25 February 1996 (the picture of model Lee Williams was disrespectfully captioned 'That's no lady, that's my waif'); 'Boy band', *Observer* 'Magazine', 19 August 2001.

Brideshead Revisited: by Evelyn Waugh, adapted for television by Granada 1981. The image of Sebastian Flyte (played by Anthony Andrews) clutching his teddy bear has become a reference point for gay imagery as well as upper-class decadence.

are images of physical punishment: James Kincaid (1992) *Childloving: the Erotic Child and Victorian Culture*, London: Routledge.

television personality Carol Vorderman: carried out a series of investigations for *Tonight with Trevor Macdonald*, ITV, 25 October 2000; 9 November 2000; 15 March 2001.

hazy images with blanked-out faces: globally, police estimated, 750,000 such images were traded. 'Candidates had to offer 10,000 new indecent images to be admitted to the club', and sometimes abuse happened live online. Although the material was seized in 1998, only 17 of the children had been identified. *Daily Mail*, 14 February 2001. See also *Panorama* on the Wonderland Club (BBC1, 11 February 2001).

The Hunt for Britain's Paedophiles: BBC2, three 90-minute programmes transmitted in June 2002. Produced by Bob Long.

p.198 **only for the eyes of criminals**: see Carole S. Vance (1990) 'The pleasures of looking: the Attorney General's Commission on Pornography versus visual images', in Carol Squires (ed.) *The Critical Image*, London: Lawrence and Wishart, p.48, on the contradictory way in which even child pornography was made available for viewing in the context of the US Commission which sought to condemn and outlaw a wide range of visual material.

A picture of a naked boy: John Hartley, 'Juvenation, news, girls and power', in Cynthia Carter, Gill Branston and Stuart Allen (eds) (1998) *News, Gender and Power*, London: Routledge.

notorious photograph of 'Rosie': 'Siding with Rosie', *New Statesman*, 20 September 1996. The outcry over pictures of naked children included the arrest of newsreader Julia Somerville and her partner when the technician at Kodak responsible for processing their pictures reported them to the police. Amidst the barrage of publicity and debate that followed, *Amateur Photographer* launched a 'Campaign for common sense'. Emily Barr, 'Snap judgements and an age of innocence', *Guardian*, 7 December 1996.

'It is an offence to take': 1978 Protection of Children Act Section 1 (1). David Newnham and Chris Townsend, 'Pictures of innocence', *Guardian* 'Weekend', 13 January 1996.

p.199 **In 2002 two policemen**: 'Soham cops are released from prison', *Daily Express*, 17 September 2002. One policeman was cleared in August 2003.

'Thirty-six hours in labour': Corinna Honan, 'The Dilemma of Schoolgirl Mothers', *Woman*, 1980.

the advent of AIDS: for a discussion of many aspects of AIDS and the media, see David Miller et al., *The Circuit of Mass Communication*, London: Sage, 1998.

'How young is too young': 'Making love in the corridors', *Daily Express*, February 1980.

'Is there anybody in this country': Barbara Jones, *Mail on Sunday*, 24 August 1986.

p.200 **report by the UK Houses of Commons and Lords**: Jessica Hodgson, 'Hello girls', *Guardian*, 2 July 2001.

have little time for romance: McRobbie (1991) above.

'There is a new breed of girl': *Observer*, 24 September 2000.

Postscript

Escape from childhood

Pictures of children have been made in a world which sees childhood as a precious quality which may be stolen or wantonly rejected. Since children are open to exploitation, some argue that their childishness must be protected above all other considerations. Yet the bitter experience of being a child is very often a continuous struggle to escape from childhood, to leave behind precisely those qualities of simplicity, ignorance and innocence that are so highly valued.

Like everyone else in Western, urban civilisation, children live in a world of meanings and of visual spectacle. They too respond to the imagery that surrounds us all, and make use of it to define themselves and account for their experiences. To be a child is not to inhabit a mythical dreamland, but to be a thinking, acting individual, with the ability to make sense of the material to hand. Yet, living through childhood means coping with continuous change. Children's bodies undergo rapid transformations and the social expectations to which they are subject are constantly re-adjusted. Some aspects of the imagery of childhood are able to draw on the richness of this resource, but all too frequently the available imagery avoids such radical instability and seeks to impose its own nervous limits.

Of all social groups, children have been the least able to explore their view of themselves in the public domain. They have found themselves trapped by received definitions, which are underpinned by powerful adult emotions. Yet, where they have gained greater access to a public voice they have been able to make a significant contribution to the broad sweep of social meanings. The result has been not a more 'childish' set of images, but a more diverse one. As adults pay attention to children's own contribution, we are forced to readjust our concept of childhood and its contexts. That means that our notion of what it means to be an adult must also become more flexible.

Children should certainly be heard as much as they are seen. We could then expect an even richer pleasure from the image.

From *Focus on Images*, 1991, courtesy of Save the Children Fund.

Index